Caste System in Modern India

Caste System in Modern India

Zafar Ahmad

AUTHORSPRESS

Publishers of Scholarly Books

Worldwide Circulation through Authorspress Global Network
First Published 2010
by
Authorspress
E-35/103, Jawahar Park
Laxmi Nagar, Delhi-110 092
e-mail: authorspress@yahoo.com

Caste System in Modern India
ISBN 978-81-7273-546-3

Printed in India at Tarun Offset, Delhi.

PREFACE

The word caste is derived from the term 'casba'. It depicts a ranking system of human groups based on hereditary and occupation. The traditional caste system in India is a rigid mode to compartmentalise society. Its functionality in society is highly surprising because it has many drawbacks. The rigid structure of the caste system in India has abided through centuries.

The Indian word for caste is 'jati'. Thousands of 'jatis' are strewn all over India. Each jati has its own governance, customs, traditions, religion, rules and style of living. The ancients divided Indian society in four groups—namely Brahmans who came from the priestly group of learning, Shatriyas who were the warrior and ruling section of society, Vaishyas who were businessmen, traders and farmers; and Shudras who comprised of labourers and humble peasants. The untouchable or Panchamas were placed below the category of Shudras. The hierarchy of the Indian caste system has been severely criticised by individuals with a humanitarian vision from India and outside India.

The leaders of independent India decided that India will be democratic, socialist and secular country. Practising untouchability or discriminating a person based on his caste is legally forbidden. Along with this law the government allows positive discrimination of the depressed classes of India. However, the caste system is still very much prevalent in India and the effects of caste system in modern India can be seen in the form of quota systems, reservations, marriages etc. There are multiple effects of caste system in modern India. Metropolitan India has started walking away from the rigidity of the Indian caste system. This is the result of co-mingling with other communities, higher education, globalisation and economic growth, while in some rural areas there is still discrimination based on castes and sometimes also on untouchability. Sometimes in villages or in the cities there are violent clashes which, are connected to caste tensions. Caste-based reservations in India have ignited the communal fire in a different way.

Caste-based violence and caste politics has opened the eyes of many people to the dangers of caste practices in modern India. Criticisms of caste system have been brought out by many liberal thinkers around the globe. It is in benefit of the people of India that they gradually remove the caste barrier from their mind to live in harmony and peace.

This book provides well-written and well-researched information on caste system and practices in modern India. In eight chapters, it describes the modern issues of Indian caste system such as caste reforms, caste radicalism, caste conflicts, caste politics, modern caste practices, reservation politics and developmental issues of backward classes, in a comprehensive way. Written in a lucid style, the book narrates new perspectives on caste system which would enliven and create an interest in historians, sociologists, anthropologists, students, researchers and layman alike.

Zafar Ahmad

CONTENTS

1

THE CASTE SYSTEM

India has a hierarchical caste system in the society. Within Indian culture, whether in the north or the south, Hindu or Muslim, urban or village, virtually all things, people, and groups of people are ranked according to various essential qualities. If one is attuned to the theme of hierarchy in India, one can discern it everywhere. Although India is a political democracy, in daily life there is little advocacy of or adherence to notions of equality.

Castes system in India are primarily associated with Hinduism but also exist among other Indian religious groups. Muslims sometimes expressly deny that they have castes—they state that all Muslims are brothers under God—but observation of Muslim life in various parts of India reveals the existence of caste-like groups and clear concern with social hierarchy. Among Indian Christians, too, differences in caste are acknowledged and maintained.

Throughout India, individuals are also ranked according to their wealth and power. For example, there are "big men" and "little men" everywhere. "Big men" sit confidently on chairs, while "little men" come before them to make requests, either standing or crouching down on their haunches, certainly not presuming to sit beside a man of high status as an equal. Even men of nearly equal status who might share a string cot to sit on take their places carefully—the higher-ranking man at the head of the cot, the lower-ranking man at the foot.

Within families and kinship groupings, there are many distinctions of hierarchy. Men outrank women of the same or similar age, and senior relatives outrank junior relatives. Several other kinship relations involve formal respect. For example, in northern India, a daughter-in-law of a household shows deference to a daughter of a household. Even among young siblings in a household, there is constant acknowledgment of age differences: younger siblings never address an older sibling by name, but rather by respectful terms for elder brother or elder sister. However, an older sibling may address the younger by name.

Even in a business or academic setting, where colleagues may not openly espouse traditional observance of caste or class ranking behaviour, they may set up kinship relations, addressing one another by kinship terms reflecting family or village-style hierarchy.

Caste-based Discrimination

Many status differences in Indian society are expressed in terms of ritual purity and pollution. Notions of purity and pollution are extremely complex and vary greatly among different castes, religious groups, and regions. However, broadly speaking, high status is associated with purity and low status with pollution. Some kinds of purity are inherent, or inborn; for example, gold is purer than copper by its very nature, and, similarly, a member of a high-ranking Brahman, or priestly, caste is born with more inherent purity than a member of a low-ranking Sweeper (Mehtar, in Hindi) caste. Unless the Brahman defiles himself in some extraordinary way, throughout his life he will always be purer than a Sweeper. Other kinds of purity are more transitory—a Brahman who has just taken a bath is more ritually pure than a Brahman who has not bathed for a day. This situation could easily reverse itself temporarily, depending on bath schedules, participation in polluting activities, or contact with temporarily polluting substances.

Purity is associated with ritual cleanliness—daily bathing in flowing water, dressing in properly laundered clothes of approved materials, eating only the foods appropriate for one's caste, refraining from physical contact with people of lower rank, and avoiding involvement with ritually impure substances. The latter include body wastes and excretions, most especially those of another adult person. Contact with the products of death or violence are typically polluting and threatening to ritual purity.

During her menstrual period, a woman is considered polluted and refrains from cooking, worshiping, or touching anyone older than an infant. In much of the south, a woman spends this time "sitting outside," resting in an isolated room or shed. During her period, a Muslim woman does not touch the Quran. At the end of the period, purity is restored with a complete bath. Pollution also attaches to birth, both for the mother and the infant's close kin, and to death, for close relatives of the deceased.

Members of the highest priestly castes, the Brahmans, are generally vegetarians (although some Bengali and Maharashtrian Brahmans eat fish) and avoid eating meat, the product of violence and death. High-ranking Warrior castes (Kshatriyas), however, typically consume nonvegetarian diets, considered appropriate for their traditions of valor and physical strength.

A Brahman born of proper Brahman parents retains his inherent purity if he bathes and dresses himself properly, adheres to a vegetarian diet, eats meals prepared only by persons of appropriate rank, and keeps his person away from the bodily exuviae of others. If a Brahman happens to come into bodily contact with a polluting substance, he can remove this pollution by bathing and changing his clothing. However, if he were to eat meat or commit other transgressions of the rigid dietary codes of his particular caste, he would be considered more deeply polluted and would have to undergo various purifying rites and payment of fines imposed by his caste council in order to restore his inherent purity.

In sharp contrast to the purity of a Brahman, a Sweeper born of Sweeper parents is considered to be born inherently polluted. The touch of his body is polluting to those higher on the caste hierarchy than he, and they will shrink from his touch, whether or not he has bathed recently. Sweepers are associated with the traditional occupation of cleaning human feces from latrines and sweeping public lanes of all kinds of dirt. Traditionally, Sweepers remove these polluting materials in baskets carried atop the head and dumped out in a garbage pile at the edge of the village or neighbourhood. The involvement of Sweepers with such filth accords with their low-status position at the bottom of the Hindu caste hierarchy, even as their services allow high-status people, such as Brahmans, to maintain their ritual purity.

Members of the Leatherworker (Chamar) caste are ascribed a very low status consonant with their association with the caste occupation of skinning dead animals and tanning the leather. Butchers (Khatiks), who kill and cut up the bodies of animals, also rank low on the caste hierarchy because of their association with violence and death. However, castes associated with ruling and warfare—and the killing and deaths of human beings—are typically accorded high rank on the caste hierarchy. In these instances, political power and wealth outrank association with violence as the key determinant of caste rank.

Maintenance of purity is associated with the intake of food and drink, not only in terms of the nature of the food itself, but also in terms of who has prepared it or touched it. This requirement is especially true for Hindus, but other religious groups hold to these principles to varying degrees. Generally, a person risks pollution—and lowering his own status—if he accepts beverages or cooked foods from the hands of people of lower caste status than his own. His status will remain intact if he accepts food or beverages from people of higher caste rank. Usually, for an observant Hindu of any but the very lowest castes to accept cooked food from a Muslim or Christian is regarded as highly polluting.

In a clear example of pollution associated with dining, a Brahman who consumed a drink of water and a meal of wheat bread with boiled vegetables from the hands of a Sweeper would immediately become polluted and could expect social rejection by his caste fellows. From that moment, fellow Brahmans following traditional pollution rules would refuse food touched by him and would abstain from the usual social interaction with him. He would not be welcome inside Brahman homes—most especially in the ritually pure kitchens—nor would he or his close relatives be considered eligible marriage partners for other Brahmans.

Generally, the acceptance of water and ordinary foods cooked in water from members of lower-ranking castes incurs the greatest pollution. In North India, such foods are known as *kaccha khana,* as contrasted with fine foods cooked in butter or oils, which are known as *pakka khana*. Fine foods can be accepted from members of a few castes slightly lower than one's own. Local hierarchies differ on the specific details of these rules.

Completely raw foods, such as uncooked grains, fresh unpeeled bananas, mangoes, and uncooked vegetables can be accepted by anyone from anyone else, regardless of relative status. Toasted or parched foods, such as roasted peanuts, can also be accepted from anyone without ritual or social repercussions.

Water served from an earthen pot may be accepted only from the hands of someone of higher or equal caste ranking, but water served from a brass pot may be accepted even from someone slightly lower on the caste scale. Exceptions to this rule are members of the Waterbearer caste, who are employed to carry water from wells to the homes of the prosperous and from whose hands members of all castes may drink water without becoming polluted, even though Waterbearers are not ranked high on the caste scale.

These and a great many other traditional rules pertaining to purity and pollution constantly impinge upon interaction between people of different castes and ranks in India. Although to the non-Indian these rules may seem irrational and bizarre, to most of the people of India they are a ubiquitous and accepted part of life. Thinking about and following purity and pollution rules make it necessary for people to be constantly aware of differences in status. With every drink of water, with every meal, and with every contact with another person, people must ratify the social hierarchy of which they are a part and within which their every act is carried out. The fact that expressions of social status are intricately bound up with events that happen to everyone every day—eating, drinking, bathing, touching, talking—and that transgressions of these rules, whether deliberate or accidental, are seen as having immediately polluting effects on the person of the transgressor, means that every ordinary act of human life serves as a constant reminder of the importance of hierarchy in Indian society.

There are many Indians, particularly among the educated urban elite, who do not follow traditional purity and pollution practices. Dining in each others' homes and in restaurants is common among well-educated people of diverse backgrounds, particularly when they belong to the same economic class. For these people, guarding the family's earthen water pot from inadvertent touch by a low-ranking servant is not the concern it is for a more traditional villager. However, even among those people whose words and actions denigrate traditional purity rules, there is often a reluctance to completely abolish consciousness of purity and pollution from their thinking. It is surely rare for a Sweeper, however well-educated, to invite a Brahman to dinner in his home and have his invitation unselfconsciously accepted. It is less rare, however, for educated urban colleagues of vastly different caste and religious heritage to enjoy a cup of tea together. Some high-caste liberals pride themselves on being free of "casteism" and seek to accept food from the hands of very low-caste people, or even deliberately set out to marry someone from a significantly lower caste or a different religion. Thus, even as they deny it, these progressives affirm the continuing significance of traditional rules of purity, pollution, and hierarchy in Indian caste system.

Background of Caste System

According to the ancient Hindu scriptures, there are four *"varnas"*. The *Bhagavad Gita* says varnas are decided based on *Guna* and *Karma*. *Manusmriti* and some other *shastras* mention four varnas: the *Brahmins* (teachers, scholars and priests), the *Kshatriyas* (kings and warriors), the *Vaishyas* (agriculturists and traders), and *Shudras* (artisans, service providers).

This theoretical system postulated Varna categories as ideals and explained away the reality of thousands of endogamous *Jâtis* actually prevailing in the country as being the result of historical mixing among the "pure" Varnas—*Varna Sankara*. All those, including foreigners, tribals and nomads, who did not subscribe to the norms of the Hindu society were contagious and untouchables. Another group excluded from the main society was called Parjanya or Antyaja. This group of former "untouchables" *Dalits*) i.e. downtrodden, was considered either the lower section of Shudras or outside the Varna system altogether. Passages from scriptures such as Manusmriti indicate that the varna system was originally non-hereditary.

Several critics of Hinduism state that the caste system is rooted in the varna system mentioned in the ancient Hindu scriptures. However, many groups consider the modern Indian caste system and the varna system as two distinct concepts. Many European administrators from the colonial era incorrectly regarded the *Manusmriti* as the "law book" of all the Hindus, and thus concluded that the caste system is a part of Hinduism, an assertion that is now rejected by most scholars, who state that it is a social practice, not a religious belief.. *Manusmriti,* was in any case a work of reference for the Brahmins of north India, especially Bengal and was largely unknown in southern India.

Although many Hindu scriptures contain passages that can be interpreted to sanction the caste system, they also contain indications that the caste system is not an essential part of Hinduism. The *Vedas* placed no importance on the caste system, mentioning caste only once out of tens of thousands of verses. Most vedic scholars believe even this to be a subsequent and artificial insertion. In fact, none other than B. R. Ambedkar concluded after a thorough study that this is a much later interpolation and gave strong scholarly evidence to support his conclusion. In the Vedic period, there was no prohibition against anyone, including the Shudras listening to the Vedas or participating in any religious rite.

In *Early Evidence for Caste in South India,* George L. Hart stated that "the earliest Tamil texts show the existence of what seems definitely to be caste, but which antedates the Brahmins and the Hindu orthodoxy". He believes that the origins of the caste system can be seen in the "belief system that developed with the agricultural civilisation", and was later profoundly influenced by "the Brahmins and the Brahmanical religion". These early Tamil texts also outline the concept of equality. Saint Valluvar has stated "pirapokkum ella uyirkkum", which means "all are equal at birth". Likewise, Saint Auvaiyaar has stated that there are only two castes in the world: those who contribute negatively and those who contribute positively. From these, it can be inferred that the caste system is more of a socio-economic class system.

Caste and Social Status

According to Fa Hien, a Buddhist pilgrim from China, visited India around 400 AD, "Only the lot of the Chandals he found unenviable; outcastes by reason of their degrading work as disposers of dead, they were universally shunned... But no other section of the population were notably disadvantaged, no other caste distinctions attracted comment from the Chinese pilgrim, and no oppressive caste 'system' drew forth his surprised censure.". In this period kings of *Sudra* and *Brahmin* origin were as common as those of *Kshatriya varna* and caste system was not wholly prohibitive and repressive.

The castes did not constitute a rigid description of the occupation or the social status of a group. Since British society was divided by class, the British attempted to equate the Indian caste system to their own social class system. They saw caste as an indicator of occupation, social standing, and intellectual ability. Intentionally or unintentionally, the caste system became more rigid during the British Raj, when the British started to enumerate castes during the ten year census and codified the system under their rule.

The *Harijans*, or the people outside the caste system, had the lowest social status. The Harijans, earlier referred to as "*untouchables*" by some, worked in what were seen as unhealthy, unpleasant or polluting jobs. In the past, the Harijans suffered from social segregation and restrictions, in addition to extreme poverty. They were not allowed temple worship with others, nor water from the same sources. Persons of higher castes would not interact with them. If somehow a member of a higher caste came into physical or social contact with an untouchable, the member of the higher caste was defiled, and had to bathe thoroughly to purge him or herself of the impurity. Social discrimination developed even among the Harijans. Sub-castes among Harijans, like *dhobi, nai* etc., would not interact with lower-order *Bhangis*, who were described as "outcasts even among outcastes".

While Caste is nowadays seen by instances that render it anachronistic, in its original form, the caste system served as an important instrument of order in a society where mutual consent rather than compulsion ruled; where the ritual rights as well as the economic obligations of members of one caste or sub-caste were strictly circumscribed in relation to those of any other caste or sub-caste; where one was born into one's caste and retained one's station in society for life; where merit was inherited, where equality existed within the caste, but inter-caste relations were unequal and hierarchical. A well-defined system of mutual interdependence through a division of labour created security within a community. In addition, the division of labour on the basis of ethnicity allowed immigrants and foreigners to quickly integrate into their own caste niches. The caste system played an influential role in shaping economic activities. The caste system functioned much like medieval European guilds, ensuring the division of labour, providing for the training of apprentices and, in some cases, allowing manufacturers to achieve narrow specialisation. For instance, in certain regions, producing each variety of cloth was the speciality of a particular sub-caste. Also, philosophers argue that the majority of people would be comfortable in stratified endogamous groups, and have been in ancient times.

Caste Mobility

Sociologist M. N. Srinivas has debated the question of rigidity in Caste. In an ethnographic study of the Coorgs of Karnataka, he observed considerable flexibility and mobility in their caste hierarchies. He asserts that the caste system is far from a rigid system in which the position of each component caste is fixed for all time. Movement has always been possible, and especially in the middle regions of the hierarchy. It was always possible for groups born into a lower caste to "rise to a higher position by adopting vegetarianism and teetotalism" i.e. adopt the customs of the higher castes. While theoretically "forbidden", the process was not uncommon in practice. The concept of sanskritisation, or the adoption of upper-caste norms by the lower castes, addressed the actual complexity and fluidity of caste relations.

Historical examples of mobility in the Indian Caste System among Hindus have been researched. There is also precedent of certain Shudra families within the temples of the Sri Vaishnava sect in South India elevating their caste.

The fact that many of the dynasties were of obscure origin suggests some social mobility: a person of any caste, having once acquired political power, could also acquire a genealogy connecting him with the traditional lineages and conferring Kshatriya status. A number of new castes, such as the *Kayasthas* (scribes) and *Khatris* (traders), are mentioned in the sources of this period. According to the Brahmanic sources, they originated from intercaste marriages, but this is clearly an attempt at rationalising their rank in the hierarchy. Many of these new castes played a major role in society. The hierarchy of castes did not have a uniform distribution throughout the country. Khatri appears to be unquestionably a Prakritised form of the Sanskrit Kshatriya.

Opposition to Caste System

There have been challenges to the caste system from the time of Buddha, and from the time of Mahavira (Jaina founder) and (still earlier) of Gosala Maskarin (Ajivaika founder).

Opposition to the system of varna is regularly asserted already in the Yoga Upanishad (of early mediaeval date); and is a constant feature of Cinaacara tantrism. The *Natha* system founded by Matsya-indra Natha and by Goraksa Natha, and spread throughout India, has likewise been in consistent opposition to the system of varna.

Many Bhakti period saints rejected the caste discriminations and accepted all castes, including untouchables, into their fold. During the British Raj, this sentiment gathered steam, and many Hindu reform movements such as *Brahmo Samaj* and *Arya Samaj* renounced caste-based discrimination. The inclusion of so-called untouchables into the mainstream was argued for by many social reformers. Mahatma Gandhi called them "*Harijans*" (children of God) although that term is now considered patronising and the term *Dalit* ("downtrodden") is the more commonly used. Gandhi's contribution toward the emancipation of the untouchables is still debated, especially in the commentary of his contemporary Dr. B.R. Ambedkar, an untouchable himself, who frequently saw Gandhi's activities as detrimental to the cause of upliftment of his people. The practice of untouchability was formally outlawed by the Constitution of India in 1950, and has declined significantly since then.

Caste under British Rule

The fluidity of the caste system was affected by the arrival of the British. Prior to that, the relative ranking of castes differed from one place to another. The castes did not constitute a rigid description of the occupation or the social status of a group. The British attempted to equate the Indian caste system to their own class system. They saw caste as an indicator of occupation, social standing, and intellectual ability. During the initial days of the British East India Company's rule, caste privileges and customs were encouraged, but the British law courts disagreed with the discrimination against the lower castes. However, British policies of divide and rule as well as enumeration of the population into rigid categories during the 10 year census contributed towards the hardening of caste identities.

CASTE SYSTEM IN MODERN INDIA

The leaders of independent India decided that India will be democratic, socialist and secular country. According to this policy there is a separation between religion and state. Practicing untouchability or discriminating a person based on his caste is legally forbidden. Along with this law the government allows positive discrimination of the depressed classes of India.

The Indians have also become more flexible in their caste system customs. In general the urban people in India are less strict about the caste system than the rural. In cities one can see different caste people mingling with each other, while in some rural areas there is still discrimination based on castes and sometimes also on untouchability. Sometimes in villages or in the cities there are violent clashes which, are connected to caste tensions. Sometimes the high castes strike the lower castes who dare to uplift their status. Sometimes the lower caste get back on the higher castes.

The Government of India has officially documented castes and subcastes, primarily to determine those deserving reservation (positive discrimination in education and jobs) through the census. The Indian reservation system, though limited in scope, relies entirely on quotas. The Government lists consist of Scheduled Castes, Scheduled Tribes and Other Backward Classes:

i) *Scheduled castes (SC):* Scheduled castes generally consist of former "untouchables" (the term "Dalit" is now preferred). The present population is 16 per cent of the total population of India (around 160 million). For example, the Delhi state has 49 castes listed as SC.

ii) *Scheduled tribes (ST):* Scheduled tribes generally consist of tribal groups. The present population is 7 per cent of the total population of India i.e. around 70 million.

iii) *Other Backward Classes (OBC):* The Mandal Commission covered more than 3000 castes under OBC Category and stated that OBCs form around 52 per cent of the Indian population. However, the National Sample Survey puts the figure at 32 per cent. There is substantial debate over the exact number of OBCs in India. It is generally estimated to be sizable, but many believe that it is lower than the figures quoted by either the Mandal Commission or the National Sample Survey.

The caste system is still very much prevalent in India and the effects of caste system in modern India can be seen in the form of quota systems, reservations, marriages etc. There are multiple effects of caste system in modern India. Metropolitan India has started walking away from the rigidity of the Indian caste system. This is the result of co mingling with other communities, higher education, globalisation and economic growth. The government of India has decided to issue job quotas to the less privileged castes and the so called backward classes. Caste based reservations in India have ignited the communal fire in a different way.

Caste based positive reservations were designed to reverse the discriminations based on caste. Inter caste marriages have served to abate the rigidity of caste culture in Indian society. Caste based violence and caste politics has opened the eyes of many people to the dangers of caste practices in modern India. Criticisms of caste system have been brought out by many liberal thinkers around the globe. It is in benefit of the people of India that they gradually remove the caste barrier from their mind to live in harmony and peace.

According to the central government policy these three categories are entitled for positive discrimination. Sometimes these three categories are defined together as Backward Classes. 15 per cent of India's population are Scheduled Castes. According to central government policy 15 per cent of the government jobs and 15 per cent of the students admitted to universities must be from Scheduled Castes. For the Scheduled Tribes about 7.5 per cent places are reserved which is their proportion in Indian population. The Other Backwards Classes are about 50 per cent of India's population, but only 27 per cent of government jobs are reserved for them.

Along with the central government, the state governments of India also follow a positive discrimination policy. Different states have different figures of communities entitled for positive discrimination based on the population of each state. Different state governments have different lists of communities entitled for positive discrimination. Sometimes a specific community is entitled for rights in a particular state but not in another state of India.

In modern India new tensions were created because of these positive discrimination policies. The high caste communities feel discriminated by the government policy to reserve positions for the Backward Classes. In many cases a large number of high caste members compete for a few places reserved for them. While the Backward Classes members do not have to compete at all because of the large number of reserved places for them compared to the candidates. Sometimes in order to fill the quota, candidates from the lower classes are accepted even though they are not suitable. Sometimes some reserved positions remain unmanned because there were few candidates from the lower classes causing more tension between the castes. Between the lower castes there are also tensions over reservation.

In the order of priority for a reserved place of the Backward Classes, candidate from the Scheduled castes is preferred over a candidate from the Scheduled Tribes who is preferred over a candidate from the other Backward Classes. As stated earlier Other Backward Classes are about 50 per cent of India's population but only 27 per cent of the Other Backward Classes are entitled for positive discrimination according to central government policy. Some Other Backward Classes communities are organising politically to be recognised as Backward Classes entitled for positive discrimination.

The Scheduled Tribes who are seen as the aborigins of India got ownership and certain rights over Indian land. Many communities in India claim also to be aborigins of India and they are claiming the same rights as the Scheduled Tribes.

The caste identity has become a subject of political, social and legal interpretation. Communities who get listed as entitled for positive discrimination do not get out of this list even if their social and political conditions get better. In many cases the legal system is involved to decide if a certain person is entitled for positive discrimination.

But with all this positive discrimination policy, most of the communities who were low in the caste hierarchy remain low in the social order even today. And communities who were high in the social hierarchy remain even today high in the social hierarchy. Most of the degrading jobs are even today done by the Dalits, while the Brahmans remain at the top of the hierarchy by being the doctors, engineers and lawyers of India.

The caste-based reservations in India have led to widespread protests, with many complaining of reverse discrimination against the forward castes (the castes that do not qualify for the reservation). The 2006 Indian anti-reservation protests are one major example. Many view negative treatment (or hatred) of forward castes as socially divisive and just as wrong.

Caste among non-Hindus

In some parts of India, the Christians are stratified by sect, location, and the castes of their predecessors, usually in reference to upper class Syrian Malabar Nasranis. Christians in Kerala are divided into several communities, including Syrian Christians and the so-called "Latin" or "New Rite" Christians. Syrian Christians, especially Knanaya Christians tend to be endogamous, and tend not to intermarry with other Christian castes. Also, very rarely are there intermarriages between Syrian Christians and Latin Rite Christians (converted in the 16th and 19th centuries) in Kerala; the latter were converted mainly from lower castes where fishing was the traditional occupation. Due to active conversion by Latin Missionaries in the coastal belt of Kerala, the new Latin converts were poor and deprived. So the Government of India gave them the social benefit of OBC status (Other Backward Classes) so that the deprived members of that community can be uplifted. It is a matter of great significance that Missionary activities were done by Western Latin rite missionaries who did not understand the significance of the caste system in India. None of the Syrian Churches ever indulged in these kinds of activities among the scheduled castes of India because they were aware of the prejudices of the caste system.

Syrian Christians derive status within the caste system from the tradition that they are converted Namboodiris and Jews, who were evangelised by St. Thomas. Writers Arundhati Roy and

Anand Kurian have written personal accounts of the caste system at work in their community.

Anthropologists have noted that the caste hierarchy among Christians in Kerala is much more polarised than the Hindu practices in the surrounding areas, due to a lack of jatis. Also, the caste status is kept even if the sect allegiance is switched.

In the Indian state of Goa, mass conversions were carried out by Portuguese Latin missionaries from the 16th century onwards. The Hindu converts retained their caste practices. The continued maintenance of the caste system among the Christians in Goa is attributed to the nature of mass conversions of entire villages, as a result of which existing social stratification was not affected. The Portuguese colonists, even during the Goan Inquisition, did not do anything to change the caste system. Thus, the original Hindu Brahmins in Goa now became Christian *Bamons* and the Kshatriya became Christian noblemen called *Chardos*. The Christian clergy became almost exclusively Bamon. Vaishyas who converted to Christianity became *Gauddos*, and Shudras became *Sudirs*. Finally, the Dalits or "Untouchables" who converted to Christianity became *Maharas* and *Chamars*.

Units of social stratification, termed as "castes" by many, have developed among Muslims in some parts of South Asia. Sources indicate that the castes among Muslims developed as the result of close contact with Hindu culture and Hindu converts to Islam. The Sachar Committee's report commissioned by the government of India and released in 2006, documents the continued stratification in Muslim society.

Among Muslims, those who are referred to as Ashrafs are presumed to have a superior status derived from their foreign Arab ancestry, while the Ajlafs are assumed to be converts from Hinduism, and have a lower status. In addition, there is also the *Arzal* caste among Muslims, who were regarded by anti-caste activists like Ambedkar as the equivalent of untouchables. In the Bengal region of India, some Muslims also stratify their society according to 'Quoms'. While many scholars have asserted that the Muslim Castes are not as acute in their discrimination as that among Hindus, some like Ambedkar argued otherwise, writing that the social evils in Muslim society were "worse than those seen in Hindu society".

The nastik Buddhists too have a caste system. In Sri Lanka, the Rodis have always been despised and they might have been out-casted by the Lankan Buddhists due to the absence of "ahimsa" (*non-violence*), which Buddhism heavily depends on. The writer Raghavan notes: "*That a form of worship in which human offerings formed the essential ritual would have been anathema to the Buddhist way of life goes without saying; and it needs no stretch of imagination that any class of people in whom the cult prevailed or survived even in an attenuated form would have been pronounced by the sangha (i.e. the Buddhist clergy) as exiles from the social order.*" Savarkar too believed that the status of the backward castes (e.g. Chamar) that performed non-violence only worsened. When Ywan Chwang travelled to South India after the period of the Chalukyan Empire, he noticed that the caste system had existed among the Buddhists and Jains.

The Jains too have castes in places such as Bihar. For example, in the village of Bundela, there are several "*jaats*" (*groups*) amongst the Jains. A person of one "*jaat*" cannot intermingle with a Jain or another "*jaat*". They also cannot eat with the members of other "*jaats*".

The Sikh Gurus criticised the hierarchy in the caste system. Where some castes were perceived by people as being better or higher than others (e.g. Brahmins being higher than others) they preached all sections of society were valuable and merit and hard-work were essential aspects of life. In Shiromani Gurdwara Prabandhak Committee, out of 140 seats, twenty are reserved for low caste Sikhs. However, the quota system has attracted much criticism due to the lack of meritocracy, where merit is considered the single most important component of winning a seat.

Caste-related Violences

Independent India has witnessed considerable amount of violence and hate crimes motivated by caste. Ranvir Sena, a caste-supremacist fringe paramilitary group based in Bihar, has committed violent acts against Dalits and other members of the scheduled caste community. Phoolan Devi, who belonged to *Mallah* lower-caste, was mistreated and raped by upper-caste Thakurs at a young age. She then became a bandit and carried out violent robberies against upper-caste people. In 1981, her gang massacred twenty-two Thakurs, most of whom were not involved in her kidnapping or rape. Phoolan Devi went on to become a politician and Member of Parliament.

Over the years, various incidents of violence against Dalits, such as Kherlanji Massacre have been reported from many parts of India. At the same time, many violent protests by Dalits, such as the 2006 Dalit protests in Maharashtra, have been reported as well.

Caste Politics

Until the mid-1970s, the politics of independent India was largely dominated by economic issues and questions of corruption. But since 1980s, caste has emerged as a major issue in the politics of India. The Mandal Commission was established in 1979 to "identify the socially or educationally backward", and to consider the question of seat reservations and quotas for people to redress caste discrimination. In 1980, the commission's report affirmed the affirmative action practice under Indian law whereby members of lower castes were given exclusive access to a certain portion of government jobs and slots in public universities. When V. P. Singh Government tried to implement the recommendations of Mandal Commission in 1989, massive protests were held in the country. Many alleged that the politicians were trying to cash in on caste-based reservations for purely pragmatic electoral purposes.

Many political parties in India have openly indulged in caste-based votebank politics. Parties such as Bahujan Samaj Party (BSP), the Samajwadi Party and the Janata Dal claim that they are representing the backward castes, and rely primarily on OBC support, often in alliance with Dalit and Muslim support to win the elections. Remarkably, what is called a landmark election in the history of India's biggest state of Uttar Pradesh, the Bahujan Samaj Party was able to garner majority in the State assembly Elections with the support of the brahmin community.

References

Blunt. E.A.H. *The Caste System of North India*. S.Chand Publishers. 1969.

Srinivas, M. N. *Religion and Society among the Coorgs of South India*. Oxford. 1952.

Aggarwal, Patrap. *Caste and Social Stratification Among Muslims in India.* Manohar. 1978.

Jogendra Nath Bhattacharya, *Hindu Castes and Sects, Munshiram Manoharlal,* Delhi. 1896.

Ghurye, G. S. *Caste, Class and Occupation.* Popular Book Depot, Bombay. 1961.

Jaffrelot, Christophe. *India's Silent Revolution: The Rise of the Lower Castes.* C. Hurst & Co. 2003.

Kane, Pandurang Vaman. *History of Dharmasastra: (ancient and mediaeval, religious and civil law).* Poona. Bhandarkar Oriental Research Institute. 1962.

Murray Milner, Jr. *Status and Sacredness: A General Theory of Status Relations and an Analysis of Indian Culture,* New York: Oxford University Press. 1994.

2

CASTE REFORMS

The 19th century is the environment where the ideas of nationalism, independence, radicalism, liberalism and etc. were first began to grow on Indian soil. So it is very important to study the Indian situation during this period in order to see the caste system against the test of time and against its strongest opponent the modernism and westernisation.

With the advent of the British as the political head of society things were bound to take on a different aspect. The British brought with them their own traditional form of government, and as Christians they could not have much sympathy with the institutions of the Hindus. As prudent foreigners wishing the consolidate their power over a strange land and people they decided to leave the peculiar institutions of the country severely alone except where they egregiously violated their cherished ideas of government. They introduced a system of education which did not demand of the learners any change of religion. Another factor that has to be considered is the practical reason that made British rulers to educate Indians. Indian was as huge as it is today making it very hard to govern. To avoid this; British rulers had to teach locals to be employed in administration in lower ranks as well as military services. The army which helped the British to control the subcontinent was more than half in percent of locals. This is not a unique solution, where the Moghuls and other Muslim rulers which conquered India found the same solution. Because of the need which the British administration felt, a class of educated Indians was born and became much bigger in number and also stronger within the Indian society.

The need for administration was the primary motivating factor in British educational policy. The bureaucracy had to be staffed by Indians, and the need for a class of clerks to help govern the Empire was what lay behind, Macaulay's famous 1852 "Minute in Education" which called for the creation of a class of Indian intermediaries who would be "English in manner and moral". Consequently, the colleges that developed overwhelmingly emphasised a classical and arts curriculum, designed indeed not to teach science or technology but to pass on English morals. The need for change was first felt by those early social reformers like the Ram Mohan Roy and others following, who were all educated by British educational system and learned to think like Westerners..

The reformists who put their marks on the nineteenth century India, were not backed by the British administration itself. Most of the nationalist Indians claim that British do nothing to change the social defects of Indian culture. This might not be hundred percent true. But we can say that those reformists were the ones who were charmed by the ideas of equality, nationalism and other ideologies. Those reform demands were not realised by the British rulers but by the Indian intellectual themselves. During the nineteenth century and under the British rule the position of the low caste Hindus did not witness a real change that can be called a reform.

Pre-British Caste Conflicts

Although it can be supposed that the caste system was a solid rock which faced no change and no challenge at all, we would be very wrong. Although some of the nationalist and religious Hindu writers claim that caste system was in reality a perfect system of division of labour conceptualised by the perfect religion of Hinduism, which also satisfied one and the all; in reality throughout the history there were challenges within the Indian society to the existence and validity of the caste system.

The motivation for challenging the caste system had been various. Caste system was a system that was integrative and stabilising just like other social orders; but at the same time included and produced movements that aimed to reform or destroy it. Who had this motivation included the groups assigned to a low status within the system had most interest in participating in movements against it, and such movements tended to take their most radical form in the more outlying region of India, the last to be "Aryanised ", that is, southern and eastern India, well as in the northwestern regions open to continuing migration and new cultural influences. Finally, these movements can be partially understood in ten of the potential lines of " dichotomisation " within the caste system itself. The most basic of these were the division between Brahman and Kshatriya, sacred priest-and secular ruler, on the one hand; and even more important, division between "twice-born " Brahmans, Kshatriyas and Vaishyas, and remainder of the population, which are Shudras and untouchables.

Just like any other place on earth, the rulers had to build good relations with the priest class. Because the legitimising force within the society was the holy men at those time. It is interesting to see that the two major movements against the classical Brahmanism were the ones leaded by Buddha and Mahavir, which were the founders of Buddhism and Jainism. These two men were both from the ruler class.

Most of the revolts against the Brahmanic priestly rule were coming from the rulers. The rulers had not to be a specific caste, where we can count a handful of rulers from the Shudras. In the 18th century, under the impact of a vigorous trade, particularly in pepper, the rule of Travancore in southwestern India led a "modernising " political in which he smashed the power of feudatory nobles allied with Brahman councilors of the biggest temple in his kingdom, annexed (not simply conquered) surrounding territory, and established a genuinely bureaucratic state manned with officials who were " gifted commoners " paid by and loyal to the king.

This is an interesting example about the upper and lower caste relations in India. A Shudra king claming for the authority but besides claming for being an upper caste. The king displayed amassive effort to build up the picture of the himself as a father to his subjects and a servant to God. Martanda Varma, In fact dedicated his entire kingdom to his tutelary deity, Shri Padmana Swami. The King of Travancore was declared to be the vassal or gent of the deity. In the thirties the powerful temple organisation had been smashed. This gesture, which came in 1750, maishalled religion behind the monarchy.What must be emphasised is that while it was not revolutionary at all, but simply a Sanskritising process for rulers to claim a high or Kshatriya status, it did represent a revolutionary opposition to the system for then to claim superiority in terms of sacred values. While this did not very frequently occur within traditional India, the case of Travancore's creative response to European commercial penetration indicates that forces of modernisation and revolt against caste hierarchy did exist within pre-British India.

Finally, it may be noted that when after British conquest a "Kshatriya ideology" emerged in Maharashtra as a conservative form of anti-Brahmanism, it did present a tradition of Kshatriya opposition that contained elements undermining the whole hierarchy and its opposition of pure-priesthood to secular kingship.

If it is to be said that economic and political revolution in India required, in the process, a religion-based revolution against caste, it is undeniable that such—revolutions have been attempted throughout Indian history. These were the great bhakti, or religious devotional movements, spread over at least fourteen centuries. They had the common characteristics of asserting an anti-caste equalitarianism (including greater equality for women), a monotheism which emphasised the devotional relationship between the worshipper and deity as opposed to Vedantic monism and priestly ritualism, and of being based primarily among low caste peasants and artisans with foundations in outlying regions such as the south (Tamilnad and later Maharashtra), the east (Bengal), and the northwest (Panjab).

Demands for Reform

The influence of the western educational institutions including the missionary schools was very strong over the subcontinent. We have to remember that British colonialists had not yet full control over the hole sub-continent when those demands for reform first introduced to society. Within the previous centuries where there was no real occupation but mostly commercial colonisation, a mutual cultural exchangehad already begun. 19th century is the period for the products to be harvested.

First reformist's demands did not come from the low castes of the society. Although there had been a hard pressure on them for almost three millenniums the first reform ideas came from the upper castes namely Brahmans and Kshatriyas. This position can be easily understood when we think that at those times not a letter were to be passed to the low castes considering them as impure and teaching them words meant insult to the sacred religion of Hinduism. Words could only be instructed to the holy people the Brahmans who were created from the head of the god Indra. So India had to wait for some low caste pupils to get through the barriers put forward by the Brahmins and reach the knowledge.

And it was the western influence and newly established western schools which gave them this chance of learning. So we had to wait for half a century to see the Dalits in action, demanding equal rights. One other reason for the upper castes to move first was the fact that they were in close connection with the westerners and facing them in their daily lives. This opportunity gave them the ability to exchange ideas and experience the western look to the problems. They were the first who felt a reform within Indian society, some triggered by the loss of his relatives to strange religious customs like the example of Ram Mohan Roy who lost his own sister. Because of the fact that the upper castes were the first ones who felt the need for a cultural reform, the issues put in the context of reform had nothing to do with the abolishment of the caste system and giving equal rights to the lower castes. What they demanded were abolishing the customs such as sati or equality for women.

Jotirao Phule and the Dalit Movement

Three factors were to assume importance for the growth of Untouchable movements as the 19th century progressed. The first was the attitude and influence of British officials. The second was the effect of missionary activities on local Untouchable communities. The third was a growing realisation among all Indians, including Untouchables that in education lay the key to future political power, as the British government prepared to extend limited representative institutions to Indians themselves. These were the factors for the start of the Dalit movement, but they were also the reasons or causes for the great Dalit leaders to emerge like Jotirao Phule.

In the biography of Phule written for his famous book "Slavery: In the Civilised British Government under the Cloak of Brahmanism" by Dr. Y. D. Phadke, Phule is desrcribed as:

> Jotirao Govindrao Phule occupies a unique position among the social reformers of Maharashtra in the nineteenth century. While other reformers concentrated more on reforming the social institutions of amily and marriage with special emphasis on the status and right of women, Jotirao Phule revolted against the unjust caste system under which millions of people had suffered for centuries. In particular, he courageously upheld the cause of the untouchables and look up the cudgels for the poorer peasants. He was a militant advocate of their right.

Phule was the first low caste reformist within India. The book indicated above was a book written in a drama style to inform the uneducated low caste population and it was published in 1873.

Phule was born in 1827 as the son of a gardener in Poona. Originally Jotirao's family known as Gorhays, came from Katgun, a village in the Satara district of Maharashtra. Since Jotirao's father and two uncles served as florists under the last of the Peshwas, they came to be known as 'Phule'. Jotirao had to leave his education after finishing the primary school to help his family work. But by the encouragement of his neighbours who were also teachers, his father accepted to send him to a Scottish Missionary School to continue his secondary school education. He was married in the age as early as thirteen. It was in his this school that he met Sadashiv Ballal Govande, a Brahmin, who remained a close friend throughout his life. Both Jotirao and Govande were greatly influenced by Thomas Paine's ideas and they read with great interest Paine's famous book 'The Rights of Man.' Moro Vithal Valvekar and Sakharam Yashwant Paranjapye were two other Brahmin friends of Jotirao who in later years stood by him in all his activities.

We can track the social changes in the Indian society just looking at the life of this reformist figure. The eye-catching things here are his education in a Scottish Missionary School and his Brahman friends who shared same ideals with him throughout his life. During those days liberalism was also a trend within Brahmin society demanding a change in the Hindu social structure. Ram

Mohan Roy and Brahmin reformists following him were demanding to clean the society from the defections of the Hindu religious and social system. In it is not a surprise to see dozens of reformists emerging from every level of society during this period. Those reformists were the ones who build the base for the real social change throughout the whole 19th and 20th century.

The first period, in which the reformation movements began, Phule was not alone as a low caste member. He had close friends from the Brahmin caste. Naturally those Brahmans who tended to become his friends or to work with him were not orthodox Brahmins. They were Brahman reformers who also had interests for changing the society. This close connection made these two groups, Brahman reformers and Dalit reformers to cooperate and sometimes to work together. Phule himself protected those Brahman reformers with his followers when they fell under orthodox pressure in various cases.

Phule's main role was to be an educator before being a political leader. He established various schools one after another to encourage education within the Dalits, a right that was prohibited by the Brahmans for thousands of years. He was also in favour of women whose position was much more problematic than the Dalit man. The first school he established was a school for girls in 1848. This school was followed by two others, which were established in 1851 and 1852. He established another school for the untouchables in 1852. During these educational efforts he saw an important help from those Brahman reformers. But in time this support faded away with the rise of Hindu orthodoxy.

Phule as a reformer stand against the cultural values of the Hindu society very clearly. Naturally his main concern was equality as a low caste member. The problem of equality was not same in the beginning when the first verses of Vedas were chanted long before the birth of Christ. This is not an exact knowledge but it is what we can understand from within the verses. What we know certain is the establishment of Laws of Manu a few centuries before the Christ. That was the turning point which defined the destiny of low castes as semi-slaves and cemented the structure of the Indian society. The caste problem became the very heart of the Indian culture from this point. And thousands of years later this problem became the main point of political and cultural discussions and the whole reform movements. It was so well established in people's mind that the upper caste reformers who encouraged the destruction of caste system, could not stand the pressures forced on them by their own caste members. So 19th century is a period where we can observe this gradual change from liberalism to extremism within the Brahman and upper caste society.

From the point of view of equality, the entire caste system and the authoritarian family structure was to be condemned. From the point of view of rationality, the whole system of superstition and religious traditionalism was to be overthrown, the whole corpus of religious writings stripped of authority. With this as his beginning point, Phule was saved from a good deal of unnecessary arguments, qualifications, compromises and logical inconsistencies. He did not, for instance, waste much breath arguing over the relative merits of different parts of the Hindu sacred scriptures. He simply treated them as legends, which may offer some insight into past Indian history, and as products of a group (Brahmans, Aryans) seeking to establish control over the minds of the people.

As the caste system interpreted as the main factor of Hindu religion there was no way for Dalit reformers to dismiss the dominant religious tradition. Although Phule accepted the assumption that something had to be put in its place: even a revolutionary culture required a moral-religious centre. At that point we can observe the affects of Semitic religions Christianity and Islam. With the inspirations of Semitic ideas most of the 19th century reformers interpreted the Hindu religion once more to clean it from deficits. Phule was not an exception just like Ram Mohan Roy. In his efforts to rationalise the religion, Phule did not reject the idea of dharma but rather attempted to establish a universalistic one.

Sarvajanik Satya Dhanrma (Public Religion of Truth) expresses this concept completely; the moral basis of society had to be centered on truth, or rationality, and it had to be one that unified all men and women as equals rather than fragmenting and dividing them into separate social groups with separate responsibilities and rights (as the traditional idea of dharma did in separating the castes). The world was seen as good and holy, in contradiction to the Vedantic idea of it as an illusion, because it is God's creation; and God as is seen in simple terms as the loving parent (in the Indian expression which avoids Semitic patriarchalism, ma-bap) of all humans who are thus equally valued as his children. Orthodox opponents claiming him to become Christian regarding his education in a missionary over expressed this point of Phule.

Phule was something more than being a mentor or philosopher. He was also a man of action, organising the people and establishing a new movement. He became the pioneer of Dalit political movement with the establishment of Satyasdohak Samaj in 1873.

But as the disillusionment with the British rule began to grow, the liberals lost their importance and militant nationalists like Tilak, Aurobindo and Lajpat Rai emerged as new leaders. Tilak or Aurobindo, unlike the liberals, drew inspiration from India's past. Not solely that. With the emergence of the militants, swaraj or self-governance became the primary agenda. Politics was becoming more and more intense. And finally, with the emergence of Gandhi (1869-1948), politics acquired an altogether different meaning. Gandhi succeeded in mobilising various sections of the people – workers, peasants, capitalists, students, lawyers and above all, women—in the nationalist movement. In this process of alienation within the reform movements between Dalit and upper caste intelligentsia. Phule was the one who build a political movement to advocate lower caste rights. Other followers continued the movement he established where Dr. Ambedkar became a striking figure in the first half of the 20th century.

ETHNICISATION OF CASTE

The caste system has been traditionally analysed as based on the notion of ritual purity. In this view, its holistic character implies that the dominant values that of the Brahmins, are regarded by the whole society as providing universal references, role models. Hence the central role played by Sanskritisation, a practice that M.N. Srinivas has defined as 'the process in which a "low" Hindu caste, or tribal or other group, changes its customs, ritual, ideology and way of life in the direction of a high, and frequently, "twice-born' caste" that is the Brahmins, but also the Kshatriyas or even the Vaishyas. Low castes may for instance adopt the most prestigious features of the Brahmins' diet and therefore emulate vegetarianism.

Such a process reflects a special coherence in society, all the groups admitting the values of the upper castes as the legitimate value system. Such coherence is not synonymous with cohesion. In fact, sanskritisation itself bears witness of an aspiration to social mobility and therefore tensions: low castes constantly try to improve their social status by imitating the high castes and contest the position, which has been assigned to them in the system. Moreover, the myths of origin of the low castes are always centered around the idea of an initial decline: even Untouchable castes claim to descend from Brahmin castes and that they have fallen from this rank often because of the malicious intent of upper caste people.

The myth of origin of the Chamars is very telling in this aspect: their original ancestor was the youngest of four Brahmans brethren who went to bathe in a river and found a cow struggling in a quicksand. They sent the youngest brother in to rescue the animal, but before he could get to the spot it had been drowned. He was compelled therefore by his brothers to remove the carcass and after he had done this they turned him out of their caste and gave him the name of Chamar. The four brothers epitomise in this narrative the Brahmins, the Kshatriyas, the Vaishyas and the Shudras.

According M. N. Srinivas, such myths do not reflect the existence of a separate, untouchable identity. They take caste for granted, and by stressing their brotherhood with Brahmans, they acknowledge the superiority of the latter. This is pure sanskritisation. For Srinivas, the mobility associated with Sanskritisation results only in positional changes in the system and does not lead to any structural change. That is, a caste moves up above its neighbours and another comes down, but all this takes place in an essentially stable hierarchical order.

While the Brahmins are the main objects of imitation, Srinivas points out that the sanskritisation process does not refer to them only. The Kshatriyas are often chosen as role models too. D.F. Pocock even suggests that there is a 'Kingly model of Hindu society'. However this style of self-promotion did not simply rely on the imitation of the superior. In fact the second varna has been one of the main avenues for social mobility because the Shudras could conquer power and replace Kshatriyas as rulers on the basis of their mere strength and because Brahmins then legitimised their rise by evolving the needed genealogies. Srinivas indeed points out that 'the Kshatriya category was the most open one in the caste system'. While this openness is a very important element in the promotion of the low castes, it does not question the system either since it has to be sanctioned by Brahmins who retain their paramount importance and whose values remain supreme.

Historically, low caste groups have also explored avenues for upward mobility through the bhakti movements and the sectarian model. Since the Buddha, gurus have recurrently questioned the caste system on behalf of the fundamental equality of men before god. Their disciples who were initiated into monastic orders forgot about their caste to form new fraternities. Srinivas emphasised that the 'protest sects' in a way 'offered opportunities for mobility to members of the so-called low castes'. However, this equality was other worldly: it did not affect the social order. Ambedkar rightly pointed out that 'from the point of view of the annihilation of caste, the struggle of the saints did not have any effect on society. The traditional caste system was more directly challenged during the British Raj.

The development of the means of communications in the 19th century led to the opening up of the jati which, till then, was confined to a reduced territory, delimited by matrimonial relations. Hence the emergence of horizontal solidarities and the territorial extension of the frontiers of caste. The members of a same jati were enabled to migrate to find jobs or even obliged to do so, if they were transferred within the British administration for instance. The State building process played an important role since it led to the establishment of an all India bureaucracy. Transfers of bureaucrats out of their native place often generated feelings of anomie and made the finding of the suitable match for endogamous marriages more complicated; hence the idea to create associations which could link members of a same caste.

These institutions were also stirred up by the census, which was a key element in the formation of the colonial state. From 1871 onwards the British enumerated the castes (like the religious groups) and therefore these 'human groups (castes) [we]re treated to a considerable extent as abstractable from the regional and territorial contexts in which they function[ed]'. This effect reinforced those of the state construction process but the census also raised among several castes the sentiment of having common interests since the British did not content themselves with enumerating them ; they also classified them.

In 1901, the Census Commissioner, Risley, decided to give the ranking of the jatis in their local context and their varna, which was a much more delicate enterprise. Castes immediately organised themselves and even formed councils to take steps to see that their status was recorded in the way they thought was honourable to them. Caste associations were therefore created also as pressure groups whose aim was to improve their rank in the census. This process was especially prominent among the low castes and therefore gives 'An indication of the widespread desire for mobility among the backward castes...'. Each census provided castes with an opportunity to petition the government for getting a higher place in the order of precedence and for being recorded under new, sanskritised, names. In 1911, 16 did so and in 1921, 20 in northern India, including Kurmis, Gadariyas, Kacchi, Ladhs and Ahirswho wanted all to be recognised as Kshatriyas. Indeed, this move was in keeping with the logic of sanskritisation since the objective was not to opt out from the system but to rise within it according to its own rules and values.

However, castes associations secularised and became gradually mutual aid structures, in charge of founding schools for the caste's children, creating co-operative movements and claiming new advantages from the state. The caste associations, from then on, tended to become interest groups. The Rudolph therefore underline their modern character – in a western sense. They behaved like a collective enterprise with economic and political objectives, in a way, which brings to mind the image of "lobbies". They had their head office, their publications, their list of members, and their organisation chart. Generally, their leaders did not come from the most prestigious clans or families but from those of the castemen who were the most educated, able to negotiate with the state and often as ambitious as the political entrepreneurs of Joseph Schumpeter. In many cases, they came from the younger generation. However, the transformational potentialities of caste associations must not be exaggerated since they were not conducive to social change per se.

The associations representing upper castes were often very conservative, as evident from the case of the Kanya-Kubja Brahmins, a jati widely dispersed across Uttar Pradesh, Madhya Pradesh and Rajasthan. In 1884, a Kanya-Kubja caste association was created in Lucknow. An all India association grew out from it in 1901 and established local branches all over the Hindi belt. It was founded for helping the Kanya-Kubja Brahmins to compete with Kayasths, Banyas and other Brahmins of North India in terms of education and administrative jobs. It supported the development of educational institutions, boarding schools, sponsored grants and newspapers which were intended to foster solidarity within the caste. The number of local branches increased until the mid-1930s when then it declined, partly because of the Congress' opposition to caste movements. However, it started to rise again in the 1950s in order to protect the Kanya-Kubja Brahmins against the "threat" that represented affirmative action measures in favour of the lower castes.

Among the non-dvijas, caste associations often merely served as vehicles for sanskritisation in North India. The Kayasths of North India were probably the first to show the way in that direction. In late XIXth century, Munshi Kali Prasad, a Lucknow-based rich lawyer from this caste, wrote Kayasthas Ethnology, a book where he showed 'to which of the four great divisions of the Aryans in India [,the Kshatriyas,] the Kayasthas belonged'. Subsequently, the Kayasths claimed that they were the descendants of the Emperor Chandragupta.

In 1873 Kali Prasad set up in Lucknow a fortnightly magazine Kayastha Samachar and a Kayasth Dharma Sabha whose main task was to educate the caste's children. A primary school – Kayastha Pathshala – was opened in Allahabad for poor and orphan children of the caste. In 1877, it became an Anglo-Vernacular middle school, then a high school and in 1895, an intermediate college.

The Kayastha Conference was founded in 1886 on the basis of the Kayasth Dharma Sabha. The first resolution it passed at its first annual meeting in 1887 stressed the need 'to improve the educational and moral status of the Community' by opening new schools for which money was raised by the association. It also tried 'to encourage the community to undertake commercial and other respectable pursuits and not to rely solely on clerical or literary avocations'. The Conference aimed at uniting the Kayasths and therefore decided 'to prepare a National Directory of the Chandraguptavanshi Kayastha community', which was intended 'to promote union and co-operation by a knowledge of their distant and scattered brethren'. It established mutual aid programmes for the neediest Kayasth families to enable them to finance the study of their sons or the marriage of their daughters, etc. Parallel to this strong emphasis on socio-economic developments, the conference did not neglect the initial sanskritisation objectives of Kali Prasad. It had a Temperance section and repeatedly—and allegedly successfully—requested the Kayasths to give up drinking.

The Kayastha Conference is revealing for the ambivalence of caste associations: on the one hand, it endeavoured to promote the status of the Kayasths in the sanskritisation logic; on the other, it was created to fight against the restrictions of job opportunities in the administration of British India. However, the Kayastha Conference still endeavoured in the 1920s-1930s to sanskritise caste rituals and invited its members to emulate the 'dvijas'. Certainly, this attitude stemmed from modern motives since the main reason for sanskritisation was to standardise the Kayasth culture and to create a homogenous social group, however, sanskritisation remained the key idiom, with its emphasis on positional mobility instead of structural changes, to use Srinivas' words. The most important social change that caste associations have achieved probably concerns the unity of the caste groups. They have successfully incited the sub-castes to adopt the same name in the Census and to break the barriers of endogamy, even if, within a caste, the members of the upper class still tend to intermarry—but then it is more economic endogamy than purely caste-based endogamy.

Ethnicisation of Caste in South India

The ethnicisation of caste seems to have begun first in South India. This process has been observed by Robert Hardgrave in the case of the Nadars of Tamil Nadu whose caste association, the Nadar Mahajana Sangam was founded in 1910 and promoted what he calls 'caste fusion', as 'the unit of endogamy expanded'. S. Barnett maintains that this kind of fusion tended to transform castes into ethnic groups. His demonstration is based on another Tamil case study, the Kontaikkatti Vellalars who do not represent a large number of people but are influential since many of them are landlords. From 1920 onwards, the caste association has encouraged them to expand endogamy in new territories and to other Vellallars in order to make up for their numerical weakness. It may then be one of the first examples of caste federations. For Barnett these innovations confront the entire ideological field of caste hierarchy, since 'blood purity', on which, according to him _ relies ritual purity has lost its importance. The relevant unit is not the original jati any more, but groups of castes, which represents the transition from caste to ethnic like regional caste blocs. "Ethniclike" because each such unit is potentially independent of other such units, defined and characterised by a heritable substance internal to the unit itself and not affected, in terms of membership in the unit, by transactions with others outside the unit. Rather than the conceptual holism of caste, we begin to see the antecedent autonomy of its component parts. In an ethniclike situation transactional ranking no longer orders the parts of the whole, and caste interdependence is replaced by regional-caste bloc independence. However, intermarriages are only one aspect of the ethnicisation of caste which also implies a collective history—at least a golden Age—and a separate, cultural identity. The subjective representation of the collective self is most important for the issue we are dealing with. Caste is partly a mindset. It is based on beliefs in hierarchies relying on purity and impurity – what Ambedhar called 'graded inequality'. Alternative social imaginaries might be conducive to the emancipation of the lower castes. As M.S.A. Rao argues: 'The problem of identity is crucial in the formation of protest groups and for collective mobilisation':

Deprived sections of society in different parts of the world have organises themselves into protest movements to fight against discriminations of various kinds based on colour, religion, caste and tribe. Their problem, however, has been one of establishing a new identity – the kind of image that they want to protect in order to gain self-respect, honour and status.

Such a change in collective identity is precisely at stake in the process of ethnic identity building by lower castes. This kind of ethnicisation of castes or caste federations are much more conducive to social change than caste associations or caste fusion pure and simple.

Ethnicisation of Caste in Western India

The ethnicisation process is well illustrated by the Satyashodak Movement developed by Phule in the Bombay Presidency in the late 19th century, which was not a caste movement since it intended to represent the 'bahujan samaj', the majority of the people, the masses. Jotirao Phule (1827-1890) was a Mali (market gardener), a cultivating caste in close contact with towns where its members sold their products. In one of these towns, Poona, Phule could attend a school of the Scottish Mission. What he learnt about the Blacks in the United States suggested to him a comparison with the lower castes—hence his book, Slavery that he dedicated 'to the good people of the United States as a taken of admiration for their sublime disinterested and self sacrificing devotion in the cause of Negro Slavery; and with an earnest desire, that my country men may take their noble example as their guide in the emancipation of their sudra Brethren from the trammels of Brahmin thraldom'.

The writings of Thomas Paine exerted a special influence on Phule who discovered the individualist values of liberty and equality in The Age of Reason and Human Rights. This source of inspiration developed in conjunction with that of Christianity. For Phule, Jesus-Christ epitomises equality and fraternity. He also regards him as the spokesman for the poor people. However, Phule did not convert to Christianity and even translated the Christian idiom into a new discourse focused on King Bali, the subterranean god who reigns in the underground world according to Hindu mythology.

Through the vernacularisation of Christian values and symbols, Phule endowed them with a new, positive identity to his people. He even gave them a new history on the basis of some of the findings of Orientalism. In 1792, William Jones had deduced from the discovery of the Indo-European linguistic family the notion of a common, original race whose branches had migrated towards Europe and India. This theory was developed during the nineteenth century by many German philologists such as Albrecht Weber, R. Roth, A. Kuhn and J. Möhl (whose books were published in the 1840s-1850s). In their writings appear the notions of 'Sanskritic race' or 'Vedic people'. These speculations reached India from the late 1850s onwards through Max Müller, who tended to be somewhat more cautious, and Muir who published in 1860 a study on 'The Trans-Himalayan Origin of the Hindus, and their affinity with the western branches of the Aryan race'.

The first Hindu nationalist ideologues of the late 19th century and early 20th century—from Dayananda to Tilak—borrowed heavily from the European orientalists. Among other themes, the one they used assiduously related to the common racial origin of the European and Indian people and its corollary, the southward migration which they interpreted to prove that the Hindus were the first race and that they once dominated the whole world. This myth helped the first Hindu revivalists to regain certain self-esteem by claiming that their ancestors were the first inhabitants of the world.

Phule used the Aryan theory to his own advantage: the fact that upper castes leaders traced their origin from Aryan conquerors could be used to argue that they descended from foreigners and that their culture, including the caste system was alien to India's original people. Phule, therefore, portrayed the Aryans as invaders who had settled in India at a rather late period to subjugate the first inhabitants of India and destroyed their civilisation. For him, the low castes were the descendents of these people. In this reinterpretation of the past, the invaders are identified as Brahmins whereas the indigenous groups are described as descending from the original ruling class, the Kshatriyas. In Phule's ideology, this category does not refer to the second varna but includes all original Indians, from peasant castes to Untouchables. For him, they formed a people, united by the bond of a common origin and of a warrior ethos:

> The Kshatriyas in India (the land of Baliraja) that is the original masters of the land here where known as Astiks, Pishachas, Rakshasas, Ahirs, Kakatas, Bhut, Kolis, Mangs,

> Mahars etc. They were extremely adept in fighting without the aid of arms (weapons) and were famed as brave and valiant warriors. They were of an epicurean (joyful) temperament and were given to the enjoyment of the goods things of life. The kingdoms of most of these rulers (chiefs) were in a prosperous condition, and it would be no exaggeration to say that the land of King Bali was literally flowing with milk and honey.

This description does not only present the original rulers of India as brave warriors but also emphasises their sense of manliness and honour while fighting (they did not use weapons) and their good nature. Such a narrative prepared the ground for the stereotype of the 'good salvage' that will be applied to the Indian aborigines. The king of these original Kshatriyas, Bali, is described by Phule as reigning over a rich country and this prosperity was the very reason for the Aryan invasions:

> The extreme fertility of the soil of India, its rich productions, the proverbial wealth of the people, and the other innumerable gifts which this favourable land enjoys, and which have more recently tempted the cupidity of the Western nations, attracted the Aryans [...] The original inhabitants with whom these earth-born gods, the Brahmans, fought, were not inappropriately termed Rakshasas, that is the protectors of the land [...] The cruelties which the European settlers practised on the American Indians on their first settlement in the new world had certainly their parallel in India in the advent of the Aryans and their subjugation of the aborigines [...] They originally settled on the banks of the Ganges whence they spread gradually over the whole of India. In order, however, to keep a better hold on the people they devised that weird system of mythology, the ordination of caste, and the code of crude and inhuman laws to which we can find no parallel among the other nations.

Phule's endeavour had a pioneering dimension since he was probably the first low caste leader who avoided the traps of sanskritisation by endowing the low caste with an alternative value system. For the first time, the low castes were presented as ethnic groups which had inherited the legacy of an antiquarian golden age and whose culture was therefore distinct from that of the wider Hindu society ; secondly, his efforts in favour of the low castes were not confined to his castemen only: he wanted to unite the Shudras and the Atishudras (dalits). As early as 1853 he opened schools for Untouchables. He projected himself as the spokesman of the non-Brahmins at large and, indeed, kept targeting the Brahmins in vehement pamphlets where he presented them as rapacious moneylenders corrupts priests eager to extort as much as they could from poor and ignorant villagers.

Phule was also the first low caste organiser. In 1875 he was attracted by the Arya Samaj, but he kept his distance from this movement because he did not trust the upper caste reformers who pretended to fight against the social system even though they observed its rules. Phule also remained aloof from the Congress, which he regarded as a Brahmin movement. Nationalism, according to him, was an illusion created by upper caste manipulation to conceal the inner divisions of Indian society. He founded the Satyashodak Samaj in 1873 in order to strengthen the sentiment of unity among the low castes. He narrated pseudo-historical episodes bearing testimony of the traditional solidarity between the Mahars and Shudras and protested against the Brahmins' stratagems for dividing the low castes. At least in the late 19 century and early 20 century, the Satyashodak idiom embraced rich peasants as well as agricultural tenants who belonged to very different castes and in some places 'the Sathya Shodhak message seemed to have reached even the untouchable'. A major spokesman of the non-Brahmin movement in Maharashtra in the 1910-1930, Mukundrao Patil, the son of Phule's colleague, Krishnarao Bhalekar, was for instance a radical defender of the Untouchables even though he was a rich peasant. He advocated 'the general Satyashodak ideology, of opposition to Sanskritisation and assertion of the " non-Aryan " unity of Maharashtrian natives'. By that time, Phule's view of the non-brahmins as non-Aryas had made an impact on the small dalit intelligentsia. In 1909, Kisan Faguji Bansode (1870-1946), a Mahar from Nagpur, warned the upper castes in the following terms:

> The Aryans—your ancestors—conquered us and gave us unbearable harassment. At that time we were your conquest, you treated us even worse than slaves and subjected us to any torture you wanted. But now we are no longer your

> subjects, we have no service relationship with you, we are not your slaves or serfs...

The Satyashodak Samaj eventually attracted even Marathas such as the Jedhe family who from Poona realised 'the futility of a purely Maratha politics'. Keshavrao Jedhe adopted 'the long-held Satyashodak view of history: Brahmans were outsiders to the country and to the ethnic community of true " Hindus "; they desired only their own caste superiority and consolidated their power through treachery, through falsification of historical records, and by weaving a web of religious slavery which set up a social hierarchy of superiority and inferiority and divided the masses'.

Maratha princes such as the Maharajah of Baroda strongly approved of Phule's ideological commitments and donated large amounts of money to his movement. A direct descendant of Shivaji, the Maharajah of Kolhapur, Shahu, who reigned between 1894 and 1922 and who was 'intensely proud of his Maratha lineage', was even more supportive. He recruited Maratha Satyas Satyashodaks in his administration. In 1902 he even reserved 50 per cent of the vacancies in the state administration for 'the members of the backward communities'.

Shahu patronised the establishment of the Satyashodak Samaj in Kolhapur in 1911. He promoted inter-caste dining and introduced the Inter-caste Marriage Act in 1918 at Kolhapur. In 1920 he appointed Maratha priests to circumvent the Brahmins and soon after established the Kshatriya Vedic School to train Maratha priests. The very name of this school suggests that Shahu was still acting in the framework of sanskritisation. Indeed, he tried to secure for the Marathas the status of Kshatriyas and in fact he broke with the local Brahmins in 1900 when they refused to recognise his family's claim to this status and accordingly refused to perform certain rituals. He wanted to 'kshatriyase' the Untouchables too. He used to give them symbolically swords and Maratha names. He called them 'Suryavaunshi', pretending that they could trace their lineage to the sun God, Surya. Shahu cannot be described as a Maratha leader also because of its efforts to federate the low castes. In the communal representation scheme that he introduced in 1920 in the Kolhapur municipality 85 castes were grouped into 20 'unions of castes'. The Marathas, the Rajputs and the Kunbis formed a constituency in themselves.

Yet, the main reason why the Sathyashodak Samaj could not become a common platform for all the non-Brahmins on the basis of a non-Aryan identity had much to do with the attitude Marathas. Most of them refused to mix with lower castes and stuck to the sanskritisation process of other with which Shahu has still affinities. For instance, Bhaskarrao Jadhav, in Marathe ani Tyanci Bhasha, displayed much ambivalence: on the one hand he admits 'the prevalence of Dravidian customs and racial intermixture among Marathas, and on the other asserts, without any qualification, (that) the Marathas are definitely " Aryan Kshatriyas "'. Therefore, even those who had followed Phule's message for some time, eventually joined hands with the Brahmins-dominated Congress, or were co-opted by it. Congress leaders such as N.V. Gadgil, who was very much aware that the nationalist movement could only acquire a mass-basis if it attracted low caste people, contacted K. Jedhe and made an alliance with him in the early 1930s. A Maratha-dominated Satyashodak Samaj, which had remained aloof from the Congress, till then, decided to join the movement. Gradually, the Maratha rose to power within the party.

In spite of this ultimate failure, from Phule to Shahu, the low castes movement of Maharashtra was characterised by very distinctive features with long terms implications. For the first time, all non-Brahmin castes were invited to unite on the basis of a common ethnic background—as the original inhabitants of India—endowed with a Kshatriya ethos and to fight the Brahmin domination. Even though the Satyashodak idiom was imbued with the symbols of kshatriya-hood, this movement escaped the sanskritisation process since the upper castes were not seen as role models but as invaders whose culture could be despised. A similar pattern developed in the South with the Dravidian movement.

Non-Brahmin and Dravidian Movements

In Madras Presidency, the Non-Brahmin movement was instrumental in engineering forms of caste fusion and succeeded in endowing the lower castes with an ethnic identity relied on two grounds: they were not only presented as the original inhabitants of India, as Phule had already argued, but also as former Buddhists. This twofold argument was first articulated in the first decade of the 20th century by Iyothee Thass, a Pariah converted to Buddhism. He pointed out that ancient India had been prosperous and most humanly governed under Buddhist kings but that they were dislodged from power by Brahmin invaders who imposed the caste system. The Buddhists were then marginalised and considered as unclean and low. Their religion had endowed them with a specific culture that eschewed violence, forbade the taking of alcohol etc. Thass even maintained that in the past India was called Indirar Desam, the land of Indirar, Indirar being the Buddha after he succeeded in controlling his five senses (indiriyams). This original civilisation was none other than the Dravidian civilisation and Thass therefore chose to call its castemates, the Pariahs, 'Dravidas'. Therefore early as the late nineteenth century, the Non-Brahmin movement claimed that the lower castes were the original inhabitants of India.

Again, British Orientalism had prepared the ground for this development. The Reverend Caldwell (1819-1891) had already suggested that Sanskrit had been brought to South India by Aryan, Brahmin, colonists and that the original inhabitants were Dravidians speaking Tamil, Telugu etc. Gradually, the non-Brahmin South Indian associations adopted the suffix 'Adi'—initial, primordial'—in their titles. The Pariah Mahajan Sabha, which had been founded in 1890, became the Adi-Dravida Mahajan Sabha, which, in 1918 appealed to the government to replace the pejorative word Pariah by Adi-Dravida, denoting the original inhabitants of Dravida land. In 1917 an Adi-Andhra Mahajan Sabha had come into existence the same way. In fact, this association was initially called Andhra Panchama Conference but the chairman of its 1917 session, M.V. Bhagya Reddy (1888-1939), in his presidential address, declared that the so-called Panchamas were the original sons of the soil and they were the rulers of the country'. Hence the change of name of the Sabha. Varma was a Mala and in the 1931 census about one Ahird of the Malas and Madhigas gave their identity as Adi-Andhras.

One of the most influential proponents of the Dravidian ideology was M.C. Rajah (1883-1947), a Pariah who became secretary of the Adi-Dravida Mahajan Sabha in 1916 and who presided over the All India Depressed Classes Association since in 1928. As a nominated member of the Madras Legislative Council since 1920, Rajah moved in 1922 a resolution recommending that the terms 'Panchama' and 'Parya' are deleted from the Government records and the terms Adi-Dravida and Adi-Andhra substituted instead.

This identity-building process was led one step further by Ramaswami Naicker, alias Periyar, a religious mendicant who had been completely disillusioned by the Congress and Gandhi while he was taking part in the Vaikom satyagraha. If Phule had drawn some of his egalitarian inspiration from Thomas Paine, Periyar was much impressed by Robert Ingersoll. Like Phule and Ambedkar, he was egalitarian in a western, individualist vein. The notion of human dignity was so central to his thinking that after quitting Congress in the mid-1920s, he launched the Self-Respect Movement, which immediately endeavoured to pressurise the Justice Party in order to make it the true advocate of the lower castes. Another of his key words was Samadharma that referred to the general principle of equality. But Periyar regarded it as a Buddhist notion. Like Thass, he presented the lower castes as descending from the first Buddhists and endowed them with a Dravidian identity, especially after his mobilisation of the late 1930s against the attempt of the Congress government of Madras at promoting Hindi in the schools of the Presidency.

The Dravidar Kazhagam (DK) that he founded in 1944, though its mouthpiece, Viduthalai, considered that the Congress was behind 'the exploitation of the northern bania and his Aryan [brahmin] mentor'. Thus, 'samardharma came to stand in for a civilisational and cultural alternative: a social order based on radically different principles from the present, which needed to rest on premises derived from a non-Aryan, non-Sanskritic ethos'. Periyar had an explicitly ethnic conception of the low castes' identity. He compared their situation to that of the blacks in South Africa. The Non-Brahmins who all shared a Dravidian identity had therefore to get united.

As a result, Periyar advocated the coming together of the Christians, Muslims and low castes Hindus, and, within the latter, of the Untouchables and the Shudras. Such a rapprochement took place indeed since Nadars and Adi Dravidas (Untouchables) were the mainstays of the Self-Respect movement and then of the DK. But there were also Vellalas, Mukkulathavar and even Chettis among the lieutenants of Periyar.

The scope and strength of this social coalition must not be exaggerated since old lines of cleavages persisted. As in Maharashtra, the 'non-Aryans' did not form a solid block at all. M.C. Rajah criticised the 'natural animosity' of the Justice Party towards the Untouchables and in 1922-23 his South India Adi-Dravida Congress broke ranks with the party. However, the ethnic ground of the Non-Brahmin discourse which, from Thass to Periyar combined Buddhist and Dravidian references had enabled its leaders to unify low caste people and mobilise them against the 'twice borns'. As early as 1920, 'a non-brahmin constituency with its own distinctive political claims had emerged in Madras' and enabled the Justice Party to win the elections. This ethnicisation process was fostered by the political reforms since the British were much willing to recognise ethnic and/or caste groups as legitimate units for representation in the political arena.

Compensatory Discrimination Policy

The formation of caste federations and the ethnicisation of caste, two inter related processes, were fostered by the British policy of compensatory discrimination based on the reservation of seats in the bureaucracy and in the assemblies. The very decision to grant such or such statutory representation to such and such group in these assemblies contributed to the crystallisation of new groups which resented their non-(or their under-) representation. The State was therefore indirectly reshaping society. Caste groups, often with low status, were prominent among those, which mobilised against the state's decisions.

The Non-Brahmin movement of Madras Presidency was especially active. In April 1920, Lord Chelmsford received a Memorandum protesting against the reservation of only 28 seats out of 65 for the Non-Brahmins in the Legislative Council of Madras. Interestingly, the signatories emphasised their caste and ethnic differences for justifying their claim:

> The Brahmins differ from the non-Brahmins in caste, manners, customs and interests and even in personal law in some respects. The former is Aryans and the latter are Dravidians and thus they differ in race. In the past the Brahmins have practically monopolised all or almost all the seats in the Local and Imperial Legislative Councils. The

> disabilities under which the Non-Brahmins have been suffering were fully set out in the Memorandum which Rai Bahadur K.V. Reddi prepared and submitted to the joint Select Committee on Government of India Bill.

The Non-Brahmins asked for more seats ir. Madras assembly because they were 'different'. During the 1920 election campaign, their leaders requested 'all non-Brahmins in this presidency to immediately organise, combine and carry on an active propaganda so as to ensure the return to the reformed Council of as many non-Brahmin as possible'. This tactic yielded dividends since the Justice Party came first in the elections. In their plea to the British, the Non-Brahmins also emphasised their marginality in the state services and the 'disabilities' from which they were suffering. This discourse fitted well too in the British approach since the Government regarded also political representation as a means for compensatory discrimination.

This policy made a similar impact on the low caste movement in Western India. In Bombay Legislative Council the Marathas showed the way in the 1920s. Their principal patron, the Maharajah of Kolhapur, Shahu Maharaj, had circulated a memorandum 'on the necessity of separate Communal electorates for the Marathas, etc., for electing members to the new Councils under the Reforms scheme', where he wrote:

> The Marathas have distinguished themselves in the [first world] war certainly not less, if not more, than the Sikhs or the Mohammedans who have been given separate electorates. They are almost given tc agriculture, military service or employment as mill-hands. Being thus not a commercial or educated community, they are poor, and without resources, influence and organisation. In this respect they are even worse of than Telis, Tilaris, Goldsmiths, Sutas, Lohars and even Mahars, Mangs and other Untouchables, to whom many a business line and handicraft are open [...] Five great monsters do a lot of mischief to the village agricultural community which mostly consists of the Marathas. The Kulkarni [Brahmin] is the biggest of them all [...] Next to the Kulkarni is the Brahmin Sawkar [money-lender] who has appropriated to himself a very large portion of the village lands. The Ahird in this order is the school-master and his brother the college-professor in big cities [...] [The fourth] is

> the Brahmin bureaucracy watered and nourished by Government themselves [...] The village priest, securely and permanently installed by Hindu religious puranas invented and developed to maintain the Brahmanic supremacy is the fifth monster.

Shahu demanded separate electorates instead of reserved seats on which, he said, he was 'sure that weak, unprincipled undesirable Marathas will be elected who would be used by Brahmins as cat's paw for them to draw the apples out of the fire', the same kind of argument used by Ambedkar before the Poona pact. However, the British were not prepared to grant a separate electorate to the Marathas. Some of them preferred to focus their demand on larger quotas and they had understood that to pressurise the British more efficiently they had to appear as representing more than one caste. They held, under the auspices of the People's Union, whose patron was the Maharajah of Kolhapur, a Conference of the Hindu Backward Classes in June 1920. The British, so far, designated the Marathas by their caste name but the conference considered that 'the term "Maratha and allied classes" should include all the Backward communities'. Maratha leaders obviously aspired to play a pivotal role in the shaping of a caste federation which would adopt the official designation 'Backward classes'. Therefore, the conference made 'an emphatic protest against the misleading statement made in public to the effect that the Marathas, Malis etc. do not belong to the Backward Classes when their percentage of education is very low'. The main demand of the conference was that the 8 seats reserved to the Marathas and allied castes in the Montagu-Chelmsford report should be extended to 15. Simultaneously, the Secretary of the Poona-based All India Maratha Mali Union made a similar representation to the British:

> The word 'Maratta' [sic] means all the backward classes. As a matter of fact not only the Marattas but all other allied communities have fought in the last world war for the Empire and all such communities are anxious to get the privilege of reserved seats in the council to be hereafter elected.

Among the allied communities of Marathas, Yadav Gavlis then opportunely discovered that they had strong affinities with the

Marathas. The President of the Yadav Gavli Association, Raghunath Vithal Khedekar, was an exceptional personality. Born in Bombay in 1873, his father had been Private secretary of the Maharajah of Bhavnagar, one of the most progressive states so far as the upliftment of the lower castes were concerned. After studying medicine in the United Kingdom, he started practising in 1902 in Bhavnagar and Kolhapur, where he met Shahu Maharaj. The first Yadav association had been founded in 1903 by a relative of his father. In the early 1920s, Khedekar protested that the Southborough Committee should consider the Yadav Gavlis as Marathas:

> The Yadav Gavli community claims descent from the Great Yadav families to one which Shri Krishna the incarnation of Vishnu belonged. The whole of the North India, Gujarat and Deccan were only ruled by the Kings of the Yadav families [...] They have kept up their Kshatriya caste traditions, customs and occupations [...] They have given considerable recruits to the government and have been regarded as Marathas and included in the Maratha regiments.

In the end, the Yadav-Gavli association demanded the 'inclusion [of this caste] in the list of the Marathas and allied communities of the Deccan for franchise purpose'. Access to political power was of course the main reason for this social rapprochement. Eventually, Khedekar was deputed by the People's Union, the Deccan Ryots Association and the Yadav Gavli Association for making a representation to the Joint Select Committee. He explained:

> If the term 'Maratha' be defined as meaning 'anti-Brahmin' in the regulation to be framed under the Indian Act, it will remove all misunderstandings and ill feelings in the Maratha castes and it will allow Jains and Lingayat castes to share the benefit of the reserved seats.

Marathas, who had already forged a 'backward' front with the Malis and the Yadavs were striving for shaping an even larger coalition including the Lingayats and the Jains under the all-encompassing label of 'anti-Brahmins'. Certainly, the loose structure of the Marathas lent itself to this kind of aggregative strategy. They have no clear-cut sub-castes, they are so 'amorphous' that 'it is hard to tell in some cases, whether a group is Maratha or of another affiliation called Kunbi'. This arrangement naturally 'facilitates incorporation into Maratha caste' of other peasant castes. But in spite of the Marathas' specificity, there is much to learn from this case study on the way state policies can indirectly refashion social groupings. The British approach of compensatory discrimination through quotas in the assemblies have accelerated the transformation of castes into interest groups and have fostered a process of amalgamation among the low castes. Leading castes such as the Marathas initiated federations whose aim was purely political. They had understood that the rules were those of the game of numbers which, alone could enhance institutional representation in the State. In Maharashtra this strategy was rather successful. Its architects could rely on the legacy of Jyotirao Phule's Satyashodak Samaj, which had established an idiom—the Bahujan idiom—encompassing all the Non-Brahmins. Another important factor laid in the pivotal situation of the Marathas who represented 20 per cent of the population. They were certainly not able to federate all the Non-Brahmins but the mere fact that the British designed a category called 'Marathas and allied' showed that they had been successful to a certain extent. Among these allies were the Kunbis, who have always been regarded as more backward than the Marathas but who appeared in the same category. Now, the Kunbis accounted for 10 per cent of the population of Maharashtra and contributed, therefore, to the irresistible rise to power of the Marathas from the late colonial period onwards.

In Maharashtra and Tamil Nadu, the ethnicisation of caste and the formation of caste federations, helped the non-Brahmins to get organised and to gradually assert themselves in the political arena. However, the most significant caste federations took shape in the South and in Gujarat.

Caste Federations

The concept of caste federation refers to a grouping together of a number of distinct endogamous groups into a single organisation for common objectives, the realisation of which calls for a pooling together of resources or numbers or both. By and large, the objectives pursued are secular and associational, although the employment of traditional symbols for evoking a sense of solidarity and loyalty towards the new form is not uncommon. The traditional distinctions between the federating groups are on the whole retained, but the search for a new organisational identity and the pursuit of political objectives gradually lead to a shift in group orientations.

This definition was evolved in the course of a study of the caste federation phenomenon in Gujarat where the 'Kshatriyas' indeed exemplified this phenomenon. Right from the 1910s the state Rajput leaders had constituted caste associations for promoting education. In the late 1930s, the descendent of one of its leaders, Natvarsingh Solanki, wanted to extend these associations to other castes which he considered as Kshatriyas. He tried to refashion the social identity of those groups in order to allow others to join hands with the Rajputs and in this way, to acquire more weight.

Gujarat's largest caste was the Kolis. They had been classified by the British as a 'criminal caste' but claimed that they were Kshatriyas and resorted to genealogists for being recognised aristocratic ancestors. In this, they purely imitated the Rajputs. Some Koli clans had been able to establish matrimonial alliances with Rajputs, as those castes practised hypergamy and/or had established small principalities before the British took over. Yet, they had retained some control over land under the Raj as landowners or rather big tenants. Many of them met the necessary conditions for being enfranchised when the British established provincial legislative councils. The right to vote therefore enabled the Kolis to use their main asset, their number" : in 1931 they represented about 20 per cent of the population, almost the double of the Patidars (12.16 per cent), the dominant caste, the main rival of the Rajputs, who represented only 4.85 per cent of the population. Solanki opened his caste association to the Kolis for this very reason: for transforming it into a mass organisation.

In 1947, the Kutch, Kathiawar, Gujarat Kshatriya Sabha was created after years of preparatory work. The word 'Kshatriya' was a useful umbrella label to bracket the Rajputs and the Kolis together. The Kshatriya Sabha is a good example of the way castes, with very different ritual status for defending common interests.

In this case, the Kolis and the Rajputs had the same enemies, viz., the Patidars. Certainly, this alliance has been legitimised in the idiom of 'tradition', by pretending that its components belonged to the same varna, but the use of the word Kshatriya was largely tactical and the original caste identity was seriously diluted.

The Rajput leaders of the Kshatriya Sabha emphasised that a Kshatriya is not to be defined by descent but by military values. Political calculations had therefore social implications. Several taboos were abolished. Rajputs and Kolis of the Kshatriya Sabha shared meals and the Kolis elite married their daughters to lower Rajputs –who practised hypergamy anyway – and this process fostered the rajputisation of the upper Kolis. Kshatriyas tended to form a new caste. The use of terms like Koli Kshatriyas and Rajput Kshatriyas certainly show that the merger was far from complete. But important dimensions of the caste system were eroded by the after-effects of basically socio-economic and political strategies.

In fact, the main demands of the Kshatriya Sabha after independence reflected a relative indifference to ritual issues in comparison to material objectives. For instance, the association claimed that the Kshatriyas were part of the "Backward Classes" and therefore should benefit from reservations in the educational system and in the administration. This claim was the exact opposite of sanskritisation.

The Kolis benefited more than the Rajputs from the Sabha, which created boarding schools, grants, loan systems etc. in favour of the poorest of their community. This development contributed to the emergence of a Koli intelligentsia of Kolis which, even though it remained small gave the Koli masses a new confidence and self-esteem as a caste. The members of this elite 'interact[ed] frequently and chart[ed] out common political strategies'. Right from the 1950s, the Kshatriya Sabha tended to capitalise its electoral support to the Congress in exchange of tickets for a number of its members as party candidates. The party was not fully responsive, especially because of the Patidars who were very influential in the Congress. The Patidars disapproved of the Kshatriyas demand regarding land reform. The Kshatriya Sabha therefore kept its distance with the Congress before the 1962 elections and the party underwent a setback. Instead, the association gave its support, against large concessions, to the Swatantra Party, which became the leading opposition party in the state. This situation persuaded the Congress to change its strategy and to give tickets to Kshatriya candidates before the 1967 elections. The Kshatriya Sabha then supported the Congress, which regained a more comfortable majority than in 1962.

Caste federations turned out to be political interest groups with more leverage than caste associations, simply because they represented more people. In Gujarat, after the Congress split of 1969, a majority of the party conservative notables remained with the Congress (O) while a larger number of Kshatriyas joined the Congress (R). They gradually gained control over the state Congress. Madhavsingh Solanki, a Kshatriya of low birth, became Chief minister in 1976 and appointed a majority of ministers with the same background. During the electoral campaign of 1977 he initiated a new caste alliance regrouping the Kshatriyas, the Harijans (Untouchables), the Adivasis (tribals) and the Muslims (hence the acronym "KHAM"). This KHAM alliance was largely responsible for the Congress success during the 1980 elections. Between 1957 and 1990 the number of upper caste Congress MLAs decreased from 33 to 6 per cent, those with a Patidar background remained stable at about one fourth of the total, whereas the Kshatriyas increased from 12 to 25 per cent and the KHAM MLAs at large from 39 to 55 per cent.

While the 'Kshatriyas' of Gujarat represent the best example of caste federation, other instances occurred in South India. In the early 1960s, the Kallan, the Maravar and the Agamudiar, three lower castes who had already close ties with each other (especially ritual ones since they clamed that they descended from the same ancestors), decided to adopt the same name, Mukkulator (lit. three castes), in order to merge and to influence local politics.

The search for new forms of caste activity did not contribute to social change and to the rise of the low castes in the same way in Maharashtra, Tamil Nadu and Gujarat but the above case studies suggest a western and southern pattern. In these areas, the development of communications, the impact of western ideas-ranging from missionaries' propaganda and school teaching, the establishment of a pan-Indian administration and census operations, fostered the formation of caste associations. These institutions had sometimes a very conservative overtone and confined their discourse into the sanskritisation framework. However, they prepared the ground for two major developments, namely the ethnicisation of castes, of which the ideology of the 'bahujan samaj' evolved by Phule and the Dravidian movement were the best examples, and the federation of castes which was epitomised by the 'Kshatriyas' of Gujarat. Both phenomena were influenced by the orientalist discourse and responses to the British policy of compensatory discrimination. They were intended to help the low castes to reach power and they were successful to a large extent.

In North India, none of these processes reached their logical conclusion even through the British Raj had generated the same context as in the South and in the West. Caste associations often followed the sanskritisation path and neither prepared the group for an ethnic discourse nor developed into caste federations.

Low Caste Associations

In North India also British policies had changed the social and political context in such a way as castes could have felt the same strong incentive to get organised. Efforts were made in this direction but they did not bear the same fruits as in the South and in the West. While caste associations took shape at an early date, they did not join hands into federations and they operated within the logic sanskritisation. For instance, in 1928, the Indian Statutory Commission received an avalanche of petitions and memoranda from caste associations, which demanded larger quotas in the assembly.

The Government was petitioned by the All India Kushwaha Kshatriya Mahasabha, 'on behalf of the kori, kachchi and murao castes'. The fact that the Kushwaha label stood for three sub-castes of castes of market gardeners shows that this caste association promoted the fusion process, but not to a very large extent : this process cannot be compared with caste federations in Gujarat. Secondly, the Kushwahas claimed the rank of Kshatriya, and another association of middle caste of peasants, which sent also a petition, the Kurmi Kshatriya Parishad Sabha, did the same. Sanskritisation continued to play a major role among the low caste associations. In the following paragraphs we will examine this issue through the case of the Yadavs and the Kurmis on the one hand and through that of the Untouchables on the other hand.

The 'Yadav' label covers a great number of castes, which had different names, initially: Ahir in the Hindi belt, Punjab and Gujarat, Gavli in Maharashtra, Gola in Andhra Pradesh and Karnataka etc. However, traditionally their common function, all over India, was to take care of bovines cattle as herdsmen, cowherds and milksellers. In their 'Tribes and Castes of the Central Provinces of India', Russell and Hira Lal note that 'In former times the Ahirs had the exclusive right of milking the cow, so that on all occasions on their must be hired for this purpose even by the lowest castes' In practice, the Yadavs today spend most their time tilling the land. In the Central Provinces, in the first decade of the last century, already two kinds of the Ahirs were cultivators and labourers and less than one Ahird were still occupied in breeding cattle and in dealing with milk and milk products.

While the Yadavs are speared several regions, as noticed above, they are more specially concentrated in the Ganges plain where they represent about 10 per cent of the population. They form one of the largest castes in Bihar and Uttar Pradesh with respectively 11 and 8.7 per cent of the population. The 'casteregious' maped by J. Schwartzberg show that the Yadavs were the largest caste in almost all the districts of northern Bihar and in much of eastern UP in 1931 But the Yadavs are not a dominant caste, as pastoral activity did not go usually hand in hand with land possession and from the ritual point of view, the Yadavs are traditionally regarded as low caste peasants:

The very mention of the community invokes, in Bihar, the image of dull, miserly and loud-mouthed people lacking in grace and culture. Besides, the Yadavs are considered as to be unusually prone to casteism and violence.

In the central Provinces, a proverb says ' A Gaoli's quarrel: drunk at night and friends in the morning'. Russell and Hira Lal note that in this region too, 'The Ahirs are also hot-tempered, and their propensity for drinking often results in affrays, when they break each other's head with their cattle-staffs'. However, their association with another image, that of placidity and peace. One of the proverbs cited by Schwartzberg says: 'The cow is in league with the milkman and lets him milk water into the pail'. Hence an ambivalent stereotype – if this phrase is not a contradiction in terms. The Yadavs reportedly descend from immigrants from Central Asia, the Abhiras, who established kingdoms in North India, the most recent of which was built in Rewari, in Haryana in the XVIIth century. The scion of the dynasty, Rao Bahadur Balbir Singh, established the Ahir Yadav Kshatriya Mahasabha in 1910. This association claimed that the Ahirs descended from the Yadu dynasty (hence the term Yadav) to which Krishna—the cowherd god—belonged, and that, therefore, they were Kshatriyas. To promote a warrior ethos and the caste unity, the association leaders could easily rely on the caste history since Ahirs were easily presented as coming from the same ethnic stock and were known for their martial valour—the prince of Rewari took part in the 1857 Mutiny for instance. This is probably why M.S.A. Rao considers that the 'term Yadava refers to both an ethnic category and an ideology'. Certainly, the Yadav leaders succeeded in their fusion project since they persuaded their caste fellows to downplay the endogamous units into which they were divided. There have even been some inter-regional marriages. Fusion was made easier from the 1930s onwards when North Indian Yadavs started to migrate from their villages to towns and especially to Delhi. But this project did not incorporate a more ambitious ethnicisation process through which other Kshatriya castes would have been merged. So far as ideology is concerned, it was dominated by sanskritisation.

The Yadavs lent themselves for such sanskritisation because they had 'a special relation to the Hindu religion, owing to their association with the sacred cow' (and with Krishna, the cowherd God). And the Arya Samaj also exerted a strong influence over the Yadav movement. As early as 1895, the ruler of Rewari, Rao Yudhishter Singh (the father of Rao Bahadur Balbir Singh) invited Swami Dayananda in his State. Branches of the Arya Samaj flourished soon after and Rewari provided a base from which Arya Samaj updeshaks (itinerant preachers) operated in neighbouring areas. The Arya Samaj was a reform movement, which has been too often regarded as purely Punjabi and confined to the urban middle class. In fact, it made inroads in the adjacent states at a quite early date and attracted then large numbers of low caste people. Dayananda even started his 'campaign against heresy and orthodoxy'—to use the words of an Arya Samajist—in the Kumbha Mela held in Haridwar. Subsequently, he toured in the United Provinces, in particular in the western part of the province. He stayed eight times in Meerut, for instance, between 1866 and 1880—the Meerut City Arya Samaj was established as early as 1877 and others followed in Farrukabad (1879), Kanpur (1879), Benares (1880), Lucknow (1880). Eventually, the Srimati Arya Pratinidhi Sabha for the United Provinces of Agra and Awadh was founded in 1886. These local branches gradually extended their influence in the countryside. The anti-Brahmin stance of the Arya Samaj was especially appreciated by the low castes of the United Provinces. In Sathyarth Prakash (The Light of Truth), Dayananda has very strong words against 'the sectarian and selfish Brahmins', 'these ignorant, sensual, hypocritical, irresponsible and vicious people' who 'often dissuade persons from learning and ensnare them into their evil ways with the result that they lose health, peace of mind and wealth. Dayananda reproached the Brahmans with exploiting the superstition of the Hindus by projecting themselves as the only intermediary between man and god, a monopoly he compares to that of the Catholic Pope and which according to him was evident from the brahminical invention of idol worship: 'These Popes fill their pockets by playing fraud upon you. In the Vedas there is not even a word to sanction idol-worship or invoking invitation and dismissals'.

Dayananda eulogised the Jats for forcefully resisting the Brahmins' 'popish' attitudes. He narrates the story of a Jat whose father was dying and who was asked to give his only cow to the priest as a 'dying gift', allegedly for helping the dying man to cross the river. The Jat had to agree since the priest had already talked to his relatives who put pressure on him. But he went to the priest's house soon after and boldly accused him of being 'a great liar' since he had not taken the cow to the river bank but was milking it. He then contested the authority of the Garuda Purana, the book the priest mentioned as dictating his conduct: 'This book has been written by your forefathers to secure livelihood for you...'. The Jat took the cow back to his home and Dayananda concludes, 'If other persons also behave like the Jat, then alone can the popish fraud be stopped'. Jats were very pleased by the way Dayananda praised one of them and they naturally shared his indictment of the Brahmins.

However, Dayananda's indictment of the Brahmins did not amount to a complete rejection of the caste system. What he condemned was the hereditary caste. He contended that in the initial varna vyavastha children were placed in each varna according to their individual 'merits, actions and temperaments'. He specifically recommended that the 'fixture of the varnas according to merits and actions should take place at the sixteenth year of girls and twenty-fifth year of boys'. Like Gandhi later on, Dayananda was not against caste as such since, according to him, provided it was not a hereditary system, the castes endowed society with a virtually harmonious structure. Moreover, he considered that marriages should 'take place in the same varnas (classes) and the varna should be based on merits, profession and temperament'. It means that not only Dayananda adds one more criterion to the definition of castes—the profession—but also that endogamy, which is a pillar of the caste system, needed to be enforced. Dayananda did not fight caste taboos either. For instance, he considered that a Brahmin needed only to eat food prepared by caste fellows because 'The nature of genital fluids made in a Brahman's body due to special kind of fooding is different from that made in chandalas body on account of bad diet. The body of the candalas is full of rotten particles due to rotten diet'. Dayananda, therefore, maintained also the hierarchy in diets which is part of the caste system. He was obviously a clear proponent of sanskritisation and the Arya Samaj exerted a strong influence in this direction over the lower castes of North India. The first anti-Brahmin movement of North India was probably the Arya Samaj. But in contrast to what happened in Western and Southern India, this movement made a very ambivalent impact since it promoted sanskritisation. The activities of the arya samajists among the Yadavs of the Gangetic plains are a case in point.

Logically enough, the most obvious implication of the Arya Samaj in the North Indian countryside lay in the sanskritisation of the Jats, as evident from the ideology of the All India Jat Mahasabha which was founded in 1905 as 'an offshoot of the Arya Samaj'. On the one hand this caste association, as so many others, asked for a special treatment from the Government; on the other hand it claimed that Jats were Kshatriyas. Arya Samajists exhorted the Jats to give up the consumption of alcohol and meat and recommended that severe restriction should be 'imposed on the movement of women'. The schools established with the association's support had often telling names—such as the Jat Vedic School founded in Rohtak in 1913—and generally taught Sanskrit in order to enable the Jats to teach Sanskrit and therefore occupy ' a profession which for centuries was the exclusive monopoly of the Brahmin'. The Arya Samajists propagated the same kind of ideology among the Yadavs.

The Arya Samaj updeshaks continuously canvassed for the adoption of the sacred thread by the Yadavs. Their campaigns were especially successful in Uttar Pradesh and Bihar. The Yadav rulers of Rewari, Rao Yudhishter Singh, true to his role as protector of the cows founded a Goraksha Sabha (association for cow protection) in conjunction with the Arya Samaj – which had started to create such sabhas all over North India. The arya samajists also enrolled the Yadavs in the cow protection movement. This movement, initiated in 1893 and relaunched at different points of time in the first two decades of the century, attracted many

Yadavs who were anxious to emulate the upper castes. In the Bhojpuri region, Gyan Pandey, who emphasised 'the special role of the Ahirs' in this movement points out that 'we have evidence here of a relatively independent force that added a good deal of power to cow-protection activities [...]—marginally " clean " castes who aspired to full " cleanliness " by emphasising the purity of their faith and the strictness of ritual adherence to it on the issue of cow-slaughter'. Such a process can hardly be presented as 'a relatively independent force'. Obsessed with an imitation of the upper castes, the Ahirs could not develop an alternative value system. Both phenomena may not be mutually exclusive, however. The same Ahirs who took part in the cow-protection movement and could also petition the Bihar Census Commissioner for being recognised a Kshatriya origin also refused to do begari (forced labour) for the upper castes. Revisiting the notion of sanskritisation, Srinivas himself points out that it 'embodies a strong element of protest against the high castes: "We dare you to stop us emulating you" seems to be the spirit underlying emulation'.

The All India Yadav Mahasabha, through which Khedekar federated regional associations based in Punjab, Uttar Pradesh and Bihar in followed the sanskritisation path under the guidance of Rao Balbir Singh, the ruler of Rewari who still played a prominent role in the Yadav movement. Interestingly, he was elected to the Punjab assembly in 1937 on a Hindu Mahasabha ticket. The programme of the AIYM is easy to summarise. It advocated vegetarianism and teetotalism. It militated in favour of the adoption of the name 'Yadav' all over India and so far as material interests were concerned, it incited the Yadavs to embrace new professional careers and put pressure on the British to make the army recruit Yadavs as officers.

While the AIYM helped the Yadavs to get united, in 1945 dissidents founded a rival caste association, the All India Yadav Sangh whose activities were even more sanskritised it took part in the 1966 anti-cow slaughter movement for instance. The main weakness of the Yadavs was their incapacity to make alliances with other castes of similar rank, like the Kurmis, who suffered from the same problem themselves!

The first Kurmi caste association was founded in 1894 in Lucknow to protest against the British decision to reduce the recruitment of Kurmis in the police. The Kurmis of Awadh then created a Kurmi Sabha and declared that other castes like the Patidars (from Gujarat), the Kapus (from Andhra Pradesh), the Vokkaligas (from Karnataka), the Reddys, the Naidus (from Madras Presidency) and the Marathas (from Maharashtra), were also Kurmis. The association gained momentum in 1901, during the census operations when it claimed that Kurmis were Kshatriyas. The All India Kurmi Kshatriya Mahasabha, which was officially registered in Patna in 1910, combined the defence of the caste secular interests and sanskritisation. On the one hand it canvassed for the use of the sacred thread among Kurmis. On the other hand, it started to ask for quotas in the administration as 'backward classes' but its action met a faint response.

Kurmis and Yadavs, even though they occupied similar social positions failed to get united. The first attempt was made in Bihar in the 1930s. It involved the Yadavs, the Kurmis and the Koeris, a caste of agriculturists representing 4.1 per cent of the state population. Members of those three castes joined hands in 1930 to contest the local district board elections. They lost badly but in 1934 formed the Triveni Sangh, a political party named after the confluence of three rivers, (the Ganges, the Yamuna and the

Saraswati, now disappeared) in Allahabad. In 1936 about one million members had allegedly paid the four-anna (one-quarter of a rupee) fee. However, at the same time, in 1935, the Congress formed the Backward Class Federation 'to counter what they viewed as the dangerous class features of the Triveni Sangh and Kisan Sabha movements'. Congressmen deprived the low caste movement from some of its leaders by co-opting Kurmi leaders and Yadavs. And then they refused to give tickets to Triveni Sangh candidates. The party suffered from a serious setback during the 1937 elections but in the few places where it won upper caste landlords retaliated violently. The Triveni Sangh and the Kisan Sabha also failed t o make an alliance because of the traditional antagonism between the low castes represented by the former and the Bhumihars who dominated the latter.

Many years later, the Kurmis tried to play a pivotal role in a similar arrangement. During the 30 session of the All India Kurmi Kshatriya Sabha, some of the delegates suggested that the word 'Kshatriya' should be removed from the name of the association and a resolution was passed to discourage the sanskritisation process. In the same way, it was decided to constitute a caste federation with the Koeris. The Kurmis leaders were not planning to create a new caste through intermarriages, but a union they called 'Raghav Samaj'—after one of the names of the Lord Ram—a choice they justified by presenting the Kurmis and the Koeris as descending respectively from Lav and Kush, two sons of Ram. This attempt reflected the weight of the Biharis within the association. While the sessions of the Sabha were often presided over by Marathas, Patidars etc., in the 1970s about 30 per cent of the executive bureau members were from Bihar. The attempt to federate the Koeris and Kurmis was rather inconclusive, no doubt because of difference in their status and economic activities ; the Kurmis were cultivators who produced staples like cereals whereas the Koeris were traditionally market gardeners.

Ambedkar and Caste Reforms

Born into a poor Mahar, then Untouchable, family, Ambedkar spent his whole life fighting against social discrimination, the system of Chaturvarna — the categorisation of Hindu society into four varnas — and the Hindu caste system.

Overcoming numerous social and financial obstacles, Ambedkar became one of the first "Dalit" to obtain a college education in India. Eventually earning law degrees and multiple doctorates for his study and research in law, economics and political science from Columbia University and the London School of Economics, Ambedkar returned home as a famous scholar and practiced law for a few years before publishing journals advocating political rights and social freedom for India's untouchables.

As a leading Indian scholar, Ambedkar had been invited to testify before the Southborough Committee, which was preparing the Government of India Act 1919. At this hearing, Ambedkar argued for creating separate electorates and reservations for Dalits and other religious communities. In 1920, he began the publication of the weekly Mooknayak (Leader of the Silent) in Mumbai. Attaining popularity, Ambedkar used this journal to criticise orthodox Hindu politicians and a perceived reluctance of the Indian political community to fight caste discrimination. His speech at a Depressed Classes Conference in Kolhapur impressed the local state ruler Shahu IV, who shocked orthodox society by dining with Ambekdar. Ambedkar established a successful legal practice, and also organised the Bahishkrit Hitakarini Sabha to promote education and socio-economic uplifting of the depressed classes.

By 1927 Dr. Ambedkar decided to launch active movements against untouchability. He began with public movements and marches to open up and share public drinking water resources, also he began a struggle for the right to enter Hindu temples. He led a satyagraha in Mahad to fight for the right of the untouchable community to draw water from the main water tank of the town.

He was appointed to the Bombay Presidency Committee to work with the all-European Simon Commission in 1925. This commission had sparked great protests across India, and while its report was ignored by most Indians, Ambedkar himself wrote a separate set of recommendations for future constitutional reformers.

Ambedkar criticised the Indian National Congress and its leader Mohandas Gandhi, whom he accused of reducing the untouchable community to a figure of pathos. Ambedkar was also dissatisfied with the failures of British rule, and advocated a political identity for untouchables separate from both the Congress and the British. At a Depressed Classes Conference on August 8, 1930 Ambedkar outlined his political vision, insisting that the safety of the Depressed Classes hinged on their being independent of the Government and the Congress both:

> We must shape our course ourselves and by ourselves... Political power cannot be a panacea for the ills of the Depressed Classes. Their salvation lies in their social elevation. They must cleanse their evil habits. They must improve their bad ways of living.... They must be educated.... There is a great necessity to disturb their pathetic contentment and to instill into them that divine discontent which is the spring of all elevation.

In 1932, M. C. Rajah concluded a pact with two right-wingers in the Indian National Congress, Dr. B. S. Moonje and Jadhav. According to this pact, Moonje offered reserved seats to scheduled castes in return for Rajah's support. This demand prompted Ambedkar to make an official demand for Separate Electorate System on an all-India basis. Ambedkar's prominence and popular support amongst the untouchable community had increased, and he was invited to attend the Second Round Table Conference in London in 1932.Gandhi fiercely opposed separate electorate for untouchables, he feared that separate electorates for untouchables would divide Hindu society for future generations.

When the British agreed with Ambedkar and announced the awarding of separate electorates, Gandhi began a fast-unto-death while imprisoned in the Yerwada Central Jail of Pune in 1932 against the separate electorate for untouchables only. Gandhi asked for the political unity of Hindus. Gandhi's fast provoked great public support across India, and orthodox Hindu leaders, Congress politicians and activists such as Madan Mohan Malaviya and Palwankar Baloo organised joint meetings with Ambedkar and his supporters at Yeravada. Fearing a communal reprisal and killings of untouchables in the event of Gandhi's death, Ambedkar agreed under massive coercion from the supporters of Gandhi. This agreement, which saw Gandhi end his fast, while dropping the demand for separate electorates that was promised through the British Communal Award prior to Ambedkar's meeting with

Gandhi. Ambedkar was to later criticise this fast of Gandhi as a gimmick to deny political rights to the untouchables and increase the coercion he had faced to give up the demand for separate electorates.

Upon India's independence on August 15, 1947, the new Congress-led government invited Ambedkar to serve as the nation's first law minister, which he accepted. On August 29, Ambedkar was appointed Chairman of the Constitution Drafting Committee, charged by the Assembly to write free India's new Constitution. The text prepared by Ambedkar provided constitutional guarantees and protections for a wide range of civil liberties for individual citizens, including freedom of religion, the abolition of untouchability and the outlawing of all forms of discrimination Ambedkar argued for extensive economic and social rights for women, and also won the Assembly's support for introducing a system of reservations of jobs in the civil services, schools and colleges for members of scheduled castes and scheduled tribes, a system akin to affirmative action. India's lawmakers hoped to eradicate the socio-economic inequalities and lack of opportunities for India's depressed classes through this measure, which had been originally envisioned as temporary on a need basis. The Constitution was adopted on November 26, 1949 by the Constituent Assembly.

References

Atal, Yogesh. *The Changing Frontiers of Caste*. Delhi, National Publishing House. 1968.

Ambedkar, B.R. *The Untouchables: Who Were They and Why They Became Untouchables?* as reprinted in Volume 7 of *Dr. Babasaheb Ambedkar Writings and Speeches,* published by Government of Maharashtra 1990; Complete Writings. 1946.

Char, S.V. Desika. *Caste, Religion and Country*. New Delhi: Sangam Books, 1993.

Ghurye, G.S. *Caste and Race in India*. Bombay: Popular Prakashan, 1990.

Keer, Dhananjay. *Dr. Ambedkar: Life and Mission*. Mumbai: Popular Prakashan Pvt. Ltd., 1990.

Mandelbaum, David M.. *Society in India*. London: University of California Press,1972.

Michael, S.M. *Untouchable, Dalits in Modern India*. Lynne Rienner Publishers. 1999.

3

CASTE RADICALISM

Caste is a unique part of India, and the Indian philosophy It cuts across every regiona! and religious denomination in India. It is the basic building block of the Indian society that can be found in any institution or organisation in any part of the world. It exists everywhere, and in every religion of the Indians. In fact it is an ethnic, and to be specific a racial factor, that continues to undermine the Indian Society, even at the twilight hours of the twentieth century.

Caste Hindus are the Brahmins (priestly castes) Kshatriyas (warrior/fighting castes), Vaishyas (business/trading caste). These three are the real caste Hindus. But they have kept with them as the fourth caste in their *Chatur Varna Dharma* (four caste system) the Shudras (working classes the artisans, agriculturists, food gatherers, hunters, fisher folk etc) as their captive slaves, with in the Hindu caste system. They have carefully kept out of the hindu fold, their caste system, *Chaturvernas* (four castes) – the fiercely independent, proud, geographically isolate Tribals; and the rebellious non-conforming 'anaryans' (uncivilised) unacceptables, who have been meticulously and carefully isolated socially, physically, psychologically, and literally kept outside the hindu society, even though living only in close proximity in the nearby and or next hamlet, as part of the same village, or area of the town and the city. Thus always, the out castes have been a different people, living separately. There are distinctly different and a separate society, nation and are clearly away from the caste Hindus and caste-non-Hindus of other Religions which in India, only for public consumption and on ideological and theological grounds claim to be unitary Religions in nature, and are non-believers of the caste-system or any other divisive factor.

The Out Castes who are today more than 250 million in India, are the third largest population in the world, next only to the Chinese and the whole Indian nation. Such a large chunk of humanity, native of India, and living in the Indian society has always been outside of the rest of the Indian Society. They have been kept thus over the ages, through the millenniums of Indian History. It has been so kept outside very carefully and systematically. It is a cleaver means of keeping out the racially different Out Castes, socially and biologically. It is so even today, even though for political purposes in a Democracy, claims contrary to this basic truth and social reality, are being made by many leader, officials and scholars in their speeches in public. They are only for public consumption. For, Caste has clearly and cleanly divided the Indian Society for too long a time.

Caste system has done immense damage to India, Indian Society, Indian people and the Indian States that emerged in India throughout the history, right from the days or after the Pre-Historic Days of the Indus-Valley Civilisations of India. Being that ancient and that problematic, its origins, roots, beginnings etc have been lost in the misty past of ancient India, even though its adverse effects and evil influences still remain for all who bother to see.

Caste has been instrumental in ending and putting a stop to the Indus-Valley Civilisation, and also to that ancient civilised culture, and the growth, evolution and further development of the technology and intellectualism of the Indus-valley Civilisation, or the knowledge of those times. Thus, all the collective wisdom of those days, right from the script of the Indus-Valley have come to an abrupt end, till the much later period of historic times beginning with the Early Vedic period of Rig Vedas. This disincentive to the growth of knowledge, and wisdom on the technological, creative and developmental side, has continued through the historic periods of middle ages, and further into the modern ages, accounting for the general backwardness of the Indian Society. Infect, the Caste System even now is oppressively acting to keep the Indian Society backward, and lagging far behind the world in almost every sphere of original development, at a time when the whole world is eagerly looking forward and moving ahead to step into the next millennium.

Caste System had frozen the Indian Society, its Social Out look, and fossilised the People, their mind and the Nation with nothing but caste and the evil influences of the caste in every sphere. Touch anything in India, you will find the impact and imprint of Caste and Caste System, if only you can recognise them. The great impact is that it had with held the development and formation of an United India, and Integrate Indian Society however small it may be in any part of this big Nation of sub-continental size. It had with held progress, development and any social evolution. It could be seen that India's progress, had come to a stop suddenly and almost abruptly. Right from the Indus-Valley Civilisation, its final destruction and fall, the scientific innovations, technological break through, engineering development, cultural evolutions, progress of the Collective Wisdom of the People and economic growth of the Nation all appear to have stopped, and with held, as if frozen on their tracks. Thus, the Native Wisdom of the Tribals in their isolated difficult distant areas, the Rural Wisdom of the other Depressed Classes, remain only with them, uncured for, neglected, and with out any out let to test them, try them, adopt them and develop them for the benefit of not only the Indian nation, but the whole Humanity.

Caste Hegemony in Maharsashtra

The Marathi non-Brahmin public sphere was distinguished by a critique of caste hegemony and the ritual and temporal power of the Brahmin. In the latter part of the nineteenth century, Jotirao Phule's writings against Brahminism utilised forms of speech and rhetorical styles associated with the rustic language of peasants but infused them with demands for human rights and social equality that bore the influence of nonconformist Christianity to produce a unique discourse of caste radicalism. Phule's political activities showed keen awareness of transformations wrought by colonial modernity, not least of which was the "new" Brahmin, a product of the colonial bureaucracy. Like his anticaste, non-Brahmin compatriots in the Tamil country, Phule asserted that permanent war between Brahmin and non-Brahmin defined the historical process. This was the foundation for politicised non-Brahmin communities identifying themselves as members of a political and ethical community, the shudra-atishudras, who shared a common identity across jati specificities, jati being the term to describe regionally distinctive caste clusters (e.g., Maratha, Mahar, Deshastha Brahmin) associated with long-term processes of state and society formation.

By the late nineteenth century, there were significant continuities between the new forms of sociopolitical critique and historical identity that Phule established for Dalit and non-Brahmin communities and a distinctively Dalit (largely Mahar) discourse of stigmatised existence. Dalit discourse, however, highlighted the instability of a collective shudra-atishudra identity (and the unique disabilities of being an untouchable) as Dalits confronted efforts to align non-Brahmin (especially Maratha) identity with the varna category, or the prescriptive pan-Indian category, of Kshatriya. Print journalism nurtured this Dalit public sphere. Between 1877 and 1929, many newspapers explicitly addressed the disabilities of caste while fashioning a new sense of Dalit identity. In their pages, Dalit reformers and publicists depicted the practice of untouchability as contingent and wrong, and associated the religio-ritual stigmatisation of Dalits with their illiteracy, poverty, and social backwardness: upper-caste perceptions of untouchability as ritual transcendental were countered by an immanent, sociopolitical critique of caste relations.

Marathas

"Maratha" was an expansive category (and an identity) that was intimately related to early modern patterns of labour mobilisation for land and military markets, and included a range of persons whose bids for political and economic power had succeeded, from the lowly kunbi peasant—cultivator to the ninety-six elite Maratha families, the shahannavkuli, who claimed a genealogical link with the Rajputs. Thus, state formation in the Deccan region was characterised both by the increased salience of the category Maratha in signifying emergent patterns of power, and by a growing number of persons laying claim to Maratha as identity. Entry into the category Maratha was possible through marriage, political economic control over land, and over time, through the fabrication of genealogical affinity with the varna-jati combination of the Kshatriya-Rajput. The inherent plasticity of Maratha social formation was tied to the redistributive economies of Old Regime polities: by embedding holders of service tenures within locality, Old Regime paradigms of land and power also enabled imperial service to function as a mechanism of localisation. The Maratha polity transformed in the eighteenth century into what the historian Hiroshi Fukazawa has termed a "Brahminical" state ruled by Chitpavan Brahmins, the Peshwai. The state-society linkages of the Peshwai produced a unique collective memory of Brahmins' political domination and not merely their ritual authority. This situation and the tripartite caste structure of the Deccan—comprising Brahmins, untouchables, and especially that loosely defined middle group, Maratha-kunbis—enabled an unusual critique of caste oppression.

The consolidation of a Maratha polity was symbolically marked by Shivaji's coronation as Chatrapati in 1674. By then, the Deccan was characterised by a sedentarised populace, monetisation of the economy, and a highly organised regime of revenue collection, though Maratha suzerainty was initially achieved through practices of social banditry and guerilla warfare. Significantly, Maratha dominance provoked challenges to Brahminical authority conducted within ritual idioms. The most famous illustration of the pattern is Shivaji's coronation as Chatrapati, or lord of the chhatra, a large parasol or canopy placed over Hindu gods and kings to signify grandeur and dignity. The controversy over Shivaji's claims to Kshatriya lineage—he came from a family of patils (village headmen) near Pune who acquired power through military service to the Nizam Shah of Ahemdnagar—arose when a section of Deccan Brahmins rejected the possibility of allowing Shivaji to be coronated with Vedic rites reserved for twice-born Kshatriyas. The belatedness of Shivaji's coronation and its ritual recognition of Shivaji's consolidation of real power over the Deccan (and other Maratha families) are noteworthy. Even more important are the multiple significations of the term "Maratha" and growing conflict around efforts to align Maratha jati with Kshatriya varna.

Brahmins

Brahmins continued to deny the Bhosle royal family's claim to Vedic rites and thus rejected their identity as twice-born Kshatriyas. Instead, they argued that the Bhosles were Shudras entitled to rites performed according to the Puranas. Symbolic insults to Maratha identity gained traction across the nineteenth century as the Chitpavan Brahmin community gained political visibility as a consequence of the Brahmin peshwa, or primeminister's increased centrality in political affairs. By 1749, the transfer of real power from the Chatrapati to his Brahmin ministers was an established fact, and Shahu I had been banished to Satara from Poona and confined to his fort, almost a prisoner of the peshwa. The declining political fortunes of the Bhosle family popularised the growing perception among upwardly mobile Maratha-kunbis, that a repetitive structure of Brahmin insult and non-Brahmin humiliation was the governing logic of history. Indeed Brahmins had long maintained that the genocide of Kshatriyas by the Brahmin Parashurama, the sixth incarnation of the Lord Vishnu, as related in the Dasavatara, or the ten incarnations of Lord Vishnu, was proof that there were only three castes in the Kali Yuga: Brahmins, Shudras, and untouchables. In 1913, Shahu challenged Brahmins' exclusive control over scriptural knowledge and ritual performance by establishing a school to train non-Brahmin priests, and by 1921 he had established an alternative locus of Kshatriya ritual authority.

By then, the Deccan had undergone significant political transformation, and both Brahmin and Maratha responses were mediated through a powerful new presence, the East India Company. The Peshwai ended when East India Company forces defeated Peshwa Bajirao II in 1818. Fromthen, the colonial state increasingly played a significant role in defining the meaning and social experience of the term "Maratha"; produced a set of affective attachments and institutional investments in history and (caste) identity, and enabled the rise of a newly salient, oppositional term, "non-Brahmin." Ironically, colonial intervention accelerated two seemingly contradictory processes: the secularisation of caste and its novel association with Hindu religion. The colonial government abdicated direct responsibility for adjudicating issues of ritual status, religious rights, and community standing, though these were important realms of state intervention under the Old Regime. While this produced new openings for challenging caste discipline and Brahminical norms, the mediation of Brahminical knowledge played an important role in colonial knowledge formation.

Colonial modernity had a twofold effect for non-Brahmin communities. It produced new investments in history and caste identity, and it provoked affinity with a new range of modern institutions—schools and colleges, law courts, hospitals—spaces through which social mobility for the downtrodden and exploited might be accomplished. Colonial infrastructure, and its multiple and dispersed effects in the form of a colonial "sensorium," was inextricably linked to new experiences of the self and enabled radical egalitarian ideology to percolate through caste radicals' discourse, from ideas of self-respect and equality among intimates to a critique of the structured political-economic inequities of Brahminism.

Mahar

A distinctive Mahar history was the ground from which other claims to social inclusion emerged and on which differences from non-Brahmins set a divergent trajectory for Dalit politicisation. In drawing on a racial theory of conquest to explain the subjugation of non-Aryan Kshatriyas, the Shudras and atishudras, by Aryan Brahmin invaders, Jotirao Phule transvalued colonial-national fascination with theories of Aryan conquest to argue that a permanent and irreconcilable hostility between Brahmin and non-Brahmin had characterised caste society from its inception. Phule never used the term "Hindu" in his writings, lest it appear that he was describing a consensual religio-cultural formation. He always wrote of Brahmin interests antagonistic to the bahujan samaj, the "majority community." However, by the time Phule was writing the terms "Arya" and "Aryan" had come to symbolise a set of associations between language and territory and between territory and religion, enabling a particular vision of the national-archaic: the civilisational history of India was now aligned with a territorially bounded, geographically distinctive protonational (Hindu) space, Bharat or Bharatvarsha.

The desire to reconstitute a glorious Aryan past in India's present was evident across the board. Phule's conception of history as caste conflict, however, recuperated a non-Aryan Kshatriya past for Maharashtra's downtrodden. Arguing that the word "Kshatriya" originated in the Sanksrit kshetra (field), he imaginatively linked agricultural labour with military service, fields of cultivation with battlefields, and the humble peasant-cultivator with a past of military prowess. Then he went even further, asserting an exceptional role for the downtrodden, the Mahars and Mangs, who had offered the strongest resistance to the Aryan-Brahmin invaders. Interpreting the term "Mahar" as Maha-ari (Great Enemy), Phule argued that the Mahars had twenty-one times freed their Dravidian brothers from conquest by Aryan Brahmins but were finally defeated through chicanery and cunning. Subsequently, the bhat Brahmins, Phule's pejorative term for these ritual specialists, composed sacred texts—the Smritis, the Samhitas, the Shastras, and the Puranas—to justify their ill treatment of vanquished Dravidian Kshatriyas.

In terms of punishment for resistance, the Mahars were defined as untouchables and banished from society, condemned to poverty, feeding on dead carcasses and wearing the black thread as a symbol of servitude.

Kondiram ended with the powerful image of Mahar children sitting on a dung heap, their bodies covered with ash, sores on their eyes, rags covering their buttocks, their stomachs "sunken and empty." Kondiram's imagery echoed the detailed prohibitions of texts such as the Manusmriti, which relegated untouchables to the very edge of human society, near graveyards and on dung heaps. While Pandit Kondiram, like Phule, agreed that the shudra-atishudras were Dravidian Kshatriyas, he presents here a very specific set of images of Mahars' destitution. Though Phule had argued that the shudra-atishudras were a political collective, he had also held Brahmins responsible for creating divisions among them. Coached by wily Brahmins to "hate the Mahars and Mangs," Shudras had forgotten that the untouchable communities were once brave Kshatriyas.

The early Dalit activists such as Gopal Baba Valangkar and Shivram Janba Kamble hitched a martial Mahar identity as Dravidian Kshatriyas to a new goal—a claim to continued employment in the British Army. Army service and its suspension deeply affected the first generation of Dalit publicists who had experienced social mobility and relatively little discrimination in the military. The significance of military service for Mahar Dalit is best understood by examining Valangkar, whose experience in the army, combined with immersion in Phule's Satyashodak ideology, resulted in a systematic Dalit critique of caste injustice.

Gopal Vithalnak Valangkar was a Mahar native of Ravadhul, about five miles from the town of Mahad. He was an active member of the Satyashodak Samaj while in the military. In 1886, he retired as army havaldar (native sergeant) and went to Dapoli in the Ratnagiri district of the Konkan to become a schoolmaster. Dapoli was a unique settlement of Mahar and Chambhar military pensioners.

However, by 1892, Mahars were collateral damage of a decision by the British government to stop recruiting untouchables. They were victims of the "martial races theory" adopted by the British Army after the Mutiny to justify reorganisation of the military along caste lines by excluding Dalits and Brahmins, who were regarded as weak, effeminate, and incapable of martial courage.

Educated up to the Normal School examination in Poona's Shri Ganesh School, Valangkar was deeply influenced by Phule's critique of Brahmin hegemony and the radical egalitarianism of Satyashodak thinking. Subhedar R. S. Ghadge, a military pensioner who later became a member of the Poona branch of Vithal Ramji Shinde's Nirashrit Sahayyak Mandal, recalled that when he was stationed in Poona along with Valangkar, they heard Jotirao Phule lecturing the Mahar regiment about the bravery of the Chambhars, Mahars, and Mangs who had valiantly fought the Aryan Brahmins in ancient times. Another member of the Satyashodak Samaj, Govind Ganpat Kale, recalled that Phule was a frequent visitor to Valangkar's home in the Maharwada in Bhavani Peth and that Phule often tested members of the Samaj by seating them in the same pangthi (row) as Valangkar, while food was served. While the Samaj might have tolerated such experiments in Phule's lifetime, Valangkar himself became a victim of caste prejudice a few years later. In 1895, five years after Phule's death, the Samaj decided to ban Dalits—Chambhars, Dheds, Mahars, and Mangs—from their meetings.

Valangkar's activism manifested both significant continuities with and new departures from Satyashodak thinking. In 1888, Valangkar wrote a Vinanti Patra (Petition Letter) in which he offered an extensive critique of caste exclusion in the form of a series of questions regarding the divine rationale for jati and varna distinctions, and for the practice of untouchability. Elaborating upon Phule's account of the defeat of the Shudra-atishudras,

Valangkar argued for a repetitive structure to the outcasting of the untouchable communities after their original defeat by Aryan Brahmins, and he historicised Dalits' social stigmatisation to the peshwa period, when lower castes and untouchables had faced severe religious exclusion and social violence. Valangkar argued that the Mahar Kshatriyas had been stigmatised after eating meat to survive the Mahadurga famine of 1396. Again during the Peshwai, the lower-caste and untouchable communities had found themselves subject to severe caste discipline under a Brahminical state. As in Phule's account, the abject position of the Dalit was historically produced through the foundational conflict between Aryan Brahmins and the autochthonous Dravidian communities of western India. In Valangkar's account, however, originary conflict was overlaid with an argument that specified a key element of Dalits' degradation, their eating of carrion. This became a recurrent theme in Valangkar's explanations of Dalit stigma, which drew on the real-life experiences of Mahar communities.

Besides founding the first Dalit organisation in the Bombay Presidency, the Anarya Dosh Pariharak Mandali (Society for the Removal of the Misdemeanors of the Non-Aryans) (ADPM), Valangkar was a frequent contributor to the newspapers Sudharak and Din Bandhu. In the 1890s, he toured western India performing kirtans (religious songs) against the ill treatment of the Dalit communities. When he was nominated to the Mahad Local Board in 1895, caste Hindus and Muslims boycotted the board's meetings. This provoked a series of reports in the Din Bandhu criticising Valangkar's treatment. Ironically, this incident occurred in the same year that the Poona branch of the Satyashodak Samaj decided to ban untouchables from their meetings.

Valangkar was adept at the organisational practices of the Satyashodak Samaj, but he was also familiar with the workings of colonial institutions such as the school, the army, and finally, the colonial bureaucracy. When faced with evidence of social exclusion and stigmatisation specific to the untouchable communities, Valangkar responded by seeking colonial intervention to safeguard Dalits' historical rights. In July 1894, Valangkar drafted a petition on behalf of the ADPM to the Bombay government demanding equal employment and civil rights for the untouchable communities. This inaugurated a spate of petitioning from other Dalit activists, including petitions from 1905 and 1910, drafted by Shivram Janba Kamble, demanding Mahars reinstatement into the British Army and employment in police forces. None of these petitions received a positive response. However, the petition became a crucial forum for writing Mahar Dalit history and for self-representation.

Phule's historical conflict between Brahmin and non-Brahmin produced the shudra-atishudra as a revolutionary subject. Like the Dalit to come, shudra-atishudra named a community that did not exist: it signalled a potentiality, but also defined that group historically by valorising their military prowess and indigeneity while challenging their defeat at the hands of wily bhat Brahmins. The power of Phule's narrative lay not only in the refusal of Brahminical hegemony but also in the claim to self representation by the bahujan samaj (majority community) of the downtrodden and toiling castes, now valued as key political actors against alien interlopers. They were the Rakshasas, the protectors of the land, who, once vanquished, appeared in Hindu mythology as asuras, or demons. History was a counter to historical forgetting, an antidote against religious superstition and ideological indoctrination. Valangkar took up the narrative of shudra-atishudra bravery and military valour and the critique of Brahmin chicanery and cunning. Unlike his notable predecessor, Jotirao Phule, whose investment in Enlightenment rationality and humanism was combined with efforts to reinterpret Hindu popular culture, especially the Puranic tradition, Valangkar turned to the Rg Veda and the Bhagavad Gita, and argued that they put forth competing views on the origins of untouchability: the former relied on a model of descent codified in the Manusmriti, while the Gita were based on a theory of karma, or doing. Valangkar's argument regarding a key contradiction between caste as religious transcendental and caste as derived from a theory of action gave the practice of untouchability a more specific history, even as it allowed Valangkar to challenge religious ethics from within the scriptural tradition.

By the early decades of the twentieth century, anti-Brahminism had transformed into political non-Brahminism with a focus on converting the demographic predominance of the non-Brahmin into political power. By the time the movement was incorporated into the Indian National Congress in the early 1930s, non-Brahminism had moved from ideological critique to political contestation. Concurrently, the once expansive, incorporative Maratha identity associated with anti-Brahminism became an exclusive identity tied to the realisation of ritual Kshatriya status, or to forms of peasant populism. As non-Brahmins poured into the Congress, Dalits' conflicts with the Congress were increasingly inflected with a Dalit/non-Brahmin antagonism. Crucially, emerging distinctions between Dalits and non-Brahmins were played out on the field of intimate life and familial relations, gender and genealogy. The regulation of sexuality, in particular, was an important axis for the politicisation of caste identity.

Anti-brahmin Politics

As per Hindu scriptures, especially the Manusmriti, defined both lower castes and women are impure, polluting, and subject to detailed regulation. It is not surprising that Phule and Valangkar equated the plights of these groups. Phule's earliest reform efforts addressed both lower castes and women. Placing gender and sexuality at the heart of caste distinctions enabled a powerful critique of the reproduction of caste through the regulation of gender.

Enforced widowhood, an important target of caste radicals' critique, focused on the inhuman treatment of the widow, who was subject to severe sartorial codes, prohibited from wearing jewellery, and forced to observe dietary restrictions to control her passions. Sexual anxieties about the widow were long-standing, but Hindu reformers' and caste radicals' renewed focus on the treatment of widows coincided with the colonial state's efforts to reform the Hindu joint family.

Caste radicals were distinctive and vociferous in emphasising the importance of caste respectability and sexual purity to the reproduction of Brahminical patriarchy. Thus, when Phule and his wife, Savitribai, opened a home in 1854 for upper-caste widows who faced intimate violence ranging from physical abuse to impregnation, they were criticising a Brahminical order that sanctioned such practices, even as they were challenging upper castes' capacity to protect "their women." Shinde attacked the hypocritical stance of criminalising women rather than challenging the sexual excesses of men and argued that all men, not merely Brahmins, were implicated in the ill treatment of women. The upper-caste widow also played an important role in Valangkar's critique. He compared the tonsure of widows with cows going to the slaughterhouse and argued that widows were deeply susceptible to sexual advances by "ascetics, mendicants, and priests" who congregated at holy places to take advantage of them. Indeed, an established trope in anticaste polemic was Brahminism's ideological reduction of women and the lower castes to beasts of burden: their sentience and physicality were inversely related to their value as persons.

Due to enforced widowhood exposed the structuring relationship between caste hegemony and control over female sexuality, the practice provided the occasion for early critiques of the caste order and of Brahminical mores in particular. A dialogue between a widow and her father in a Satyashodak jalsa (folk drama) uses the widow's physical disfiguration to stage a broader critique of enforced widowhood and to challenge its growing acceptance among non-Brahmin communities where pat (second marriages) had previously predominated.

During the first decades of the twentieth century, Satyashodak jalsas were the main vehicles for spreading the Samaj's message to the rural populace. Traditional tamashas, renowned for their word play and sexual innuendo interspersed with song, typically began with an invocation to Lord Ganapati. The stories centered on the theme of Lord Krishna's dalliances with his gopis (milkmaids). Instead, the Satyashodak jalsa invoked the gana (the people) as leaders (pati, or "the source of rule"). Satyaji's dialogue with Brahmin women on the irrationality of Hindu ritual, discussions about the exploitation of the peasantry, and critiques of the Brahmin-moneylender (shetji-bhatji) were popular. The use of coarse and insulting language was standard. Bhimrao Mahamuni from Otur is credited with having staged the first jalsa with the support of Shahu Chatrapathi and Krishnarao Bhalekar. Ramachandra Ghadge (Kale, Satara district) started his famous jalsa troupe in 1915.

Satyashodak activists experimented with new social forms and countercultural strategies to challenge Brahmin hegemony and exploitation of female suffering. Like the jalsa, another important effort centered on politicising Hindu marriage as the hinge between intimate and public political life, and as the site where ideologies of caste purity and gender respectability were articulated as caste power. Thus the Satyashodak marriage eliminated the need for a Brahmin priest and emphasised self-respect and equality within marriage. This challenge to the social reproduction of caste through religious exploitation of the non-Brahmin communities, and the sexual regulation of (their) women, inspired Ambedkar, who urged Dalits to perform Satyashodak marriage. He even presided over one in Vidarbha in 1927.

Though caste radicals were preoccupied with challenging caste ideology by rethinking marriage and sexuality, they were by no means immune to the extension of novel patriarchal practices into their own households. In the last quarter of the nineteenth century, enhanced regulation of women became a mechanism to resolve anxieties about social status among upwardly mobile, politicised Marathas. Sociocultural practices such as Marathmola percolated down from royal families and landed gentry to young women from upwardly mobile families. This partial segregation of women involved withdrawing their labour and physical presence from public space and became a status marker for Maratha families claiming elite Kshatriya status. Meanwhile, Dalit publicists and reformers underlined the susceptibility of Dalit women to sexual violation according to "custom" and focused on enforced sexual servitude through womens' ritual dedication. Even as Dalit publicists launched a severe critique of the interdependence of sexual compulsion and the material deprivation of Dalit communities, their efforts to modify Dalit intimate relationships also enhanced the authority of male Dalit reformers.

The contradictory effects of the social reform of gender by caste radicals can be explained by the fact that Dalit and non-Brahmin political subject-formation increasingly involved the politicisation of Dalit and lower-castemen through the reform of family and female subjects. Earlier, colonial paradigms of social reform had intersected with (and enhanced) Brahminical models of caste and sexual purity to produce hegemonic ideologies of domesticity, female enfranchisement, and companionate marriage. They had been vigorously criticised by anticaste radicals, who drew attention to the supplemental relationship of gender and caste and the reproduction of caste norms through sexual regulation. In the first decades of the twentieth century, however, non-Brahmin critiques of the gendered character of caste were muted by emergent forms of caste conflict that increasingly framed the modernisation of gender as dependent on the reconstitution of caste masculinity.

An important consequence of the discrete, if mutually entailed, trajectories of gender reform and the politicisation of caste by anticaste radicals was that the subject of non-Brahmin and, later, Dalit politics was imagined as male. Bourgeois ideologies of femininity carried a very different valence for stigmatised communities, since coerced sexual labor constituted a key site of collective humiliation. While such developments speak to divergent genealogies of the feminist subject, they also help to explain the specific conditions that set the ground for a masculinist anticaste politics.

By the early decades of the twentieth century, Jotirao Phule's resonant narrative of Brahmin invasion and political usurpation was redirected to serve an argument regarding the impure, miscegenated origins of the Chitpavan Brahmins. Maratha masculinity was directly engaged in the resulting narratives, while Dalits—excluded from Kshatriya status—were rendered marginal to the conflict. The emphasis on Dalit and Maratha masculinity was the result of caste radicals' initial emphasis on the importance of gender and sexuality in the constitution of the (political) community of caste. Their divergent trajectories can be explained, however, through caste radicalism's intersections with the institutional contexts of colonial modernity and the discursive logics of an emergent cultural nationalism.

In Maharashtra, it was said that there were only Brahmins and Shudras in the Kaliyuga. This indicated a Brahmin centric view of the degradation of the all intermediate castes to Shudra status. Constant conflicts over Shudra status were in evidence from the 1700s, if not earlier, and became especially virulent by 1830 with regard to Chitpavan Brahmins' determination to downgrade the Kayastha Prabhus to Shudra status. Phule had framed them as aliens and interlopers. Valangkar embellished Phule's account: the Konkani Chitpavan Brahmins were Semitic people who had fled the Barbary coast, were shipwrecked off the Malabar coast, married low-caste women from the Konkan region, and became a caste of fishermen. They won power and Brahmin status through cunning. Valangkar went further to explain the distinctions between Mahar and Maratha. He described the Mahars as varnas of mixed jatis who shared the lineage of other Dravidian Kshatriyas—Surya, Chandra, Shes, and Yadu. However, he defined Rajputs and Marathas as Turks who had been sent to annihilate Buddhism and Jainism in India. If Valangkar distinguished the Marathas from other Dravidian Kshatriyas, it is because this was a pronounced theme of Maratha genealogies produced in the early decades of the twentieth century, which sought to redefine Marathas' status as Aryans and as Kshatriyas.

However, Dalits and Marathas past felt compelled, to engage with the Chitpavan Brahmins' genealogy related in the Sahyadrikhand, a caste origin myth that referenced an act of genocide in the Dasavatara to explain the disappearance of Kshatriyas from the Deccan. In the Dasavatara, the axe-wielding Brahmin Parashurama, an incarnation of Vishnu, is said to have exterminated all Kshatriyas during the *Treta Yuga,* in retaliation for his father's murder. To extirpate his sins, Parashurama tried to perform penance. Unable to find Brahmins in the Konkan, he created the Chitpavan Brahmins by purifying a group of sixty fishermen at a funeral pyre. The Chitpavans were rendered pure (*pavana*) through funereal ashes (*chitta*).

If this genealogy rendered Chitpavan Brahmins of dubious distinction, it created an even more compromising account of non-Brahmins. The Shudra-Kshatriyas of Kaliyuga, it was said, were the product of illicit intercaste unions between Brahmin sages, rishis, and enslaved Kshatriya women. The term "Shudra," in both popular discourse and legal texts, conjured the dishonour of impure origins, a bastard identity born out of bondage, sexual degradation, and servitude. Indeed, Maratha assertions in the early twentieth century challenged this foundational narrative of sexual violence and caste miscegenation by addressing the Brahmin's miscegenated identity.

In order to align themselves with region and nation, Marathas asserted that they were the original inhabitants of Maharashtra and thus true nationalists. To make their case they drew on colonial racial typologies inflected by regional caste conflicts and made sometimes confusing and inconsistent distinctions between

Aryans and Dravidians, and Hindus and Brahmins. By the turn of the century, Maratha purity had become a sensitive issue for Maratha activists and elite Maratha families alike. The latter distinguished themselves from Marathas of uncertain status, referred to by a range of terms—*kadu*, *akkarmashe* (lit. "miscegenated," "bastardised"), and *kharchi* (semi-legitimate)—and sought to legitimise status through ritual incorporation into varna hierarchy. Marriage advertisements seeking pure alliances between elite, wealthy Maratha families began to appear in the pages of the Kolhapur newspaper Vijayi Maratha (Victorious Maratha) and the more conservative, Belgaum-based Rashtraveer (Patriot).

Such practices were doubly inflected by the desire to challenge Brahmin hegemony and to claim for Marathas a distinctive Kshatriya identity by aligning jati with varna status. The net result was a shift away from Phule's tradition of radical egalitarianism and critique of religious orthodoxy toward an embrace of Aryan identity for Kshatriya Marathas, now increasingly represented as Hindus with full access to Vedic rituals in contrast to Brahmins, who were portrayed as being of questionable origin. Notable exceptions to this tendency are Mukundrao Patil, editor of the Din Mitra (1910-30), who repeatedly urged an expansive identity for non-Brahmin castes as non-Aryan Hindus ranged against Brahmin domination; and the non-Brahmin activists Keshavrao Jedhe and Dinkarrao Javalkar.

The reconstitution of the Maratha self (and of Maratha masculinity) was inherently unstable. At one level it constituted a challenge to Brahmin power (and Brahmin-centric history) across the *longue durée*. However by positing a direct correspondence between the uneven political regimes that produced Maratha as a resonant caste identity in western India and the ritually exclusive varna status of Kshatriyas, Maratha assertion relied on a genealogy that denied salience for Phule's imagined collectivity of shudra-atishudras. The rewriting of Maratha history left little room for Marathas of questionable status and increasingly rendered alliances between Dalits and Aryan-identified non-Brahmin groups difficult. As debates over caste identity intersected with narratives of sexual violence and structural analyses of the sexual reproduction of caste, complex political tensions between Brahmins, non-Brahmins, and untouchables were also staged. Between 1922 and 1926, an aggressively masculinised counter discourse became a major node of conflict for non-Brahmin challenges to Brahmin superiority.

In the 1890s, Ganpati and Shivaji melas [festivals], started by radical Hindu nationalist Bal Gangadhar Tilak (1856–1920), had countered Muharram processions by politicising public space and religion through everyday cultural symbols and historical figures associated with intimate practices of Hindu religiosity. Themelas included street marches, singing, and the staging of plays that created a context for displays of anticolonial rhetoric and patriotic fervour. They also accommodated inflammatory anti-Muslim rhetoric and derogation of women and anti-Brahmin radicals.

In turn, Chatrapati melas counter staged Maratha masculinity. Participants wore warrior costumes, carried spears and javelins, sang mela songs criticising Brahmin hegemony, and asserted the true national patriotism of non-Brahmins. The Peshwas were blamed for losing Maharashtra to the British. Insults were common. By 1924, nightly fracases between Tilakites and non-Brahmin activists brought the melas under extensive police surveillance and caused the banning of many songs and publications by both sides.

This aggressively masculinised non-Brahmin political culture exacerbated caste antagonism through a sexual politics. Popular pamphlets made sexual innuendos about Brahmin women and represented widows as symbols of Brahmin tyranny. They cast aspersions on the sexual purity of Brahmin communities, characterising them as the illicit offspring of Marathamen and Brahmin women. Brahmins were routinely described as *dasiputras* in polemical texts, thus reversing the Brahmins' narrative of the Marathas as Shudras and the offspring of *dasis* (enslaved women). Indeed, Brahmins complained that one of the taunts employed by the activists was, "the Chatrapati mela has come; Brahmin women better run."

Gender and genealogy were discursively central to this emergent non-Brahmin public sphere. Non-Brahmin activists emphasised the history of concubinage and Brahmin men's sexual exploitation of lower-caste women (and their own wives) through popular-cultural representations of the Peshwai as a period of sexual debauchery. To suggest that Brahmins were foreigners and the offspring of caste miscegenation threatened the Brahmins' claim to caste purity and, therefore, to ritual authority. Government censorship of "inflammatory" or "obscene" texts illustrates the growing significance of a public sphere of print and performance in exacerbating Brahmin/non-Brahmin conflict in Poona, hotbed of Tilakite activism.

The deep-rooted resistance of Brahmins and conservative non-Brahmins—including Phule's relative, Baburao Phule—who accused Phule of being a Christian convert who destroyed Hindu religion, intensified friction and set the stage for a spirited response. The Oriental Translator described the book as "written in the most intemperate and objectionable language; in places the violent fury of the writer has so carried him away that his whirling words are barely intelligible."

Shivaji's protection of Brahmin women from the depredation of Muslimmen was mentioned in conjunction with Brahmin hypocrisy about the behaviour of their women—"the Bhatmind thinks religion is destroyed when a Shudra is crowned king but cannot comprehend when a Brahmin woman comes jumping from the bed of a Shudra. Brahmins, it was noted, had the vile tendency to "suspect their mother's chastity," "shave women," and to allow widows to throw their illegitimate children on "crossroads eight times a week." At the same time, the Brahmin priest "who calls the non-Brahmins Shudras an enemy is a badmash dacoit [bandit] who casts evil glances at their women." Equating Brahminism with slavery, the text noted, "it is a sin to give alms to a Brahmin who smokes ganja, drinks wine and ascends the staircase of houses of ill repute. To get marriage solemnised by Brahmins is tantamount to polluting an auspicious occasion [and] writing the horoscope of a future slave generation."

Given the centrality of gender and sexual regulation to the discursive hegemony of Brahminism in western India, the Brahmin woman had long personified elements of non-Brahmin critique, even as she became the rallying point for a renewed politics of Brahminism. Here, the historic conflict between Brahmins and non-Brahmins was staged through competing narratives of caste masculinity and differential claims over women. Despite this public, explicitly confrontational, masculinist politics, Dalit reformers' masculinity was predicated on the reform of gender within their community and the defense of community honour against the disdain of outsiders. In 1908, the Somavanshiya Mitra published a letter from Shivubai Vallad Lakshman Jadhav-Sonkamble, who identified herself as a murali. Muralis were young girls from the Mahar, Mang, kunbi, and so-called nomadic communities who were married off to the god Khandoba at his temple in Jejuri in fulfillment of a vow. Muralis wore a mangalsutra of seven cowrie shells and, although human marriages were denied them, as nominal wives of the god they were obligated to provide sexual services to men. Murali dedication was among a range of regionally distinctive practices involving women of all statuses, which came to be glossed by the colonial state as ritual "prostitution." The lives of dedicated women, however, were more complex. Many remained with one partner all their lives. As temple servants, others acquired property in the form of tax-free inam lands. Women from Dalit and nomadic communities were historically associated with the traditions of courtly performance, especially the erotic lavani. By the twentieth century, they were more closely associated with tamasha performance, now depicted as a lewd and raunchy popular cultural form.

The legendary Pavalabai was dedicated as a murali, though her exquisite beauty and performative skills brought her to the attention of the famous Brahmin tamasgir (tamasha performer), Patthe Bapurao, born Sridhar Kulkarni. Pavalabi joined Patthe's troupe and became his companion. Though she was a famous performer, Pavalabai's career mirrored the reduced significance of traditional popular culture to an emergent Dalit politics and the growing presence of a reformist critique of (Dalit) female sexuality.

Shivubai's letter was written against this backdrop of male reformers working to abolish stigmatising practices, especially ritual dedication and sexual servitude. She responded to a letter written by a Mahar panch (religious head) castigating muralis as social evils whose sexual promiscuity was ruining Dalit men and their families. Shivubai objected that she was forced to do her job by the men of her community. She noted that many women converted to Islam and Christianity to avoid prostituting themselves. Indeed, Shivubai held the men of her community responsible for perpetuating the practice and called for a campaign against fathers who dedicated daughters. Shivubai's indictment of the men who perpetuated the practice was distinctive. Her point was overwhelmed, however, by multiple and overlapping efforts to criminalise the practice.

The practice of murali dedication was strongest near Jejuri and in southern Maharashtra, where it was associated with a distinctive inheritance practice among the Mahar and Talwar communities. In 1906, the collector of Bijapur argued that "the prevalence of the practice of dedicating girls to prostitution among the Mahars is partly attributed to the fact that the male issue of prostitute daughters are allowed to succeed to a Mahar watan" when a man dies without male offspring. Bomanji argued that even if the practice was customary, "this recognition of illegitimate children should be stopped." What Bomanji failed to mention, however, was that the decision to allow a murali's male heirs to inherit their mother's property had been reached after a decision to disinherit muralis from directly owning ancestral property.

The then Revenue Commissioner for Alienations, Sir Barrow Ellis, noted that "though prostitution was not expressly a condition for tenure, it was customary to retain one unmarried daughter to hand down watan to illegitimate offspring." Government Resolution no. 6788, passed on January 22, 1858 barred ownership through illegitimates. Locally, however, the practice was clearly condoned.

A complex case from 1873, involving a Talwarki watan in the name of "Vianki Talwar," brought up questions of whether a prostitute's adopted son, or her prostitute sister's biological son should inherit her estate. In this case, as with all other cases originating in the Dharwar district, it was decided that inheritance should skip the prostitute and go directly to her male illegitimate offspring. Thus the depiction of the practice of ritual dedication as a form of sexual servitude (and social scandal) was only partially true: murali reform gathered steam after female inheritance was stigmatised and Mahar and Talwarmen had become beneficiaries of governing paradigms that privileged patrilineal inheritance. By the 1890s, various missionary groups had taken up the issue and suggested punishing parents and priests who enforced the tradition and recommended the transfer of dedicated women to orphanages. N.G. Chandavarkar, a social reformer, famous justice of the Bombay High Court and a member of the Society for the Protection of Children, made similar recommendations. By the time the noted Indologist R.G. Bhandarkar sent up a memorial from prominent Indian and European citizens of Poona in August 1906, it was found that an extensive discussion of the devadasi issue had already taken place in Madras in 1903. The figures for dedication in southern Maharashtra for the period 1905–9, when the murali controversy reached its height. The Bombay government's inquiry into the practice encompassed more than four hundred pages of testimony by district magistrates in Bombay, extensive debate on whether murali dedication could be criminalised, as well as far-reaching transformations of Hindu law to prevent illegitimates from inheriting—whether male offspring of muralis or dasiputras customarily entitled to a half share from a Shudra father's estate. The opinion of Dalit male reformers was not solicited, let alone the muralis.

Public attention to the practice of muralis' dedication shifted power within the community toward the viewpoint of male Dalit reformers and publicists. The degradation of Dalit women became a powerful issue around which they mobilised to demand gendered respectability through the abolition of customary practice. As much as intervention into murali practice was a means to reform the Dalit family, it was also the lever to move power away from figures such as the panch and male heads of household and toward Dalit publicists who wielded a normative conception of sexual vulnerability. Debates over ritual dedication—now recast as prostitution—became crucial to the reconstitution of Dalit masculinity even as it secured the social power of publicists, pedagogues, and community spokesmen.

Shivubai's letter launched a furious debate in and beyond the Somavanshiya Mitra. Efforts were made in Jejuri to educate families against dedicating their daughters. Shivram Janba Kamble held a meeting in Jejuri where he made a speech against the practice. Muralis like Shivubai held fathers responsible for pushing their daughters into the practice and criticised male customers for creating a market for muralis' sexual labor. Butmen castigated muralis for seducing them and breaking up families, thereby assuming muralis' "consent" to their dedication. This was tricky given the normal age of dedication and its representation as customary practice. And yet, muralis (and their families) were blamed for perpetuating a practice that stigmatised the entire community.

Dalit reformers—like missionaries—suggested criminalising murali dedication. A 1909 reformers' petition demanded the registration of muralis and the prosecution of parents who performed new dedications. This produced a climate among Mahars that was responsive to criminalisation of the practice. By then, the Bombay government had reached a consensus that criminalising the practice was the most direct means of curtailing it. No new legislation was passed, but a proclamation banning the practice and reiterating the punishment for dedication was issued. Subsequently, the Somavanshiya Mitra carried news of two men, Kisan Sadhu Mahar of Jejuri and Mahalu Mahar of Bombay, prosecuted for dedicating their daughter and sister, aged eleven and thirteen, respectively.

Although some muralis supported criminalising the practice of dedication, their primary focus was on redefining their position within the Dalit community. In addition to prosecuting muralis, Dalit reformers like Kamble also promoted murali marriage and sexual monogamy as the route to gendered respectability. Shivubai argued that marrying muralis acknowledged men's responsibility for the practice, even as it enhanced muralis' self-respect and community standing. In fact, on April 18, 1909, the Somavanshiya Mitra noted that Shivubai had married the social reformer, Ganpatrao Hanumantrao Gaikwad. Marriage offered protection in a context where men were actively involved in acquiring, dedicating, and frequenting muralis. For the women who chose to remain muralis, however, emphasis on marriage further stigmatised the practice and pushed it into a zone of shameful secrecy. Murali remarriage continued to have great public support.

As the reform of the traditional practice of murali dedication came to be allied with the reform of the Dalit intimate, sexual monogamy and the production of family became appealing alternatives for Dalitmen and women to whom this held out a recognisable model of respectability. Sexual respectability was achieved, however, through the stigmatisation of "custom" and ritual servitude or dedication.

The fraught position of female subjectivity "between community and state" is an enduring binarism in South Asian historiography. An adroit colonial move allied women with caste and religious communities and simultaneously castigated communities for reproducing female backwardness and preventing female emancipation. As the relationship between women and community deepened, first in reaction to colonial intervention and later as a form of nationalist glorification, the possibility of gender equality was also precluded. By the turn of the century, uppercaste nationalists had recuperated women as symbols of a modernised "tradition" and relegated them to the inner recesses of community life, arguing that women would be enfranchised from within community rather than through colonial state intervention. An issue taken up largely by Christian missionaries and later by Dalit reformers, murali reform was distinct from this colonial-nationalist association of women with tradition. Here, the issue was the over determined association of Dalit female sexuality with sexual availability and degraded female value. The ill treatment of the upper-caste Hindu widow by scriptural injunctions is an apt comparison, although Dalit reformists differed in their efforts to create a set of secular associations between femininity and domesticity.

As the work of regulating Dalit women continued in more dispersed forms, the degraded status of women was seen to be closely related to the emasculation of Dalit men. Fifteen years after the murali issue died down, an editorial by the Dalit activist and thinker B.R.Ambedkar asked why Brahmin and upper-caste women enjoyed an exalted status as mothers when Dalit women's children were subjected to humiliation and denied basic recognition.

The right to a new habitus, to good clothing, footwear, jewellery, and bodily comportment—standing erect while speaking, refusing to contort the body in an obsequious fashion—was critical to Dalit self-fashioning. Though discourses of sexuality and of female enfranchisement were caste-specific, the focus on the feminised body—how it was experienced and represented—was central to a range of political processes. Women, marriage, and family remained irreplaceable sites for reproducing caste ideas and practices. Thus emergent forms of a caste specific female subjectivity were directly implicated in the production of a social field where transformations of the non-Brahmin and Dalit habitus could occur, and they deeply affected emergent forms of caste masculinity. The politics of caste and gender complicated modes of political participation and of subject-formation associated with masculinisation and community modernisation. In a very real sense, however, the stage was set for a Dalit public sphere rendered male.

Agitations for Equality

As a distinctive identity for Mahar Dalits was clarified in the late nineteenth century, so too were the emerging tensions of village life intensified—conflicts between Dalit and Maratha groups over provision of services, the exploitation of caste labor, and friction between claims to Brahmin proportional representation and anti-casteism increased. The situation made escape from the village highly desirable for Dalits. Indeed, the liberatory potential of machine and metropolis exerted a profound hold on the Dalit imagination and the Dalit modernity that developed in concert with the urbanisation of Dalit communities.

Mahar Dalits migrated to cities like Bombay and Nagpur in disproportionate numbers. Mahars performed unskilled labor under difficult and exploitative working conditions—40 percent of them were considered to be performing "coolie" labor, and they constituted more than 45 percent of the total workforce. They were concentrated in particular industries: more than 60 percent worked in the railways or textile mills—the railways were the first and most significant mode of Mahar employment and drew a majority of workers from the Nasik and Ratnagiri districts. Significant numbers worked for the municipality, for factories, and for public works companies such as Bombay Electric Supply and Transport (BEST). Mahar migrants from Satara comprised the bulk of dock workers and coalminers. Urban migration and urban infrastructure—especially everyday technologies of travel and communication that appeared to shrink, even obviate, social distance—provoked key transformations of Dalit selfhood.

Din Bandhu's commentator on urban life was clear that modern travel— "sitting with thighs and shoulders touching"—obliterated caste distinctions, because it was impossible to maintain caste taboos or regulate contact in public conveyances.

Lower-caste use of steamboats, trains, and trams opened a new dimension where touch was rendered anonymous even as it was secularised. However, these new spaces were in constant danger of being overwhelmed by social pressure to reproduce hidebound Brahminical beliefs and practices.

Valangkar's abhang was publicising the Din Bandhu Sarvajanik Sabha. Valangkar drew on a set of gendered associations between social stigma and public intercourse to challenge Dalits' civic exclusion. Like a woman naturally "shy of her husband and public gatherings" when she was menstruating, Dalits also experienced "shame" and self-revulsion. One was never to see a Mang or a Mahar in public. Valangkar's abhang challenged the Dalit's internalisation of pollution and proposed that without equality between Brahmin and Mahar, between the excessively fortunate and the excessively stigmatised, there could be no true "public." For Valangkar, the organisation of the world through the phenomenology of touch and smell also enabled an extension of stigma from biological bodies to the metaphorical collective of the body politic. In the interplay between literal touch and the imaginative democratisation of the body he saw possibilities for self-fashioning and political transformation. Going further, Valangkar also suggested that only with a caste mind cleaned of impurities could the Sarvajanik Sabha accept the Dalit castes.

Ironically, then, the institutional spaces and amenities of colonial urbanity exacerbated the experience of the caste body by highlighting the irrationality of caste segregation. As Dalit publicists—Valangkar, Kamble, and others—denaturalised the caste order, they also motivated caste Hindus to justify caste distinction in new ways that utilised the regulatory power of colonial institutions to produce new instruments of caste hegemony. Both dimensions, Dalit emancipation and new forms of subjection, were played out in schools and temples.

Access to education was a long-standing demand of Dalit publicists, as it had been for Satyashodak activists. Education was central to self fashioning because it demystified the Brahmin trickery at the heart of the continued dehumanisation of Dalits and non-Brahmins. There was also the material fact of Brahmin preponderance in colonial administration. Conflicts over access to colonial schooling emphasised the built-in contradictions of colonial education. In 1882, the Hunter Commission asserted the government of India's commitment to untouchable education, reaffirming Wood's Dispatch of 1854, which opened government-funded schools to all castes in response to missionary pressure. The record of government-funded education for untouchables was poor, however.

The most famous case is of the Christian Mahar convert from Dharwar who petitioned the government in June 1856 after being denied admission into the government school. The Bombay government refused to compromise the education of the majority of caste Hindu students at a government school for the sake of "a single individual" by making caste Hindus associate with a Mahar student. Caste Hindus' right to exclusive education was thus reinterpreted as the colonial administration's respect for the religious sentiments of the majority.

The Free Church of Scotland and the American Marathi Mission had supported Phule's Society for the Promotion of Mahars and Mangs, which established schools in Pune between 1848 and 1852. The extensive involvement of missionaries in the field of untouchable education was viewed as blurring the line between proseletysation and social service, compromising the colonial state's explicit commitment to religious noninterference after the 1857 Mutiny. Colonial officials held missionaries responsible for politicising untouchables who showed "independence and self-sufficiency," by inciting them to "claima right" even when untouchables themselves chose not to exercise it, thus exacerbating conflict between the majority of caste Hindu students and a few untouchable students.

Conflicts over equal education in the 1880s and 1890s confirmed government fears of unrest. Often, the government's anxiety to maintain (and enhance) the population of students attending publicly funded English schools undercut the commitment to education for untouchables.

Increasingly, the colonial government faced a spate of petitions as untouchable students—who faced informal boycott by caste Hindus or the active enforcement of segregated education by colonial officials—petitioned for civic inclusion, while the parents of caste Hindu students wished to exclude untouchables from classrooms. The Bombay Education Department had considerable leeway in deciding issues on a case-by-case basis in this contentious atmosphere. As government's general commitment to native education confronted its specific commitment to untouchables' education, a novel resolution arose: Dalit students were placed on the school's verandah at a distance from both caste Hindu classmates and the classroom, to fulfil the colonialmission of educational access.

Sitting on the verandah obstructed the untouchable students' vision and hearing and left them vulnerable to the adversities of climate. In 1916, Communist activist R. B. More attended classes on the first floor of a school in Tale, in the Mangaon district, sitting on a scaffold erected by school authorities. Like the scaffold, the school verandah preserved the illusion of equal education even as it emphasised the liminal status of those Dalit students who had managed to secure a right to government education. Reinterpreting the caste Hindu position as the majority sentiment, colonial officials made the verandah a new technology of segregation that reproduced caste exclusion.

Dapoli, the hub of early Dalit activism, was also a significant site of struggles for equal education. After the Society for the Propogation of the Gospel closed down its primary school, military pensioners petitioned the government on July 1, 1892, to enrol fourteen of their children in the municipality's primary school. After asserting that admitting Dalit children would cause caste Hindu students to leave the school, the Dapoli municipality agreed to open a separate class with a separate teacher if the Mahar and Chambhar pensioners could collect enough boys. B. R. Ambedkar, who attended that school between 1894 and 1896, described how all the Dalit students sat in one room, placing their slates on the ground so teachers could examine them. The children were barred from the common water supply. The right to education, when combined with new practices of segregation, paradoxically intensified untouchable students' experience of stigma.

The Mahar community's growing refusal to countenance socioritual stigmatisation produced new sites of contestation. Like separate educational facilities, efforts to build separate temples reflect an arc of Dalit critique. The economic enfranchisement of an important group of Mahar elites in the Vidarbha region enabled the institutionalisation of a separate religious authority for Mahars. The 1877 opening of Empress Mills in Nagpur had provided a new source of livelihood for Mahar Dalits. In addition, a Mahar petty bourgeoisie of malguzars (landlords) financed the move into an industrialising cotton economy. This educated elite maintained links with rural areas, endowing schools and hostels and playing a role in shaping early Dalit politicisation.

Born in 1864, Vithoba Raoji Moon Pande typified the new Mahar "small scale capitalist" first mentioned in an 1899 settlement report for the Nagpur district. Educated in a mission school and influenced by critiques of caste hierarchy and Hindu superstition, he took advantage of his frequent travel as a cotton trader to act as a pracharak (preacher) for the Gorakshan Sabha (Organisation for Cow Protection) which had links with the Arya Samaj. In 1906, Moon Pande established the Antyaj Samaj (Society for the Outcastes), renamed the Loyal Mahar Sabha in 1912 and presided over by his close associate, the Reverend G.D. Philips. Before he died in 1924, Moon Pande had requested nomination to the Central Provinces Legislative Council. Like Valangkar, Moon Pande's life coincided with the emergence of the Dalit public and publicists in the crucible of colonial modernity. Unlike Valangkar, however, Moon Pande's challenge to caste discrimination instituted an alternative source of religious hierarchy.

Moon Pande responded to the Brahmins' exploitation of Mahars at the Ramtek temple by establishing a separate Mahar priesthood to minister to the community's religious needs. To counter the Gorakshan Sabha's failure to build separate Mahar ghats, Moon Pande asked—and received—permission from the Ramtek Temple Committee to build a separate temple for Mahars on January 24, 1905. In March 1906, he acquired land for the purpose at a high price. That same year the Antyaj Samaj committee took over management of the new Mahar ghats, established an independent Mahar priesthood, and gave Moon Pande pandeship, the right to perform rites and receive dakshina (charities) from Mahar pilgrims at the ghats.

By 1907–08, this parallel structure of religious authority protected Mahar pilgrims from paying extravagant sums for shraddha (funeral) rites. Moon Pande's use of Mahars' growing economic strength to assert a positive Hindu identity went further. Along with the Reverend G.D. Philips, he collected funds for a separate temple, a Shivalaya, near the Mahar ghats. Construction began on October 27, 1920, and was completed in 1924, shortly before Moon Pande's death.

Separate institutions signalled failed efforts at civic and religious equality. They also indexed the changed discursive and political contexts of Dalit self-fashioning. Unlike the establishment of separate schools, Moon Pande's temple and Mahar priesthood reproduced religious hierarchy by legitimising the priest's role. Instead of criticising Hinduism in toto and envisioning a complete excision from Hindu religiosity, Moon Pande's critique of religious exclusion produced a mimetic structure of religious authority, a Mahar priesthood. At the same time, his work underscored the growing economic strength of an emerging Mahar elite whose power as reformers within the community allowed them to challenge the Hindu hierarchy. Moon Pande's actions were radical and reformist, and indicated the ambivalences of Mahar religiosity and the limits to Hindu inclusion.

References

Ainapur, L. S. *Dynamics of Caste Relations in Rural India*. Rawat Publications. Jaipur. 1986.

Bandyopadhyay, Sekhar. *Caste, Culture, and Hegemony: Social domination in Colonial Bengal*. Sage Publications. New Delhi. 2004.

Bayly, Susan *Caste, Society and Politics in India from the Eighteenth Century to the Modern Age*. Cambridge University Press. 1999.

Benjamin, Joseph. *Scheduled Caste in Indian Politics and Society*. Ess Ess Publishers, New Delhi. 1989.

Kothari, Rajni *Caste in Indian Politics*. Orient Longman. 2004.

Shah, Ghanshyam (ed.) *Dalit Identity and Politics*. Sage Publications. New Delhi. 2001.

4

CASTE CONFLICTS

Caste conflicts are intense, sudden, but not necessarily wholly unplanned, lethal attacks on the civilian members of one caste by civilian members of another caste, with the victims chosen because of their group membership. Such riots are vicious events that involve not just killing and maiming but also mutilations and other atrocities. These riots usually lead to numerous deaths, even more refugees and internally displaced persons and greater caste homogeneity in the area as a result of the violence that has occurred.

In India, caste conflicts have risen in prominence because factors like land, employment and resources have increasingly come under pressure with increasing population but the level of resources has remained stationary. Usually such riots are more common in the East and the North of India where employment opportunities are scarce outside of the traditional avenues of agriculture and more recently, the swelling government bureaucracy. Typically, caste conflicts arise in a situation where there is a feeling that one caste community is being edged out by the other community or communities.

The caste-based riots commonly seen in states like Bihar and Uttar Pradesh in particular, where the issue has been domination of a different kind. Egged on by radical left groups and also by mainline political groupings like the Bahujan Samaj Party, the established feudal systems were challenged. This rebellion was violent in its manifestation. Unfortunately, the established feudal classes like the Bhumihars and the Muslim landlords reciprocated equally violently and brutally—the former by constituting the Ranbir Sena and the latter by constituting the Sunlight Sena.

There are many opinions underlying the emergence of the Senas in Bihar. Some consider that the Senas came into being in response to Naxalite terrorism. Some attribute the rise of the Senas to the fallout of the green revolution. According to them, higher productivity could not remove the basic inequalities that existed between the landlords and the land-less. The demand of the peasants for fair distribution led to the formation of the Senas to suppress the landless labourers.

The increase in the physical manifestation of violence also owes it to the hitherto-subordinated communities asserting their rights. It is only when such communities seek to transgress the boundaries drawn by society that we see eruptions of this kind. The spurt in brutality should not be read as a mere collusion between civil society and the State. The widespread violence inflicted on Dalits across the country, particularly in the North, owes also to the Dalits publicly asserting their rights, especially in the wake of the Mandal Report and the Ambedkar Centenary in 1990.

Besides the Dalits, several communities—sub-castes, religious minorities and tribes are organising themselves as identity movements The secular and liberal intellectuals are uncomfortable with such assertions on the part of caste and religious minorities, but these struggles are significantly reshaping democracy in India. The violence we see today results from these contests.

Pattern of Caste Conflicts

In India, the caste system has resulted in highly stratified societal structure with a hierarchy of castes. In traditional and formal sense, the caste system is based on three interrelated principles. These are predetermined social, cultural and economic rights of each caste based on birth; the unequal and hierarchical (graded) division of these rights among the castes and provision of strong social ostracism supported by social and religious ideology to maintain the Hindu social order. While the first two of them defined and laid down the framework of the caste system, the third prescribed the social mechanism of its enforcements. Third feature of caste system relating to the provision of strong ostracism for the enforcement of the system is quite important and crucial in providing the continuity of the system despite the changes in the in legal framework of social behaviour of the Hindus in contemporary India. The social ostracism normally takes the form of numerous penalties, supported by social and religious ideology. The form of social ostracism varies from social and economic boycott to various types of physical punishments to the low caste untouchables who challenge the traditional rules. The violation of the customary rules and practices invite violent conflicts between the dalit and the dominant castes.

The conflict between the dalits and other dominant caste are not a new phenomenon. The social behaviour by the dalit contrary to the customary rules and norms or assertion in some form by them for human basic human rights—to be treated equally have invited the violence reaction and atrocities by higher caste. It is very clear from the field results that the atrocities committed on Dalits presents a pattern, which is reflective of the continuing influence of the customary rules and norms on the behaviour of the Hindu toward dalits. The extent and the magnitude of various crimes committed against Dalits certainly reflect the incivility and violent character of caste system. What has come out of this study is that discrimination and untouchability is still being practised and the traditional machanism in the form of social ostracism and numerous penalties is used by the high caste on large scale. Dalits predicaments are such that the provision of equal citizenship guaranteed by the Constitution has become a farce in several spheres, if not in all.

The magnitude of atrocities is measured in terms of number of cases registered by the dalit with police under Indian penal code, Protection of civil right act and prevention of atrocities Act. This statistics is picked up from the annual report of the SC/ST Commission and Crime in India for eleven states.. Official data are supplemented by the survey data on the nature and pattern of violence and atrocities. Survey information is qualitative in nature, with case studies from about 550 sample villages in eleven states The case studies, which are collected through field survey and in close interaction with the dalits, indeed is a mirror of the present state of Hindu society with respect to the continuing influence of caste system in rural India.

A total of two and half lakh (precisely 252370 cases) cases of various crimes were registered countrywide by the dalits during

1990 to 2000. Of the total crimes about 94 percent is accounted by the eleven sample states. Four BIMARU states however accounted bulk of the crimes and atrocities. In fact in 2000 Uttar Pradesh, Rajasthan, and Madhya Pradesh account for about 65 percent of crimes and atrocities against SC in the country, and this is far higher than their in the total SC population in the country which is 65 percent. Southern States: Andhra Pradesh, Karnataka, Tamil Nadu and Kerala are no less good. Gujarat and Maharashtra also accounts for worst cases of crimes reported against Dalits.

After having presented the magnitude of crime and atrocities based on the official statistic we try to get insight in to the pattern of violence and atrocities based on the field survey which again the Commission have been conducted in eleven states. There are a wide range of violence—varying from psychological humiliation/ torture to physical assault, and sexual violence against Dalit. The range of violence is indeed widespread and indicative of the oppressive character of the caste system. There are also regional variations in the pattern of atrocities.

Regional Variations

In the state of Andhra Pradesh caste conflicts take numerous forms. It include Murder, Rape, Naked Parading of a Dalit woman, Social Boycott, Grievous Hurt, Beating, Attacking of Dalit Bastis, Destruction of Properties, Causing Serious Injuries, Death in Police custody, Encroachment on Dalit lands, Bonded Labour, Forceful Eviction from House-sites, Harassment due to love relationship with Caste Hindu, Suicide due to humiliation & excessive beating by the Police, Beating up for riding a cycle; wearing nice cloths; for sitting in the Bus, Harassment of Dalits Sarpanches and Panchayat members, and Resentment and insult over winning of Dalit. Attempts by the Dalits to assert their self-respect and to break the taboos imposed by the high castes are viewed with hostile suspicion and met with violence of various types. Whenever Dalits have tried to organise themselves or assert their rights, there has been a backlash from the high caste feudal lords resulting in mass killings, gang rapes and arsoning of Dalit.

Bihar represents one of the leading states in term of magnitude and intensity of violence on the dalits. Massacres after massacre and endless list yields obnoxious results—the number of Dalits killed are extremely high. The nature of atrocities that are committed on the Dalits vary in forms but there has been a single underlying logic of demeaning them and forcing them into retreat a passive and submissive existence. They range from a macro level organised violence and repression through formation of Senas (private armies) to the micro level, ban on entering village temple or discriminatory use of ghats (river banks/lake sides) and a forceful implementation of these discriminatory unwritten rules by non-Dalit castes. The other quite commonly encountered forms of atrocity have been intentional acts designed to demean the community through challenging the notions of izzat (dignity/respect) that exists in the community. These have been the common theme in all the regions of Bihar.

In Karnataka, the atrocities took number of forms like Murder, Rape, Grievous injuries, Arson, Abuse and insults, illegal occupation of Dalit lands, Bonded labour, foisting of false cases & unlawful arrests/detention by Police, Prevalence of Devadasi system, discrimination in Hotels & Tea stalls, No access to wells and other drinking water sources, Outraging the modesty of Dalit women, naked parading of Dalit Women, Forcing Dalits force to consume human waste. Brutal repression is unleashed when Dalits refuse to carry out the traditional work related to all kinds of menial and degrading jobs. The Dalit entering a temple, or even entering a restaurant for tea or food is considered as an assertion for equality by Dalit, which invite violent reaction on the part of high caste.

In Madhya Pradesh, there are various types of atrocities being committed which include, Murder, Attempt to Murder, Rape, Arson, Hurt, Abuse; insult & beating, wrongful confinement & arrests, Attack on Dalit houses and outraging the modesty of Dalit women, Eviction from houses, Forceful driving away from villages, etc. In the recent past the atrocities against Dalits in the state have increased due to various reasons. Among other reasons the decision of the state government to distribute land to the Dalits previously marked as grazing land and state policy to ensure reservation in Panchayats and to ensure participation of Dalits, tribal and women in local governments are most prominent. Opening of avenues for the Dalits, has provoked the high caste to violence.

In Maharashtra, which is known for social movement, does not have good record with respect to atrocities against. In 2000, a total of 489 cases of crimes, untouchability and atrocities were registered by the dalits and this include 2 murder, 16 cases of hurt, 49 rapes, 98 cases of untouchability and 128 cases of atrocities.

In Orissa, the atrocities relate more generally to land disputes, payment of low wages, utilisation of common property resources and enforcement of caste based discrimination and untouchability. In most cases, the police or the State have had minimal role to play and never been sited as having given any justice to the Dalits. It might be said clearly that the State's responsibility to protect the dignity and livelihood of Dalits has been violated in many instances. There are also innumerable instances of caste violence that go unreported due to the fear of backlash by the upper castes. Since dalit is dependent on them for survival they bear and absorbed the insult and anger quietly.

The cases of atrocities against Dalits in rural Punjab are not all that glaring. Of all the 51 villages studied, there was only one village in the Malwa region from where a case of social boycott of Dalits by the dominant castes was reported to have taken place during the last five years. Boycotting no longer works as an effective method of controlling Dalits in rural Punjab. However, there have been a few cases of "individual oriented" atrocities. Though the caste factor remains important in these cases, so far most of these cases did not lead to the involvement of the entire caste communities in the conflict. Most frequent cases of atrocities reported from rural Punjab are those of physical beatings. And nearly all of them emanate from the prevailing structure of agrarian relations, viz., the Dalit labourers being assaulted by their dominant caste employer farmers.

The Dalits in Rajasthan face far more hostile situation than in Punjab, given the feudal and deeply caste ridden character of the society. Rajastan account for about 20 percent of all crimes committed against dalit in the country. This ratio of crimes against dalit was much higher than their share in the countries SC population, which was about only 5.5 percent. In fact Rajastan's share in the crime was four time higher than its share in SC population. The atrocities in Rajastan takes various forms and include insult & abuse, Beating, Grievous Hurt, Foisting of false cases; wrongful confinement/arrests, etc.

The raising trend in the atrocities in Tamil Nadu is closely associated with growing assertion among the dalit in the state. These atrocities are brutal in nature leading to grievous hurt and murder of dalit. They are aimed at generating scare, and fear psychosis so that Dalit would be forced to accept their subordinate status. These violent acts are, more often than not, accompanied by a massive destruction of properties, such as arsoning of the houses, breaking of household utensils and setting fire on crops in the lands owned by Dalits. The purpose behind most of the atrocities is to root out Dalit resistance, socially, psychologically and economically. The destruction of properties assumes more importance as aggressive non-Dalits recognised that the assertion of dalit is closely associated with their economic well-being.

The state of U.P rank first both in term of absolute number of crimes against SC and in term of U.P.'s share of crimes against SC in the total crimes committed against SC in the country. U.P account for almost one third of the total crimes committed against the SC in the country and this ratio was much higher than the U.P. SC population's share in the total SC population in the country. The SC population in U.P constitute about 17 percent of SC population in the country, but its share in the total crime against SC was about one third (or 30 percent). The high number of cases registered under the atrocities is a grim reminder of the continuing and unabated violence and atrocities against the Scheduled Castes in the state Information from the field study in the form of sample case studies across the villages indicated cases of atrocities related to bonded labour, depriving of government housing scheme, false cases for theft, restriction on the use of public roads and discrimination in wage payments.

Gujjar Agitation in Rajasthan

Gujjars — a farming, royal, worrier and trading tribe — are classified by the government as an "Other Backward Class". They are part of the caste system that do not face as much exclusion or discrimination in society. The Gujjar community feels it has been economically and educationally left behind and it wants to be reclassified as a Scheduled Tribe. They demand scheduled tribe status so that they can qualify for government jobs and state college seats reserved solely for such groups. The Indian government has put in place an affirmative action plan that sets aside job and educational quotas for the disadvantaged groups that it classifies as Scheduled Tribes and Scheduled Castes. These tribes, the government believes, need extra assistance to overcome centuries of neglect.

The state government however has so far declined to change their status. Instead has announced to spend Rs. 2.82 billion ($ 67 million) for improving schools, clinics, roads and other infrastructure in Gujjar-dominated areas. However, Gujjar leaders have said that they "do not want money".

Even in 2007, Gujjars in Rajasthan had fought police and members of the powerful Meena tribe that already qualifies for Scheduled Tribe benefits and is opposed to Gujjars sharing the benefits it has cornered for itself. At least 26 people were killed in that violence. In wake of the ongoing Gujjar agitation in neighbouring Rajasthan, high alert had been sounded in the border districts of Madhya Pradesh to check any spread of violence. The agitation finally ended after Rajasthan Chief Minister Vasnundhara Raje agreed on a 5 per cent reservation under a new special category.

The violence erupted in the state of Rajasthan in India on 23 May 2008 when protesters belonging to the Gujjar caste who were demanding a lower scheduled tribe status,instead of their current, higher OBC (Other Backward Class) status, lynched a policeman in Bharatpur district in Rajasthan. In response, police shot at protesters as they tried to damage railway lines and government property. At least 15 were killed on the spot.

On 24 May, the Indian army was called in to help calm the violence as another 15 people were killed when police shot at a mob protesters trying to torch a police station in Sikandra.

Thousands of protesters blocked a rail route between Delhi and Mumbai. Highways had also been blocked, and state authorities cancelled many buses.

Police in Sikandra town fired at protesters who torched a police station and two buses and shot and wounded a policeman, said Amanjit Singh Gill, Rajasthan's director-general of police. Protesters also burned down a police station in the nearby village of Chandra Guddaji, Gill said. Fifteen demonstrators died Friday when police fired live ammunition and tear gas to halt rioting, said Singh. A police officer was also beaten to death. At least 70 injured people were hospitalised in Jaipur, the state capital, and the town of Dosa.

Demonstrators blocked a major highway linking Jaipur to Agra — site of the world famous Tejo Mahalay or Taj Mahal monument — stranding thousands of people. Thousands of army, police and paramilitary forces patrolled villages to control the violence.

26 May witnessed sporadic violence when more than 36 towns observed a bandh to protest against the police firing. Six wagons of a goods train on its way to Agra derailed near Bandikui station in Dausa district due to tampering of rail tracks, allegedly by the Gujjars. Northern railway cancelled nine trains passing through Rajasthan and diverted several others to different routes.

The Indian Army, the Rapid Action Force, jawans of the Rajasthan Armed Constabulary, besides the Rajasthan police, carried out patrolling in the troubled districts of Bharatpur, Karauli and Dausa as at least a dozen places, including Alwar, Kotputli, and Kekri in Ajmer, Pali and Rayla in Bhilwara observed *bandhs*.

Government's Response

Rajasthan Chief Minister Vasundhara Raje on 25 May said there is a limit to everything and that her government will not allow Gujjars to take the state to "ransom". "It is shocking that notorious dacoits and goonda elements, wielding arm and ammunition, have joined Kirori Singh Bainsla and are indulging in arson and violence. Such things will not be tolerated," Raje stated. The government will not allow anyone to take the state to ransom and law and order into their own hands, she warned. Raje alleged "a political party from a neighbouring state was instigating and pumping money" to fuel the violence in the state. She said the government is open for talks to resolve the issue in a peaceful manner and regretted that Bainsla has been rejecting her appeals. Expressing anguish over the violent incidents that have rocked the state since the past two days resulting in death of 37 people, Raje said there is limit for "bearing such violence and arson" and warned of stringent action against those who take the state to ransom. She said it was very unfortunate that the violence comes in the wake of the Jaipur bombings which claimed 66 lives.

On 26 February, the Chief Minister announced that she would write to the Prime Minister of India recommending placing Gujjars in the category of de-notified tribes, setting aside a reservation of 4-6 per cent for them. With post-mortem examination and the last rites yet to be performed on the bodies of 18 persons killed in police firing, the Rajasthan government on made it clear that a commando operation would be the "last option" for the recovery of the bodies now in the custody of large congregations of Gujjars at Karwadi village in Bayana tehsil of Bharatpur and at Sikandra in Dausa district. "We could have recovered the bodies in less than two hours using force. However, we will not do that considering the chances of further bloodshed," Home Minister Gulab Chand Kataria said. Parliamentary Affairs Minister Rajendra Singh Rathore told journalists here that the "Gujjar reservation is a national issue. The Cabinet has decided to write to the Prime Minister requesting him to convene a meeting of Chief Ministers to review the National Scheduled Tribe Policy document of 2006."

However, on 27 May Kirori Singh Bhainsla rejected Chief Minister Vasundhara Raje's proposal for additional reservation for the agitating community. Bainsla's rejection of the proposal was unexpected, as he had earlier welcomed Raje's move to recommend in a letter to the Prime Minister four to six percent special reservation for the community.

Madhya Pradesh, another state with a large Gujjar population was put on alert after the violence. Delhi was also affected for 2 days. Community members, who have decided to assemble at Gwalior in Madhya Pradesh along with the bodies of those killed in the agitation. To keep control of the situation, additional police forces have been deployed in Morena and Chambal, keeping in view large number of Gujjars residing in the region. Police were also keeping a strict vigil on the Rajghat bridge on the highway of Rajasthan border.

Caste Violence in Bihar

Bihar has seen conflict between the upper castes (the landowning feudal classes and business contractors) and the lower castes (usually powerless sharecroppers and agricultural labourers) ever since independence. The gradual empowerment of these lower classes has provoked a bloody reaction from the gangs (sena) surrounding upper-caste criminals. The ever-present repression and retaliation escalated in the second half of the 1990s, when the entire populations of a number of hamlets were massacred in outbursts of Naxalite and sena violence.

Lack of effective state intervention and the political patronage of the upper-caste militias have worsened the situation described above. Patronage along caste lines by various political parties and organisations has exacerbated the problem of suppression and violence. In Bihar, civil society is organised along caste lines to a far greater degree than in other Indian states. This caste orientation reinforces the strong nexus between the landlords, contractors, criminals, politicians, and administrators. Bihar, apart from being one of the biggest states (with 83 million inhabitants in 2001, after Jharkhand had been split off to form a separate state), is also the poorest state in terms of both per capita income and human-development indicators. Whereas India as a whole, and the surrounding states with a similar feudal past (Uttar Pradesh and West Bengal), have considerably reduced the percentage of people below the poverty line, Bihar has not. Male and female literacy in 2001 were as low as 60 percent and 34 percent respectively, which is far below the average of 76 percent and 54 percent of India as a whole.

This continuing poverty is due partly to the feudal rigidity in the agrarian structure of Bihar. The hold of the landlords has distorted the modernisation of social and political structures. In addition to the Brahmins, the Bhumihar and the Rajput are the dominant landed elite. For a long period in the history of the state, these zamindars (landlords) have dominated politics and have exploited their sharecroppers and agricultural laborers. Popular resistance was formerly organised by the communist parties, which had a strong presence in many areas. From the late 1960s onwards, their role has been taken over partially by the Naxalites and partially by assertive low-caste politicians. Particularly, the emergence of the movement led by Jayaprakash Narayan in the 1970s and the promotion of low-caste politicians in the 1980s and 1990s to prime ministership (Laloo Prasad Yadav and his wife Rabri Devi of the Rashtriya Janata Dal [RJD]) has changed the political landscape in the state. The RJD (National People's Party) has risen to political prominence by championing the interests of traditionally repressed lower castes, but has remained largely inactive on the issue of land reforms and the implementation of minimum wages.

The emergence of the low caste as a political force has provoked a reaction among the landlords. Ever since the Rajputs in Bhojpur district formed the Kuer Sena in 1979, all upper castes and even some middle-caste groups have formed their own sena, mainly in order to suppress the lower castes and classes. In the 1990s their role was extended to defending the political interests of the caste, namely the defeat of the RJD. As such, the senas continue a long feudal tradition. Earlier, the zamindars had men called lathaiths (those armed with sticks) whose main job was to execute the orders of the landlords, keep the peasantry and sharecroppers under control, ensure that "taxes" and other payments were paid regularly, and enforce the settlement of local disputes. Bihar has regularly experienced gruesome murders of entire hamlets when impoverished labourers dared to stand up for their rights. In May 1977, for example, eleven people in Belchi village in the Patna district were stabbed to death. Today's senas however, are more powerful because of their structure and political patronage.

Three reasons could be cited for the emergence of senas in Bihar. First, the negative fallout of the "green revolution," which in the 1970s and 1980s resulted in greater agricultural productivity. It also resulted in increasing basic inequalities that existed between landlords and the landless. The poor and landless, mainly belonging to the lower classes, increased their demands for fair distribution of land and its produce, which led to the formation of senas by landlords to suppress them. Second, the growth of the Naxalite movement in Bihar resulted in the lower caste and class openly challenging the age-old domination of the upper castes and classes. With the Naxalite groups openly advocating and indulging in armed activities, the landlords began cultivating senas to counter the opposition from both the Naxalites and the landless.The third reason was the politicisation of caste, especially through the "reservation policy" for the lower castes, which was introduced in 1990. While education and employment have not reached the entire lower-caste population, a small segment of the lowest castes and of the backward castes has benefited, however. This lower-class elite has begun mobilising the lower castes for their own political ends, sometimes with the help of the Naxalites. The powerful upper-caste landlords could not tolerate this defiance by the low-caste elite and formed various senas to resist the gradual emergence of the lower castes in politics.

Conflict Dynamics

Besides Ranvir Sena, which is basically the private army of the landlords, there are a number of other armed gangs who represent the interests of the other castes. The Sunlight Sena is controlled by the Muslim Pathan landlords of Garwah, Palamau, and Gaya in alliance with the Rajput landlords of Palamau. The Bhoomi Sena was initially formed as the Kisan Suraksha Samiti in early 1980. Rich Kurmi landlords (a middle caste of the region), corrupt gentry, and professional criminals accumulated a huge quantity of arms, recruited some Kurmi youths, and launched a professional armed gang. The Bhoomi Sena is still powerful in some blocks in Patna district, but in other districts it has been eliminated by the armed squads of Maoist organisations. The Lorik Sena, of the backward-caste Yadavs, was formed in 1983 in Nalanda district but soon extended its activities and it is still powerful in Gaya and Dhanarua block in Patna. It appears to have degenerated into a gang that thrives on extortion from Yadav peasants.

Ranvir Sena, the most dreaded of all senas, is an organisation of the upper-caste landlords. It came into existence in August 1994 in Belaur, a village with a population of twelve hundred in the central Bihar district of Bhojpur. The leader of the organisation is Bharmeshwar Singh, who is also a Bharatiya Janata Party (BJP) activist, having previously been with the Congress Party during its period of national and regional government. Estimates of the strength of the Ranvir Sena range from a few hundred to tens of thousands. The gangs are armed with knives, sickles, and home-produced guns and revolvers. Landlords finance it through "generous" contributions and subscriptions and members of the squads are reported to be drawing a monthly salary. The Ranvir Sena has also opted for the legal path by creating the Rashtravadi Kisan Mahasabha (RKMS), a peasant union that fields candidates for the elections, in alliance with the BJP and the Samata Party, both ruling parties in New Delhi.

The main objective of the Ranvir Sena and the RKMS is to intimidate the Dalits (the lower castes) and wipe out Naxalism. Ranvir Sena represents the Bhumihar and the Rajput, two major upper castes who have, in the past, been at loggerheads. The name Ranvir is actually associated with a nineteenth-century Bhumihar folk hero who fought against the Rajput landlords in Bhojpur. The common objective of oppressing the Dalits and the Naxalites and protecting their class interests has led them to heal their differences.

Since its formation in 1994, the Ranvir Sena has been involved in more than twenty-five massacres, in which, according to different reports, between three hundred and one thousand persons have been killed. The raping of women is a common tactic employed by members of the Ranvir Sena and other caste militias to spread terror in lower-caste communities. In 1992, more than one hundred Dalit women in the Gaya district of Bihar were reportedly raped by the Savarna Liberation Front. Pregnant women and children have also been killed. Some of the more gruesome murders in the years thereafter are the following:

- Within weeks after its formation, the Ranvir Sena was involved in clashes in the Bhojpur district. The first major incident occurred in Bathani Tola (Sahar block) on 11 July 1996, when nineteen CPI–ML supporters were killed by around sixty Sena activists armed with homemade firearms and cutting weapons. In previous months, numerous exchanges of fire took place leaving both sides with casualties. Two months earlier, nine Sena supporters were killed in a village in the same area.
- In late March and early April 1997, the Ranvir Sena killed ten Muslims in one village and eight Dalits in another village. On 20 April, two hundred armed persons belonging to the CPI–ML Party Unity attacked the village of a BJP member of the legislative assembly, allegedly responsible for the earlier attack, blew up his house, and killed six hard-core supporters of the sena.
- On 1 December 1997, sixty-three Dalits, including sixteen children, were killed in Laxmanpur Bathe village in Jehanabad; five teenage girls were raped before being shot in the chest. The village was raided in an overnight attack

by two hundred and fifty Ranvir Sena members. The victims were sympathizers of the CPI–ML Liberation; in the area there had been an argument about the capture of government land by Bhumihars.

— In January 1999, twenty-two lower-caste men, women, and children were killed in Shankarbigha (Jehanabad district) when a Ranvir Sena gang entered their eight thatched huts and shot the inhabitants at point-blank range. The village is only 10 kilometers away from Laxmanpur Bathe.

— In April 1999, two groups of fifty men, each carrying sophisticated arms, attacked two hamlets in Sandani in Gaya district, killing twelve Yadavs, including a ten-year-old child; the killings were possibly a retaliation for the Bhumihars killed in Senari village one month earlier. Squads of the Maoist Communist Centre (MCC) then slit the throats of thirty-four Bhumihars in retaliation for two massacres carried out in MCC strongholds earlier in the year, claiming a further thirty-four lives.

— In June 2000, thirty-five Yadav men, women, and children were killed in Miapur, Aurangabad district, by a gang of two hundred Bhumihars. One week earlier, thirteen Bhumihars had been killed in Newada district, at a distance of 200 kilometers, in retaliation for the killing of three Kurmis.

The above list of massacres perpetrated by the Ranvir Sena reveals two trends. First, the scale of the killings has increased. There have been instances, in which the entire Dalit or Muslim population, including women and children, of one hamlet was slaughtered. Second, the geographical reach of the sena's activities has been extended. Whereas initially, they focused on the Bhojpur district of Bihar, their operations are now spread over many other districts of Bihar and Jharkhand, especially Jehanabad, Patna, Gaya, and Aurangabad.

The political support of the upper castes to the Ranvir Sena and the RKMS has unfortunately also increased. The Ranvir Sena, as alleged by the Dalits, has the support of the major political parties in the state—the BJP, Congress, and even some sections in the ruling RJD. These allegations were raised in the press and by human-rights organisations. In October 2001, the Justice Amir Das

Commission, constituted by the government three years earlier to investigate the nexus between political parties and the Ranvir Sena, confirmed the allegations. Notices have been issued to two federal ministers—including the powerful BJP minister Murli Manohar Joshi—and to twenty-two other politicians, of whom only two belong to the RJD.

The continuation of the conflict is also due to the involvement of local police officers, most of whom belong to the upper castes. The police are often on the scene of incidents but remain inactive. In his report on the 1996 attack in the Sahar block, the then home office minister Indrajit Gupta (a communist) remarked during the debates in the Lok Sabha (national parliament), on 19 July 1996 that "the failure of the district machinery was the immediate reason for the tragedy. In fact, it has been admitted by the state administration that despite the availability of intelligence about the impending tragedy and even the positioning of forces in the area, the massacre could not be averted due to connivance or lack of courage on the part of the law enforcing agencies."

Government's Response

Ministerial responsibilities in the Indian constitution have been divided between the union government and the state governments. Law and order is a function of the state, and as such, it is primarily the responsibility of the Bihar government to deal with the issue. Unfortunately, Bihar is one of the few states in India with a defective system of governance. Bihar banned all caste-based private militias as long ago as 1986, resulting in the disappearance of a number of such groups in the first half of the 1990s. However, the government is finding it difficult to tackle the Ranvir Sena for various political and social reasons. In 1996, the state government, then headed by Laloo Prasad Yadav, banned the Ranvir Sena after the latter's involvement in the killing of six Dalits in Sarthna village in Bhojpur. But the government has not been able to control it.

The state government's response over the last six years has been reactive and short-term. After every major massacre, it has announced financial compensation to the families of the deceased, and the concerned officials have been either suspended or transferred. Occasionally, a new post was also created in the police to deal exclusively with this issue. After the Laxmanpur Bathe massacre (in which sixty-three people were killed in December 1997), the state government transferred the home secretary, suspended the superintendent of police in the district, and created a new post of additional director general of police to focus on the law-and-order problems. Similarly, the state government directed the administration to take up the construction of roads on a war footing. The absence of roads keeps the poor people in the remote areas in a precarious position and hinders the swift deployment of police forces.At the judicial level, the state has appointed special courts for speedy trials. After the Sankarbigha massacre in January 1999, Chief Minister Rabri Devi announced the creation of a special court. A major problem is that many of the arrested sena members are known to be quickly released on bail and to have many sympathizers within the police and justice departments. Committees have been formed at state and district levels, and they have come forward with various ideas, particularly stressing the need for the restoration of local self-government, the implementation of land reforms, and a meaningful development of the affected areas.

At the police level, the handling of the situation has been dismal. It is alleged that in several cases the police were unconcerned in dealing with the situation. For example, three police pickets were present during the attack in Bhatanitola in 1996, but they appeared to ignore the shots being fired. After an attack in Narayanpur where twelve Dalits were murdered by the Ranvir Sena in February 1999, it took the police twenty-four hours to reach the scene. They then told the villagers that, although their station is just two miles away, the complaint had to be lodged at another police station, which had jurisdiction over the particular village. The major efforts by the police are focused on the creation of new pickets in the affected areas. These pickets are insufficiently manned and their weapons are obsolete. During the massacres they either remain silent spectators or have even fled from the scene. During the attacks in March and May 1997, Ranvir Sena men were allegedly accompanied by members of the police force. Three days after the retaliatory Maoist attack, six communist extremist were killed by the police in a "fake encounter," i.e., after they had surrendered.

The state government has continually demanded the deployment of paramilitary forces by the central government. Five companies of the Central Reserve Police Force were sent to Bihar by the left-wing government in New Delhi after the Laxmanpur Bathe massacre in 1997, but they were withdrawn soon after the right-wing BJP government came to power.

After an incident on 13 February 1999 in Narayanpur, where twenty-one Dalits were massacred, the union government, rather than sending extra police forces to Bihar, dismissed the state government and imposed presidential rule, i.e., direct administration from New Delhi. However, a majority in the New Delhi parliament rejected the interference and the RJD government was reinstalled. The episode illustrated that party politics aimed at dislodging a state government were considered more important than a joint intervention against terrorist violence. Instead of helping to resolve the problem, the government of India has always condemned and criticised the state government for its failures. Massacres, and the reports of the "high-level" teams after visits to the area, have been misused in a partisan manner in order to increase the stranglehold of the union government on the state government.

Multi Track Diplomacy

The response from society and from nongovernmental organisations—domestic and international—to the caste violence is mixed. The role of NGOs in Bihar in creating awareness of the problem is commendable, but they have failed to make any impact on the government.

The caste/class conflicts in a polarised and backward society such as Bihar have set in motion a vicious circle of caste politics and caste consciousness, with various political parties stimulating the mobilisation of caste for political purposes. Consequently there has been a tendency for the elite sections within each caste to set up their own senas to protect their socioeconomic and political interests. The Dalits were the last group to form their own sena. The Dalit Sena was the initiative of a right-wing politician, Ram Vilas Paswan, and was undertaken "in order to form a unit for the self defense of the Dalit community." By forming caste-based organisations, these leaders attempt to wean their electorate away from the more radical, class-based organisations in the state.

Political calculations and expediency have determined the response of the political parties to Ranvir Sena's activities. The ruling RJD has always blamed the Congress and the BJP (which has the support of the upper castes) for financing and guiding the Ranvir Sena to destabilise the RJD rule. In the aftermath of the massacres, political parties usually send a fact-finding team for an on-the-spot study of the massacre.

The right-wing opposition, especially the BJP, sees the growth of the Ranvir Sena as representing the failure of the Bihar government under Laloo Prasad Yadav and Rabri Devi. The killings are seen as the result of the encouragement of criminal gangs by a government that wants to remain in power rather than the manifestation of a caste war.

The CPI–M regards the non-implementation of basic land reforms, nonpayment of minimum wages, and the nexus between the landlords, people, and criminals as the main reasons behind the vicious circle of violence. The CPI–M, like the other communist party, the CPI, is critical of both sena and the Maoist party organisations. The poor villagers "caught between the warring groups, spend sleepless nights," it says. The CPI–ML, the main opponent of the Ranvir Sena, has been more severe in its opposition. It organises bandhs (strikes) both at state and national levels against its activities and the failure of the state and central governments to take any effective steps. Both parties see the sena more as a private army of the bhupatis (the haves) in a struggle with the have-nots, rather than as a Bhumihar caste party. Gandhian organisations in the state have been active, working on relief projects and organising communities in the tradition of nonviolence and tolerance. They, however, are not effective in the remote rural areas.

The People's Union for Democratic Rights (PUDR), like most political parties, has sent fact-finding teams to investigate the caste-based violence in Bihar, and has published various reports with recommendations. Also, the People's Union for Civil Liberties (PUCL) has published a couple of reports on violence in Bihar. Both the PUDR and the PUCL are ideologically aligned with the proponents of agrarian revolt and do not command any siginficant influence over the governments. Their championship of the Naxalite cause has weakened their position as a human-rights watchdog.

At the international level, Human Rights Watch (HRW) has been monitoring the problem for a long time and has made recommendations to the state and central governments. It has carried out a number of studies and investigations, and has approached the state government directly with a list of suggestions. These include the prosecution of senior officials found to be complicit in the attacks, the provision of full security to villagers, placing police pickets away from upper-caste areas, and creating independent commissions of investigation. It has been alleged by human-rights organisations that some politicians are members of the Ranvir Sena and that the police have sometimes accompanied the sena during their attacks or have conducted raids after attacks by the senas. The purpose of the raids is often to terrorise Dalits as a group, whether or not they are members of guerrilla organisations. Sena leaders and police officials have rarely been prosecuted for such killings and abuses. There is, in this respect, a clear difference between the response of the state to militant activity by Naxalite groups and by the senas. Whereas a large number of Naxalites are killed in "encounters" with police, not a single Ranvir Sena member has suffered this fate. The administration is noticeably slow when it comes to tackling these armies. Evidence of police collusion with the Ranvir Sena has led to charges that the sena is being backed by the state administration and nonleftist political parties in order to check the growing leftist movement. Police have frequently operated as agents of the landed upper castes, conducting raids on Dalit villages and disguising killings as "encounters."

To combat the caste violence and the growth of caste-based militias, efforts need to be made at both the macro and micro levels. Land reforms must be effectively implemented, the state police need to be modernised, developmental programmes should be implemented, and political parties must function autonomously of caste influence.

The Minimum Wage Act, the land reform legislation, and the poverty alleviation programmes have to be implemented urgently. The new government proposals to make sharecroppers the legal owners of land should be enacted as soon as possible, before sharecroppers are turned off the land and the question of landlessness and polarisation is made even more intractable. The state administration should implement its own legislation. Lack of educational, health, transport, and communication facilities have precluded the participation of the impoverished masses in civil society. Although there have been various development packages devised in the past by the central and state governments, they have not sufficiently reached the target groups due to poor governance and widespread corruption. Only a better economic deal for landless labor and sharecroppers may turn the scales. The restoration of democracy may lead to more transparency and influence from below. The holding of village council elections in June 2001, after a gap of twenty-four years, is a good first step in the restoration of democracy at the village level. The institutions, however, continue to be controlled by the village elite or their agents. Unless the poor people can free themselves from economic slavery, empowerment will remain difficult.The Bihar police force needs to be urgently revamped to effectively handle the caste militia.

- The police force needs to be augmented in terms of numbers. Arming the police with better weapons would increase their prestige and morale and also instill fear in the private militias. The police also need to be provided with better transport and communications, enabling them to reach trouble spots more easily and quickly.
- Most importantly, steps need to be taken to recruit officers from the lowest ranks of society (Dalits and poor Muslims) into the police force. Caste is an important factor in the police and the administration of the state, particularly in some districts.
- The rules of conduct should be redefined. Care should also be taken that the police remain physically separate from the contending groups and do not accept upper-caste hospitality.
- A judicial body should be set up to investigate the role of the police in villages during and in the aftermath of massacres.

Peace committees, bringing together influential righteous citizens, Gandhian organisations, and other NGOs as well as the secular political parties, including the parties on opposing sides in the conflict, will have to be formed in order to maintain peace and restore sanity when conflicts have taken place. Such joint committees will also have an important function in overseeing the constitutional behaviour of political parties, i.e., documenting and protesting against the political patronage of caste militias and caste organisations in general.

Successive governments in India have had reason enough to rely on the unending patience of the neglected and deprived millions in India, who have not risen in fury about illiteracy, hunger, illness, or economic insecurity. The stubborn persistence of these deprivations has much to do with that lack of fury. This, however, does not negate the point that it is poverty in its different forms – absolute deficiency in the supply of the minimum survival needs, relative deprivation, marginalisation in access to resources, denial of the benefits of development – that produces, more persistently than any other cause, the conditions in which political conflagrations occur, albeit with a pronounced element of stochasticity in their location and timing. In the situations of 'agrarian unrest' or of 'caste resistance', poverty is seen to be converted into violent conflict mainly as a consequence of the correspondence of prevailing socioeconomic inequalities with differentiations in caste and tribe, with the infiltration of external influences in the form of ideological inspiration. In order to bring about a major change in the life of Dalit masses, social and economic opportunities have to be opened up in a big way to a whole lot of people belonging to these groups.

References

Akerolof, George. "The Economics of Caste and of Rat Race and Other Woeful Tales", *Quarterly Journal of Economics,* XC.4, November. 1976.

Banerjee, Biswajit and J.B. Knight, "Caste Discrimination in Indian Urban Labour Market" *Journal of Developing Economics.* 1985.

National Commission for Scheduled Castes and Scheduled Tribes. Fourth Report 1996-97 & 1997-98, vols. I &II, Delhi. 1998.

Parvathamma. *Scheduled Castes and Tribes: A Socio-economic Survey,* Ashish, Delhi. 1984.

Thorat S.K., "Passage to Adulthood : Perceptions from Below", in Sudhir Kakar (ed.), *Identity and Adulthood,* Oxford University Press, Delhi. 1979.

Gurr, T.D. *Minorities at Risk: A Global View of Ethnopolitical Conflicts,* Washington DC, Institute of Peace Press. 1993.

5

CASTE POLITICS

India is quite undeniably the most stratified society in the world. Over and above huge income disparities, there are caste, religious, and community differences that are deeply engraved into everyday social relations. No doubt, the nature of caste and community interactions has changed over time, but considerations along ascriptive lines still remain important markers both at the public and private domains.

Although tribes and religious distinctions exist in other societies as well, what sets India apart is the prevalence of the caste order. There are really no phenotypical differences between castes, but it is presumed that Hindus have specific coded substances in them that set them apart from one another. Commingling of substances led to becoming polluted, and therefore social relations had to be finely calibrated to make sure that people did not compromise their inherent and inalienable substances by being in close physical proximity with members of different castes.

Even this is not that difficult to comprehend. Physical separation is a dominant diacritic of racism: Indeed everyday interactions at the level of community, religion, and linguistic affiliation often partake of this prejudice. But what makes caste stand apart from other forms of stratification is that in this case there are elaborate and ritualised rules that ordain not just how distinctions should be maintained, but also prescribe sanctions should the norms be violated.

This too, one might take as a quantitative exaggeration of a principle that is not unknown in other societies. Perhaps, it is an extreme form of stratification with cognate likenesses in racism, religious separation, and so on. In which case, the problem of comprehending caste is not difficult as all one has to do is to enlarge the scale and deepen the grooves of ascriptive prejudice. This is primarily because of the popular belief that castes that are considered impure according to the Brahmannical hierarchy, nevertheless participate willingly in their own degradation

The most systematic and influential proponent of this position can be found in Louis Dumont's *Homo Hierarchicus*. It was not as if Dumont was saying anything that has not been said before. Butinthe course of his exposition on caste as a state of mind, he gave the term "hierarchy" a technical and sophisticated meaning. According to Dumont, a pure hierarchy allows for economics and politics only surreptitiously, but only in the interstitial levels. Otherwise, the hierarchy stands firm as its two poles stand in opposition to each other. At one extreme of this hierarchy is the Brahman (or the most pure), and at the other stands the untouchables (who are positively polluting). The castes in between are encompassed by this pure hierarchy, which is obsessively ranked on the purity/pollution principle.

Contemporary evidence indicates that caste identities cannot be strait jacketed within an unrelenting hierarchical grid where the status of the pure and the impure are empirically and unproblematically firm in their interactional nexus. In fact, this feature was noticed long ago by Senart, Bougle, and Blunt. For example, Senart argued that castes should be seen as units, and one should not rush into arranging them in a hierarchy. Even Bougle, who otherwise believed that hierarchy was an important characteristic of caste, nevertheless forcefully demonstrated that castes also mutually repel one another. That these two formulations were mutually contradictory did not strike Bougle with any degree of analytical force Blunt was perhaps the most incisive of them all when he observed that "if the caste system was devised with the object of preserving 'the purity of belief and ceremonial usage,' it has been a singular failure". And yet, the dominant Brahmannical view so dominated the intellectuals that it was Dumont's understanding of caste that swept Blunt, Bougle, and Senart under the carpet.

The fact is that the caste order is characterised by contesting notions of hierarchy and that is why we find competitive assertions of caste identity. Nor is it that status concerns in these multiple hierarchies are always linked to purity and pollution issues. They may also be associated with power and wealth, as among the merchant Jain castes, much more directly than what caste purists would have us believe. A general insensitivity toward this aspect of caste has led to the over valuation of the Brahmannical version of hierarchy, both in scholarly works and in popular imaginations. This has also contributed to the general intellectual puzzlement as to how one should conceptualise the relationship between caste and politics because here we have tension and competition in place of ideological acquiescence.

If castes do not contest their positions in the hierarchy, then where does the symbolic energy to compete for power in the political arena come from? Each caste should be content with its lot, and its members should calmly accept the superiority of those who are placed above them in terms of purity rankings. Indeed, Leach once said that when castes begin to compete, then they no longer function as caste. The truth, however, is that the caste system sans competition and conflict never really existed on the ground. There are different rankings in different locales depending upon who has the power and the wherewithal to make a particular ranking system, or hierarchy, work to their advantage. In some cases, the Brahmans were able to realise their favored hierarchy in practice; in other cases, it was the Jats, or the Rajputs, or the Marathas, or the Marawas, or the Lingayats, and so on. This is why it is important to factor in the notion of caste identity; otherwise tensions within the caste order will never be fully understood.

Not only are we now confronted by identity assertions of earthy peasant castes, which were earlier ranked as lowly shudras but also of those who, until recently, were called untouchables. Now we also know that none of these castes had ever ideologically accepted their degraded status. Yet they lived out their humble lives quietly for generations for fear of offending the privileged strata. We now know more of their origin tales that boast of the elevated positions they once held before an unsuspected chicanery, a lost war, or a mercurial god, demoted them to lowly rungs in popular perceptions Jotiba Phule, the nineteenth century leader of the non-Brahman movement in Maharashtra, put forward the claim that the so-called "shudra" lower castes of today were actually Kshtriyas in preAryan times. They were the kind and genial rulers of the land before the Brahmans and then the Muslim "robbers" from across the Himalayas took over by deceit and cruelty. In this rendition then, the origins of the authentic Kshatriyas predate Vedic Hinduism.

It is true that all these tales of the past are just tales, not unlike myths, but so are Brahmannical justifications of their superiority. As myths, all of these origin tales occupy an identical logical position. It is another thing that intellectuals tend to prefer stories that Brahmans tell us over those that are related by less privileged castes. This is particularly so when we examine the relationship between caste and politics, and the move from caste as a system to caste as identity.

Study of Caste and Politics

The study of caste and politics can be analytically justified only when we accept that castes are, first and foremost, discrete entities with deep pockets of ideological heritage. As they are discrete phenomenas, it is both logically and empirically true that there should be multiple hierarchies as each caste always overvalues itself. The element of caste competition is, therefore, a characteristic of the caste order and not a later addition. This implies that the caste system, as a system, worked primarily because it was enforced by power and not by ideological acquiescence. Only when we are armed with this perspective are we conceptually prepared to study the relationship between caste and politics. First, the relationships between castes were played out within the confines of the closed natural economy of the village. This left no room for maneuver for the subaltern communities and castes. Second, in precolonial times, caste hierarchies were contested and renegotiated episodically following the philippics of a war or a major social upheaval. As such instances were rare, it gave rise to the illusion that castes have never competed and have been politically inactive.

The tranquility that this vision of the pure hierarchy inspired should have been shattered irreparably when certain castes began to clamour for a higher status following the census operations conducted by the colonial regime. According to O'Malley, during the 1911 census enumeration, a number of castes objected to being placed at inferior levels in the hierarchy or wanted to be known differently from the traditional term assigned to them. Such petitions came fast and thick because the impression had gone around at that time that the census was not just about putting down numbers but also about assigning rank and prestige. Around this time caste associations, or sabhas, began to proliferate to press for higher status both in census records as well as in everyday interactions. Some enlightened Rajas, such as the ruler of Tranvancore, also helped in this regard by elevating certain castes. The Baroda prince gave scholarships to bright students from "low" caste families. Dr. B.R. Ambedkar, the legendary leader of the Scheduled Castes and one of the founding figures of independent India's Constitution, was one such beneficiary.

British authorities intervened in the caste order in three significant ways. First, it gave the Brahmans extraordinary precedence by taking their advice on what was the correct custom. This gave Brahmans in certain regions, particularly in South India and Maharashtra a lot of supralocal influence of the kind they did not enjoy hitherto. Resentment against this growing Brahman dominance resulted in anti-Brahman movements in South India and Maharashtra from the latter years of the nineteenth century. There are two mainstream political parties in Tamilnadu that can legitimately claim to be descendants of the original anti-Brahman Dravida Kazagham movement. Also in North India, traditional peasant castes that were classified as lowly shudras, according to Brahmannical ranking, were forming their own associations to press for their rightful status under British rule.

Second, the Moreley-Minto reforms of 1909 introduced separate electorates that gave a fillip to non-Brahman castes in their quest for self-respect. They now began to organise themselves as "Depressed Classes." This gained momentum from 1917 onward, and various Depressed Caste Associations began in different parts of India. In fact, the concern for the lower castes and untouchables was evident in the colonial administration from the 1880s onward. This was initially with special reference to education, so that the poor would find a ladder to climb from "the gutter to the university". Nevertheless, such a policy also demanded the enumeration of backward classes. This process began from 1883 onward, and the list of castes included in it began to grow rapidly. As the backward class rubric also included the untouchables, there was a move initiated in Madras in 1917 to separate them for the rest for special treatment.

Third, British presence also made a difference as a number of laws were enacted to lessen the weight of untouchability that the so-called polluting castes had to bear. For example, the Madras Government passed the Removal of Disabilities Act in 1938; this was soon followed by Mysore in 1943. There after, between 1943 and 1947 a number of states enacted similar laws to free those traditionally deemed as low castes from the incubus of traditional disprivileges. The Yadavs, Kurmis, and Koeris of North India formed the Triveni Sangh to contest the 1935 elections. Though they lost that round to the Congress, the Triveni Sangh held and gradually increased its size. It incorporated other castes from similar backgrounds into its fold to form the Backward Class Federation. The members of the Backward Caste Federation were generally tenants and small cultivators, and they used their organisation to fight for their economic interests against the landlord classes, many of whom were close to the Congress.

Recent studies, therefore, clearly demonstrate that it is not as if castes are warming up to power considerations only after India became independent. The process of questioning established hierarchies through means other than war began with the establishment of British suzerainty in India. Caste and politics were always related, but the relationship was manifested differently at different periods of time. The establishment of democracy in independent India has introduced one major change in the way caste and politics interact, and that is by making all castes legally equal. This combination between law and economic change has allowed castes that were hitherto considered low to take the fight to the traditional superior communities and even to thumb their noses at established symbolic and ritual systems. As Beteille rightly remarks, outside the domain of the family, caste is most active at the level of politics in contemporary Indian society. If this aspect of caste was not noticed in the past, then it was primarily because political upheavals of the medieval age were few and far between.

Quite clearly, castes were never outside politics; only the connection is much more transparent today. Whereas in the past ambitious castes had to "wade through slaughter to a throne," caste tensions today are a daily grind. Further, unlike colonial times, castes in contemporary India are not concerned about official rankings. Caste identities have evolved to a much higher level, and it is now a question of self over others and not self in relation to others. Thus, no matter which caste is in question, its involvement in politics is primarily to stake a claim to jobs, educational opportunities, as well as to positions of power in government bodies in direct competition against other castes. Unlike the agitations regarding the census operations in 1911 and later, caste assertions today are not just to feel good in an attributional way but to make it good in a highly competitive environment that disregards the interactional setting that the pure caste hierarchy recommends.

The break down of the traditional caste system and the emergence of caste identities that energise contemporary caste politics can be explained in a variety of ways. Weiner believed that the repeated ideological exhortations of the Congress party brought an end to "the self-imposed barrier to protests by caste, that is, the acceptance of their place in the hierarchy". It may be recalled that India's struggle against British colonialism was lead by the Congress, and quite naturally this party also controlled the government uninterruptedly for 20 years after independence. According to Weiner, the charisma of Congress leaders, combined with the success of the freedom movement, led to the downgrading of the moral basis of castes. According to Kaviraj this resulted in a "democracy of castes in place of a 'hierarchy'". Although it is certainly true that the political representation and the impact of the Congress have played a significant role, they need to be placed in the context of the significant shifts in the structural plates of agrarian India. As the power of the erstwhile big landlords waned, the middle farmers and the former untouchables grew in stature and became politically more assertive.

Political Ascendance of Castes

In the years following independence, the traditional upper castes continued to rule inmost parts of India. For example, until 1977, upper castes continued to hold prominent elected positions in Uttar Pradesh, the most populous state in the Indian union. Untill 1962, as many as 63 per cent of ruling Congress members of the Legislative Assembly came from elite castes. Soon, however, traditional peasant castes such as Ahirs, Kurmis, Koeri, Lodh Rajputs, and Jats began to dominate the political scape of northern India. In the southern state of Tamilnadu, the Vanniyars and Thevars have become assertive, and in Karnataka, control was wrested in the mid-1950s from the traditional rural elite within the Congress party by the Vokkaligas and Linagayats. In the North Indian Hindi-speaking belt, upper caste members of parliament fell below 50 per cent for the first time in 1977. The challenge to the established Congress was mounted in Uttar Pradesh rather effectively in the late 1960s by a coalition of peasant castes led by Charan Singh. In Bihar, also, there was a significant decline of upper caste members of the legislative assembly after 1977

In Bihar and Uttar Pradesh, the Yadav caste has gained a great degree of political salience. In Uttar Pradesh, the Samajwadi party is headed by Maulayam Singh Yadav, and in Bihar, the Rashtriya Janata Dal has Laloo Prasad Yadav at its helm. It may also be noted that Maulayam Yadav is today the chief minister of Uttar Pradesh and Laloo Prasad Yadav's wife, Rabri Devi, is chief minister of Bihar. It is not always the case, however, that other peasant castes such as the Kurmis and Koeris always rally behind either the Janata Dal or the Samajwadi party. According to Jaffrelot, Kurmis are not as widely represented in these parties as the Yadavs are. In 1996, only three percent of Samajwadi party members of the legislative assembly were Kurmis. In Bihar, the numbers were higher but still not more than around eight percent of MLAs were from the Rashtriya Janata Dal.

The decline of the traditional elite castes in Indian politics has been discussed quite frequently in academic literature. Rudolph & Hoeber characterised the newly ascendant peasant castes as "bullock capitalists" who challenged the hegemony of the traditional Kshatriya castes, such as the Rajputs and Bhumiyar. These peasant castes constitute 34 per cent of the population but control about 51 per cent of land, more than any other agrarian class. As a category they are closer to "yeoman farmers" than to kulaks. Hence, the appellation "bullock capitalists" is an apposite term for their economic operation is a mix of "capitalist, preindustrial, and non-capitalist features"

The political emergence of these bullock capitalists coincides with the emergence of the backward class movement in large parts of India. To put the matter in perspective, it needs to be recalled that feudal landlordism, or zamindari, as the Indian variant was known, was abolished after independence in India. This seriously undercut the economic and power base of the traditional rural elite, many of whose members also had an established urban foothold. Although there were attempts by this class to conceal the extent of their holdings by registering their possessions in the name of fictitious owners, the writing was on the wall.

In 1963, Srinivas wrote that landownership was "a crucial factor in establishing dominance. Generally, the pattern of landownership in rural India is such that the bulk of the arable land is concentrated in the hands of a relatively small number of big owners as against a large number who either own very little land or no land at all". The picture has obviously changed a great deal since the 1960s. The bullock capitalists of Rudolph & Hoeber are small owners of land, and yet they exercise considerable political power in contemporary India as can be gauged from the successes of Samajwadi party and Rashtriya Janata Dal in Uttar Pradesh and Bihar, respectively.

It is not as if these peasant castes have suddenly become much richer. The more crucial fact is that the patrons of the past have become poorer. They can no longer wield the kind of power or influence they used to take for granted. Naturally, the idea of vote banks in the control of dominant factions does not quite apply today. According to Sharma, the new dominants of rural India are not necessarily those who are economically at the top. They must, of course, have a viable economic standing, but they should also have sufficient numbers as well as political connections. Karanth puts this idea across rather nicely when he says that "it is not always necessary for a caste to have all the attributes of dominance...but one or two are enough to ensure a modicum of dominance". Indeed, a modicum of dominance is more prevalent today than decisive dominance because very few castes can simultaneously claim unchallenged superiority at the economic, political, and cultural level.

The morphological features of contemporary agrarian structure inhibit cumulative inequalities and decisive dominance. It needs to be remembered that 85 per cent of land-holdings in India are below five acres and 63 per cent below three acres. Given this ground level situation, owner cultivators can hardly be expected to behave like the power wielders of yore. In addition, a large number of rural people are seeking rural non-farm employment. Today, 44.5 per cent of rural net domestic product is non-agricultural. The 50th round of the National Sample Survey held during 1993–1994 shows that 32.9 per cent of rural households were outside agriculture. By the 57th round of the NSS during 2002–2003, the percentage increased to 35.2 per cent. In states such as Punjab, Jammu and Kashmir, Kerala, and Haryana, the number of non-agricultural households in rural India is above 50 per cent. This has not only led to rural exodus, but even for those who stay back in the village, it is not agriculture that solely contributes to their earnings. The poorer villagers participate in a host of occupations that require a narrow band width of skills, ranging from construction labor, to coolie, to rickshaw puller, to vegetable seller. Of course, for all of them getting a regular urban job has the highest value.

All of this suggests a picture of rural stratification that cannot uphold the earlier prestige that was accorded to the landed elite in a noncompetitive caste hierarchy. It is obvious that if the earlier hierarchy held, with all its idiosyncratic nuances, it was primarily because it was but stressed by the economic power of the agrarian rich. As that is no longer the dominant feature in rural India, castes compete out in the open. The fact of caste competition in politics should not lead us to believe that this is a restatement of the caste system. The obverse side of this collapse is the assertion of caste identities. Castes that could not project what they had always believed for fear of reprisal can now boldly assert their pride and status claims.

Numerous field studies also demonstrate that conflicts between castes are rarely resolved at the village level. In the past, the village panchayat used to mediate tensions of various kinds, but, as Karanth demonstrates, the caste panchayat, or council, has lost its importance. Sahay finds that in Bihar tensions between castes are not adjudicated at the local level. In some cases, the tensions remain unresolved; in other instances, the matter is taken to court where the decision it is not always satisfactory. In one instance, Sahay recalls from his field notes, "members of the Chamar caste were beaten up by the Brahmins. The case was not settled at the village level. The chamars went to the police and to the court for justice. When they realised that the court was not going to punish the Brahmins immediately, they beat some of the Brahmins up and withdrew the case from the court"

It has been frequently pointed out that caste politics is not to end caste but to "use caste as an instrument for social change". Democratic politics has brought about aggressive caste assertion, but this has not resulted in contesting the category of caste as such. As Sheth points out, the vertical consolidation of caste along the purity hierarchy has been replaced by a "horizontalisation". Political alliances in this horizontal scheme of caste relations are not enduring, and they are "openended entities". They are made keeping in mind the coalescence of secular interests, and they fade away when a better and more appropriate bargain is struck with other castes and caste clusters. For example, alliances such as KHAM and AJGAR had their best days in the 1980s and are now defunct.

Rise of Dalit Politics

The Constitution of independent India not only abolished untouchability but also made provisions to reserve jobs and seats in government undertakings and educational institutions, respectively, for Scheduled Castes and Scheduled Tribes. With independence, and the abolition of untouchability, the untouchables became known as Scheduled Castes because they were listed for special privileges in the Schedule of the Constitution. Untouchability had diverse manifestations in different parts of India, so it was far from obvious as to which castes should be included in the Schedule of the Constitution

It is not just the owner cultivators or bullock capitalists, who are aggressively using caste as a vehicle of self-assertion, but so also are those who were earlier considered to be untouchables in the traditional Hindu caste hierarchy. This phenomenon too has an India-wide character from Tamilnadu in the south, to northern states such as Uttar Pradesh. The Republican party in Maharashtra and the Bahujan Samaj party in Uttar Pradesh are the two most widely acknowledged political organisations forwarding the aspirations of the former untouchables.

The Republican party was founded by the legendary Babasaheb Ambedkar in 1957. He later led his people to renounce Hinduism and embrace Buddhism instead. It is true that most of the votaries of the Republican party of India belong to the Mahar caste because other formerly untouchable castes of the region, such as the Mangs, Matangs, and Chambars, have stayed away from it. In fact, they often veer toward supporting the Bharaiya Janata party which is, ironically, a rightwing Hindu organisation. This is because many members of these other castes believe that the RPI is a vehicle of upward mobility for the Mahars alone.

Nevertheless, Babasaheb Ambedkar's shadow looms large even today in the politics of the former untouchables. They resent the term "Harijan" that Gandhi used for them as they consider it too patronising. They would rather be known as "Dalits," or the oppressed. Ambedkar was the first to use this term to denote the Scheduled Castes for its obvious combative edge. Ambedkar, today, has been deified among the Buddhist Mahars of Maharashtra and has a similar iconic status to Buddha in many Mahar families. Ambedkar's death anniversary in 1981 provided the occasion for Kanshi Ram to inaugurate the Dalit Shoshit Samaj Sangharsh Samit. In its attempt to attract as wide a range as possible, the DS-4 also called out to Muslims to help fight the privileges of the traditional elite castes.

In 1984, this time in celebration of Ambedkar's birthday, the DS-4 transformed itself into the Bahujan Samaj party. Since then, it has been a vital force in North India. It may not have won the elections outright in the several polls that it has faced, but by clever political manoeuvring, it has managed to propel Mayawati as the Chief Minister in U.P. on two occasions with the most unlikely political allies. The first time Mayawati's ascendance was supported by the Congress and then later by the Hindu rightwing Bharatiya Janata party.

Neither do the Dalits constitute a homogenous group. They contest for superiority among themselves. Middle class Dalits are more concerned about identity and often project themselves as indigenous people, Buddhists, and or another group. But the poor Dalit marginal farmer and landless laborers are more concerned about questions of economic exploitation, but these issues are not adequately attended to by their middle class leaders. For instance, Burra found that Buddhism had not made a significant impact upon rural Mahar Dalits. Strict observance of Buddhist norms and a singular identification with Buddhism were more common among urban Mahars. According to Vora, no Dalit leader after

Ambedkar paid any consistent attention to economic issues. Dalits are, however, very active when it comes to voting in elections. As Yadav notes, the turn out of Scheduled Caste voters was as high as 62.2 per cent in the 1998 elections.

Although the Constitution also provides for reservations for Scheduled Tribes (STs), their situation is in many ways quite different from that of the Scheduled Castes. It is difficult to arrive at a formal definition of tribes in India; many of them are in transition, and many more are already peasants and far removed from a life in the forests. In addition, there are the tribes of Northeast India, such as the Nagas and Mizos, who are not backward because they were the ruling communities in their respective regions and not under the hegemony of the Hindus in the rest of the country. But as with other tribes in India, they too worshipped gods that were not part of the Hindu pantheon. However, stratification between classes was quite marked in many of these northeastern peoples, and that is why they do not fit our usual understanding of "tribes" though they are categorised as such in the Indian Constitution. True, the term "tribe" has been a contentious one in anthropology, and instances from India only confirm its somewhat dubious status. Incidentally, those designated as tribes would rather be called "adivasis" instead. In addition, the tendency to romanticise tribes can also be highly misleading. The belief that tribes spontaneously sacralise nature and that they are primarily hunters and gatherers certainly do not hold true for the majority of STs in India

In general, tribes are considered to be deprived communities because of their geographic isolation. In the northeast, they are in a majority, but in certain belts in east and central India, they are in substantial numbers, although never over 50 per cent of the population of those regions. This is why tribal mobilisations, such as the Jharkhand movement, as well as those in the northeast are regional in character. Scheduled Caste organisations do not have regional autonomy or control on their agenda because their members are embedded in Hindu society and dispersed all over the country.

In recent years, two states have been formed in recognition of the numerical strength of the tribal population in those regions. This does not mean that the leadership in these states is exclusively in tribal hands. This is not possible because the tribes are not in a majority in either of these two states. Yet, by carving these separate states it is hoped that greater attention will be paid to the specific claims of the tribes that live there. The most important demand that tribes make is that non-tribes should not take away their lands and the forests from which they made a living in the past. In addition, they have also stepped up their claims for more jobs in factories and other state enterprises, with particular emphasis on those organisations that have been established on what was once tribal land.

Thus, although it might seem at first sight that the politics of tribes and castes are cognate phenomenon, the two are really quite different. In fact, SCs have been more successful in getting their claims recognised in practice than have STs. This is because of the latter's geographical isolation from the larger Hindu society. As SCs were always within the interactive nexus of the caste system, they were more adept at using the levers of power than the STs. Be that as it may, the logic of caste politics is certainly very different from that of tribal politics and therefore deserves to be understood separately.

Symbolic Rebelliousness

No caste really thinks of itself to be inherently inferior to any other caste. It is another matter that they were never really able to espouse this point of view with the facility with which they do so now primarily because the subaltern communities were locked within a closed village economy. Because agrarian economic relations and land ownership patterns have undergone major transformations in recent times, earlier dominant castes are not as powerful as they once were.

This change in agrarian class relations, coupled with the provisions in the Constitution, has allowed for the proliferation of caste associations all over the country. It is true that this process began in the early decades of the twentieth century when caste competition at the political level first began to manifest itself.. Through *gaurav gathas* and *jati puranas* these associations seek to instill a sense of pride in their primordial identities without which it would be difficult to use caste identities for political aims.

It is interesting to note in this connection that the origin tales of the non-scheduled castes rarely question established norms and customs other than staking their claim as to an exalted past. There are some exceptions such as in the case of the Khandelwal Jains of Rajasthan, who pointedly distance themselves from Kshatriya practices and consider them to be abhorrent. Otherwise, non-SCs do not, as a rule, contest Hinduism or the various practices associated with it. The Yadav association exemplifies this rather nicely and, at the same time, demonstrates how caste loyalty can be used to forward sectional interests in the name of democracy.

Yadav associations were established as early as in the opening decades of the twentieth century. In 1933, the formation of the All India Yadav Mahasabha brought together various disparate Yadava associations under one roof. The AIYM traces the history of the Yadavs to Lord Krishna. He plays the role of a sagacious warrior priest in the *Bhagvat Gita* as a supreme exegete of Advaita and the laws of karma.

By relating the Yadavs to Krishna, the cowherd, the AIYM is able to portray its followers as descendents of a mighty progenitor with Kshatriya status. As Michelutti records, the AIYM believes that the Yadavs are not just "natural politicians" but they are also the best custodians of democracy. Therefore, if one is to keep democracy alive and well, then it is the Yadavs for whom one should vote.

SCs too have their own organisations, which speak of their proud pasts. Although many SC associations are content in claiming Brahman or Kshatriya status, those that are politically active are keen to point out their alienation from established Hindu myths, beliefs, and rituals. When Ambedkar converted to Buddhism, he made it clear in his vows that he did not consider Buddha to be an incarnation of the Hindu god Vishnu as many Hindus claim. Nor did he follow any of the rituals of Hinduism and abided strictly by the Buddhist code.

Dalit politics today symbolically defy Hinduism by either promoting conversions to Buddhism or by claiming that Dalits belong to the original Kshatriya orders before Vedic Hindus entered the geographical space of India. As mentioned above, Phule of the Satyashodhak Samaj in Maharashtra argued that the so-called low castes of Maharashtra were the original and real Kshatriyas before the Brahmans and then the Muslims overwhelmed them. Many SC organisations now project their culture as the origin of all cultures in Indic civilisation. These Dalit communities believe that they are the *adi* of all other cultures in the Indian subcontinent, although the Aryans, who came later, did their best to undermine this fact. This adi theme helps further the Dalit claim that social and political supremacy should rightfully belong to them and not to the Brahmans who, by deceit and treachery, have worked their way to the top. By legitimising their cultural supremacy in terms of historic priority, Dalits gain the necessary symbolic confidence in their quest for political power in contemporary politics.

Such instances of symbolic defiance are not limited to Hindus alone. Jodhka incisively highlights how the Sikh leather workers have also challenged the established norms of the mainstream Gurudwaras and their styles of worship. These Sikh leather workers now call themselves Ad-Dharmis and refuse to bow down to the dictates of the dominant Jat Sikh community. The Ad-Dharmis have set up their own Gurudwaras and refuse to go to those run by Jat Sikhs. It is true that SC Sikhs have often felt alienated and unwanted in local Sikh Gurudwaras, although Sikhism is officially against casteism. Ad Dharmi Gurudwaras also give the Sikh holy book the pride of place but have a bust or engraving of Ravidas, the devotional medieval low caste saint who challenged Brahman orthodoxy. Although Ravidas' contribution is acknowledged fulsomely in the Sikh holy book, his image is not to be found in any mainstream Jat Sikh Gurudwara. Ravidas is an important figurehead among former untouchables, especially in North India, and by installing his image in the Gurudwara, the Ad Dharmis were reaching out to other SCs elsewhere, even those outside Sikhism.

The fact that castes are politically active should not give the impression that the equation between caste and political allegiance is unequivocal and unproblematic. It is not as if all members of a certain caste vote unanimously with utmost primordial loyalty. Unfortunately, this view has not been challenged as strongly as it should be. In many scholarly works it is uncritically assumed that the political fortunes of parties depend primarily upon the caste composition of constituencies. When castes align politically, it is not as if the bond is informed by considerations of hierarchy or tradition. Wehave found that formations like the Bharatiya Lok Dal or the KHAM and AJGAR alliances were not very stable fixtures in the political firmament. When castes come together, they do so because they believe that their secular interests coincide, which is why it makes good political sense to cement an alliance. Otherwise, members of such alliances do not always think well of their political partners, and in many cases, they have developed oppositional folklores. The KHAM alliance, to take another example, comprises Kshatriyas, Harijans, and Muslims.

Further, the predominance of a certain caste in a defined region is not because it has superior numbers that can carry it through elections but rather because it is better organised. This is the case with Jats of West Uttar Pradesh as well as the Ahirs and the Marathas to give but a few examples. In the case of the Marathas, it is true that they constitute about 30 per cent of the population of Maharashtra, but this caste is politically divided into numerous political affiliations. There are Marathas in the Congress, in the Communist parties, in the Bharatiya Janata party, in the Shiv Sena, and so forth. This negates the possibility of Marathas acting as a united political lobby. As Michelutti points out, the number of Yadavs in politics is proportionately much higher than among any other community in the Sadar Bazaar area of Uttar Pradesh where she conducted her study. Likewise, Jats used to dominate west Uttar Pradesh, although they never constituted more than 8 per cent of the population anywhere in that region. Inspite of this, the Jats were so powerful because they were the best organised and were economically the strongest peasant caste of the region.

SCs do not always vote for parties, such as the RPI or the BSP, that are slated as Dalit organisations. In fact, Congress party still polls the largest share of SC votes across the country. Although the BSP secures mostly Dalit votes, it is not as if the percentage of votes from this community is assured. Occasionally, it has also been noticed that non-SCs also vote for parties such as the BSP. Jaffrelot brings to our attention the fact that in the 1996 elections about 25 per cent of Koeris voted for BSP, and not, as one might expect, for the Samajwadi party of the middle peasants. However, it must also be said that the BSP has striven to attract Muslims and other peasant castes to its cause. Even though it may have won over a section of Koeris, there is no marked Yadav preference for BSP over the last few elections.

If one were to study the relationship between caste and elections then there would indeed be many instances of mismatch and of marked fluctuations in political loyalties. This is true not just of peasant castes or the SCs but holds for the traditional upper castes as well. Incidentally, there is no constituency in Bihar where the Yadavs are over 20 per cent of the population. Yet, if the Yadav-controlled Janta Dal continues to rule in Bihar, it must be something more than just caste loyalty that one needs to consider. Therefore, the popular assumption that caste arithmetic is all that matters in determining political behaviour is clearly in need of revision. Empirical data do not substantiate this argument beyond a point.

Politics of Reservations

When the Indian Constitution provided reservations for Scheduled Castes and Tribes, it also added that in due course of time similar legislations ought to be devised for the Other Backward Castes as well. The population of these so-called Backward Castes is difficult to estimate, and the figures range from 25 per cent to 52 per cent of the total population of the country. In terms of their social and economic standing, they are placed between the traditional elite castes such as Brahmans, Banias, Kayasthas, Rajputs, other lower castes, and the SC and STs.

These Backwards are now known as Other Backward Castes (OBC) and, in general, comprise largely peasant and other agrarian communities. These castes are not untouchables but are considered backward as they lack a culture of learning on account of their lowly peasant status. Thus though they did not have to bear the burden of untouchability, their depressed economic position contributed to their general cultural backwardness. In recognition of this fact, the Constitution of India recommended that the state intervene and help these communities by legislating some measures that would break this cycle of poverty and backwardness.

In pursuance of Article 340 of the Constitution, the Kalelkar Commission was set in 1955, but it could not come to any satisfactory conclusion about who should be legitimately considered as OBCs. The Mandal Commission came into existence in 1980, and it promptly came up with a long list of 3743 backward castes on the basis of social, economic, and educational backwardness. The Mandal Commission's recommendations were implemented in 1990 by the then Prime Minister V.P.Singh.

The implementation of reservations for OBCs set off a furor of protests, including a few suicides, all over the country by those who are considered to be members of forward castes. Many felt that reservations for OBCs were not warranted for two reasons. First, this would make India a caste society by law, and second, many of those who are considered as OBCs are really quite powerful and dominant in rural India, both economically and politically. The obvious reference was to Jats and Yadavs. A number of social anthropologists wrote against reservations for OBCs primarily on these grounds.

Beteille's criticism of the Mandal Commission recommendations was widely commented upon. He distinguishes between reservations for OBCs following Mandal recommendations and the reservations that were already grantedinthe Constitution for Scheduled Castes and Tribes. Although provisions for Scheduled Castes and Tribes were with the intention of reaching toward greater equality, reservations for OBCs were really to bring about a balance of power on the calculus of caste. The kind of deprivations that former untouchables and *adivasis* encountered for centuries can in no way be compared to the traditional condition of the OBCs. In fact, the Mandal Commission recommendations were actually giving in to a powerful rural lobby that did not really care for equality of opportunities as much as it did for equality of results. It can also be said that Mandal recommendations are not out to extirpate caste as was the aim of instituting reservations for SCs and STs, but to represent castes, and thus make this ascriptive marker a perennial political resource to be flogged in perpetuity.

Another major justification for upholding reservations for SCs and STs came from the acknowledgment that these communities lacked viable marketable assets that would allow them to pursue a life of dignity in a democratic society. The SCs were kept away from education, could only perform menial and polluting jobs, and suffered from a variety of other deprivations. In the case of the STs, it was their physical isolation that put them at a disadvantage with respect to others in society. Reservations for these communities were therefore meant to raise their marketable skills and educational standards to compensate for their historic lack of privileges and to facilitate their participation as equal citizens Reservations, Mandal style, only helps them to convert their political and economic assets, which are currently rural, to urban jobs and related skill assets. These they could develop on their own without the necessary intervention of national level reservation policies.

If one were to look closely at the criteria for social backwardness, then it would become quite apparent that the considerations that went into the reckoning of who were the OBCs were politically weighted. The Mandal Commission listed three categories of backwardness, e.g., social, economic, and educational. In all a caste can score a maximum of 22 points but needs only 11 to qualify as backward. Each of the four indicators of social backwardness carries three points, the three indicators of educational backwardness just two points each, and each of the criteria for economic backwardness, which should have been the most important, are given only one point.

As social backwardness is given the greatest weight, we examine that more closely. The four indicators of social backwardness are performing manual labor, what other castes think of a particular caste, do the women in that caste work outside the home, and if 25 per cent of females and 10 per cent of males get married above the state average before the age of 17.

Each of these indicators carries three points, and it is not at all difficult for a well-to-do rural caste to score on each of them, earn 12 points, and thus qualify as an OBC. Educational and economic backwardness need not come into the picture at all. All landowning peasant castes are proud to call themselves farmers who perform manual work, whether or not they actually do so. The criterion of women working outside their homes is not a good indicator either as they need not necessarily be toiling on others' fields or as coolie labor.

It is interesting how the Mandal recommendations provoked anthropologists to debate issues such as citizenship and equity in the context of Indian society, perhaps for the first time. Policy concerns, at the all-India level, received a kind of urgency in several anthropological writings in, and on India, on a scale that was never witnessed before. The governing assumption in all such works is that caste identity, and not the system, underpins and informs caste politics. This point of view is gradually gaining ground among anthropologists who are now explicitly beginning to acknowledge the discrete nature of caste identities and the consequent clash of multiple hierarchies. Dumont's prestigious *Homo Hierarchicus* for long stood in the way of realising this phenomenon, but the pressure of social facts has forced anthropologists to look for a different analytical perspective.

Politics and Caste-region Nexus

Cast as a system of vertical division, sustains on the basis of localisation. Caste hierarchy may invoke the ideologies of *chaturvarnya* and of purity-pollution. But the hierarchy makes sense operationally, only when it is concretised in a local situation. Studies concentrating on *Jati* by sociologists and social anthropologists, have always pointed out how hierarchical ranking of *Jati* makes sense in the context of village or small localities. Similarly, cultural, ritual life of members of *Jati* is organised around village or locality. It is only in comparison to some other caste within a locality that the higher or lower status of caste can be experienced. A statement that 'carpenters dine with ironsmiths' does not carry any meaning unless it is specified as to where this interdining took place. In other words, *Jati* as a unit of social relations, ritual status and cultural universe is firmly based within the framework of well-defined territorial boundaries. As much as vertical, horizontal separateness of a caste, too, has a locality as a point of reference.

Often, we find distinct 'pockets' of various castes. Most castes are not only specific to a certain State but also specific to a particular area. This means that a caste, which has a concentrated existence in one area, may also constitute numerically large or significant group in that area. In a study of north India, Schwartzeberg has shown how caste concentration takes place at village and district level. He shows that more than fifty percent of Ludhiana's population is Jat, and Chamars and Majahabis have separate pockets in Punjab. The same applies to UP, Bihar, Orissa, etc. He argues that both in the case of peasant castes and Dalits, exclusivity seems to be the rule. This means that if in one village, Jats are the largest group; other peasant castes would almost be non-existent. Similarly, in districts where Majahabis are numerous, other Dalit castes are rarely seen. In the case of peasant castes, the regional base is considerably expansive while non-peasant castes are often confined to smaller pockets. This pattern is evident in State after State: In Tamil Nadu Vanniyars belong to North and South Arcot, Salem and Chingleput; Thevars in Ramnad Nadars earlier belonged to Tirunelveli. Similarly, Izhava sub castes belonged to different parts of Kerala – Tiyyars to North, Izhavas to central parts and Tandans to south. The Vokkaligas of Karnataka are concentrated in the Mysore region, Constituting around 29 percent of the population of Mysor State. In Maharashtra Agris are concentrated in one district of Konkan-Raigad, Leva Patils in Jalgaon district of North Maharashtra, Vanjaris in Nasik, Ahmednagar and Beed district. Iravati Karve and Dandekar have given a detailed sketch of the residential pockets of different castes of Maharashtra.The Malis of Rajasthan belong to Jodhpur region, and most smaller castes are concentrated in specific areas. The case of Jats of Western UP is too famous to require a mention. In Bihar, Bhumihars have a concentrated strength in the south while Rajputs have in the western parts. Kammas belong to Andhra region and Reddis to Rayalseema. One can keep multiplying this list of examples. M.N. Srinivas observed in 1957 "this kind of relationship between a caste and a region is widespread in India...". More specifically, as Washbrook observes in the context of TN, most endogamous Jatis extended over no more than a few adjacent villages

This association of many castes with specific territorial 'pockets' has produced two political results. One is the rise of 'locally dominant' castes. Srinivas' early use of the term 'dominant caste' was specifically with reference to a small locality or village or group of villages: In his 1955 essay 'The social system of a Mysore Village' Srinivas mentions that "The concept of the dominant caste is important for understanding intercaste relations in any local area.". Elaborating on the concept in 1957, he uses the phrase 'locally' dominant and then adds, "Occasionally a caste is dominant in a group of neighbouring villages if not over a district or two, and in such cases, local dominance is linked with regional dominance.". As far as 'local dominance" is concerned, there seems to be a direct link between domination and numerical preponderance. Large size of population, though, has one other implication. Often, a caste has numerical advantage when it also has a high degree of control over resources—at the village level, land. Thus, economic power and size combine to produce patterns of local domination. If one carefully follows Srinivas' account of locally dominant caste in Mysore, two things can be drawn from it: a) this political effect of caste-region interface is an outcome of local hierarchy based on caste and b) Just as dominance of one caste the subordination of other castes is a result of 'localisation'. Castes, which are 'trapped' by circumstances into that locality, face subordination.

The other, more commonly noted political result of caste pockets relates to electoral politics. Localised pockets of castes have come to mean that candidates of a particular caste will always get elected from certain areas. The study of Maharashtra gives ample evidence of this: The Maratha-Kunbi caste cluster, which is spread almost over the State, manages to send largest number of MLAs to State legislature irrespective of political upheavals. In 51 constituencies, the elected candidate has always been a Maratha, consecutively for six elections since 1978. In other 19 constituencies also, a candidate of the same caste has been elected since 1978. Thus, in one-fourth constituencies, the caste of the MLA has been the same since 1978. More specifically, Agris always get elected from Raigad district, Leva Patils from Jalgaon district, Telis from Wardha and Bhandara districts, Lingayats from Solapur and Kolhapur districts, Malis from Amravati district, etc. It is clear that there exists a tendency among parties to match caste by caste in selection of candidates. But the case of Maharashtra suggests that local pockets of castes have an important implication for the phenomenon of regionally dominant castes. It is only through such localised pockets that smaller and non-dominant castes get an opportunity to stake their claims to power. If smaller, non-dominant castes are not concentrated in one area, they are not likely to get any representation on their own strength. In Uttar Pradesh (UP), the Kurmis and Binds have formed their separate parties, Apna Dal and Pragatisheel Manavsamaj Party respectively and it has been observed that in 1999 Apna Dal did get large number of votes in five Lok Sabha (LS) constituencies although no candidate of the party was elected. The Binds, one of the more backward castes, rallied behind their caste candidates and made their presence felt in seven LS constituencies. This clearly shows that the Kurmis and

Binds can draw upon their localised demographic 'resource' to at least protest against the domination of Yadavs; just as Maratha domination in Maharashtra can be contested through localised pockets of other non-Maratha castes.

Construction of Regionally Dominant Castes

Localised concentration leads to localised domination and possibilities of some representation. One the other hand, throughout the twentieth century, certain Jatis evolved into castes spread over a large territory. This gave rise to the regionally dominant castes. From mid-fifties onwards, politics in most states centered around one regionally dominant caste(s). In most cases, middle level castes sought to contest the ritual superiority, material ascendance and political domination of 'upper' castes—mostly Brahmans, and in the north, Kayasthas and Thakurs. In the first half of twentieth century, the middle-caste protests took the form of non-Brahman movements in Maharashtra and in the south. In the second half of twentieth century, the middle castes extended their claims to state power at the regional level.

The non-Brahman movements in Maharashtra and south were concerned with creating 'regional' non-Brahman identities. In Maharashtra, the invocation of Shivaji and Maratha rule by the non-Brahman movement was crucial in bringing various peasant castes together. The movement also facilitated the emergence of Maratha politics on a larger scale geographically. In Tamil Nadu, the non-Brahman movement was built upon the collapse of caste and region. The Brahmans were excluded from Dravid identity. In Karnataka, the Vokkaliga 'Caste' came into being by the fusion of various peasant Jatis such as Morasui, Hallikar, Halu, Nonabad, and so on. In Gujarat, Kanabis of different areas came together in 1931 to constitute themselves as 'Patidars', although, Saurashtra Kanabis are still looked down upon by Gujarat Patidars. Also, the Leva and Kadvi divisions of Patidars are supposed to refer to sub-regional differences. Yet, from 1931 onwards, the 'Patidar' identity has evolved as a regional or State level identity. Similarly, despite internal tensions, Kshatriyas of Gujarat have been organising themselves as one group. Rajputs, who are in the forefront of the Kshatriya mobilisation, are regionally differentiated. Gujarat Rajputs being mostly tenants or landless, sought to align with Kolis and Bariyas (also landless) as

Kshatriyas. Saurashtra Rajputs being landowners resisted the claims of non-Rajputs to Kshatriya status. However, over the years, the Kshatriya group of castes in Gujarat as a whole has provided a counterpoint to Patidar politics. The Kshatriya Sabha took an initiative in bringing together Rajputs and Kolis and shaping their politics. The Jats are probably the most regionally structured caste. Various Khaps of Jats span specified villages and a meeting of all Khaps, the Sarvakhap meets to discuss common matters. But alongside Khaps, Jats of western UP as well as adjoining Haryana are also organised through the all India Jat Mahasabha, which always extended support to Charan Singh.

It can be argued that both the rise of non-Brahman movement and rise of middle caste as dominant caste in many States follow a similar pattern. A protest against castes ranking high in the hierarchy gives an impetus to these processes. But these processes gain momentum when small, localised, endogamous Jatis overcome their localisation by seeking either in mythology or history a link with a larger territorial unit. This development is accompanied by formation of territorial or even 'all-India' associations—Mahasabhas or Mahasanghas—of the newly evolved caste group. A moderately reformist posture follows vis-à-vis intra-caste practices, particularly marriage practices. Since the process is ideologically rooted in opposition to upper castes, the claims of such 'castes' relate to share in power, opportunities for material uplift and amelioration of tradition-inflicted disabilities. Central to this whole process is the journey from locality to region. Once a caste crosses the threshold of locality, the possibilities of realising political claims become very real. A geographical expanse allows the concerned caste to make claims on representational basis besides the basis of caste injustice. In fact, most dominant castes, as also proponents of non-Brahman movement, claim that the heritage of that region belongs to them; they are the true and authentic bearers of symbols associated with the particular region; they represent the culture of that region; the non-Brahmans are true Dravids, the Marathas are bearers of the symbol of Shivaji, Patidars exemplify the essence of Gujarati culture or Jats represent the true Kisans.

Linguistic States

If a caste claims that it represents the regional culture better than others, if follows that there will be a strong connection between such dominant castes and regionalist movements. These States constitute a region not only in just a geographical-administrative sense, but in socio-cultural and political sense also. Hence the link between dominant castes and States.

One can come across many examples of different patterns of relations between caste and regional identity. These include assertions by upper castes, convenient collaboration between upper and middle castes, the rise of contending middle castes, exclusion of upper castes, etc. Probably the latest example would be Uttaranchal where caste played an indirect role. When the union government decided to implement the policy of reservations for OBCs, stiff opposition came from upper castes of Uttaranchal. It was argued that this region did not have OBCs – at least not in large numbers. From the point of anti-reservation movement, the issues of separate identity of hill people distinct from plains people, came to the forefront. Without much exaggeration, it could be said that formation of Uttaranchal is an instance of upper caste assertion where 'regional' distinctiveness was indirectly claimed on the basis of different caste composition of the population. When the Oriya speaking territory was part of Bengal, Brahmans and Karans came together to shape Oriya opposition to Bengali domination. In 1912, this same social force invoked Oriya nationalism to protest against Orissa's annexation to Bihar. Since the creation of Orissa State, the upper castes have generally retained their hold over the State's politics, culture and economy.

As far as collaboration between upper and middle castes is concerned, Maharashtra can serve as a very good example. Although the non-Brahman movement had considerably villainised Brahmans, the Samyukta Maharashtra Movement saw the Brahmans and sections of Marathas collaborating and mobilising the masses on the basis of regionalist sentiments. This collaboration had a major long-term effect. While formation of Maharashtra State ushered the Marathas into position of power, the sharpness of non-Brahmanism was almost lost. The Brahmans, of course, were not in a position to make a comeback to politics, but nor were they hounded out of politics in particular or the public domain in general. On the contrary, Brahmans continued to dominate culture, education, media, under the benign auspices of 'Maharashtra Dharma'. More tangentially, the regional assertion led by Brahmans and Marathas displaced the main focus of non-Brahman movement, considerably weakening anti-caste discourse. Instead, Maratha domination became legitimised in the name of non-Maratha lower castes, identified in the sixties as Bahujan Samaj– the contemporary OBCs.

Just as the Gujarati-Marwari baniya was the cause of Marathi Brahmans and Marathas coming together, the prominence of Tamil Brahmans resulted into the unity of Telugu Brahmans and non-Brahman castes of Andhra. Although initially the non-Brahman Telugus joined Justice Party, they were not enamored by the anti-Brahman rhetoric. This weakened the non-Brahman movement in Andhra. It has also been argued that cooption of elite Reddys into the congress facilitated a less acrimonious relationship between Brahmans and Reddys.. The examples of Maharashtra and Andhra show that regionalism can intervene in the competition between upper castes and middle castes. Secondly, these examples suggest that regionalism can help a smooth transfer of State level political apparatus to middle castes. Often, in this 'smooth' transfer, radicalism as a basis of political claims is lost and claims of lower castes get a short shrift through symbolic gestures and tokenism.

Starting off from limited collaboration between upper and middle castes, Maharashtra and Andhra Pradesh witnessed the rise and assertion of middle castes. A similar assertion was witnessed in UP once the Jats of western UP became politically organised. The Jat assertion took the form of a demand for 'backward' status. From this, Charan Singh also attempted to project himself as representative of backwards. However, following Jats' association with land, their leaders, Charan Singh earlier and Tikait later, harped on a farmer identity as the identity of Jats in particular but of Gujjars as well. Interestingly, during Takait's farmers' agitations, at one stage, activists of Bharatiya Kisan Union proposed that they should ask for a separate state for western UP. Thus, the caste of Jats is an example of middle caste assertion at the regional level. Politics of Haryana is another instance of Jat assertion at State level while in Rajasthan; the Jat assertion took the form of a concerted effort to claim backward status. The Jats of Rajasthan deviated from pro-congress politics to vote for BJP in 1999 for the sole purpose of getting their backward status recognised. The Jat Mahasabha decided to vole for BJP once Vajpayee promised to concede their demand.

Many States have witnessed keen competition between two castes or caste clusters. In instances of such competition, the contending castes usually belong to a middle status. In Rajasthan, the competition between the Jats and Rajputs has been rather neatly transformed into a bipolar party situation. Gujarat and Karnataka are the other two examples of contending middle castes but politics there is not organised so neatly. The Patidar caste also gained control over resources and sought to displace the Brahmans and baniyas from political power. However, Gujarat politics is characterised by congress efforts to attract Kshatriyas, Swatantra Party's efforts to forge an alliance of Patidars and kshatriyas, Patidar alliance with Brahmans and Banias in opposition to reservation and growing affection among Kshatriyas towards the congress. These developments have led to the emergence of BJP as a Patidar force in the nineties. Karnataka witnessed a tussle between Vokkaligas and Lingayats right from the time of creation of a Kannada speaking State. Therefore, two Kannada speaking States were demanded. This has been recorded by the State Reorganisation commission. Thus, here is an example of a large caste cluster opposing a unified linguistic State for fear of loosing its numerical advantage. Vokkaligas dominated Mysore politics between 1947 and 1956. Since 1956, although Lingayats did get an upper hand, political dominance was shared by these two contending caste clusters till 1972. It was noted by Ambedkar that linguistic States would only lead to consolidation of the 'upper' castes, jeopardising the interests of scheduled castes. In Punjab, for instance, the scheduled castes were not very supportive of the demand for a separate State of Punjab by reorganising the State on linguistic communal lines. Even Sikh untouchables kept away from that demand fearing that a reorganised Punjab would facilitate domination of Jat Sikhs.

Tamil Nadu manifests a pattern of caste region relationship, which is distinct from other States in many respects. It did not throw up any single dominant caste although Vellalas and Nadars benefited the most from the Dravid non-Brahman movement. Secondly, the non-Brahman movement dealt with the issue of regional identity right from the beginning in the second decade of twentieth century. Non-Brahmanism was identified with

Dravidianism. While attempting to unite all non-Brahman castes on the Dravid platform, the Dravid movement refused to recognise Brahmans as part of Dravid society. Just as this movement sought to effect a fusion of many non-Brahman castes, it also aspired to build a 'Southern' identity opposed to 'north'. In 1937 the movement led by Periyar waged an anti-Hindi agitation. The logical culmination of anti-Hindi, anti-north Dravidian non-Brahmanism was reached in 1939 when Justice Party demanded 'independent' Dravidsthan. Thus, caste-region interaction in Tamil Nadu strengthened an exclusionary regional nationalism.

However, this exclusion did not last long. Once the regional claims were realised through formation of Madras State and non-Brahman claims were translated into an extensive policy of reservations, Brahmans were incorporated as members into the Tamil society. Brahmans are accommodated as ideologues and legitimizers of the regional legacy of Dravid movement. It is indeed ironical that a strong non-Brahman movement, through its regionalism allowed a re-entry of the Brahman caste both into the elite and into the political arena in general. In the nineties, the political assertion of the Vanniyars marked the political scene in Tamil Nadu. However, Vanniyars have a long history of separate political organisation.

In spite of the efforts of non-Brahman movement to bring together all non-Brahman castes, Vanniyars were organised through Tamilnad Toilers' Party and Commonweal party. Although DMK supported the latter in 1952 with a view to defeating Congress, Kamraj was successful in bringing both Vanniyar parties into congress fold. Another backward caste, the Thevars, backed the forward bloc for a long time. These details suggest that in spite of very vocal non-Brahman movement, Tamil politics did not throw up any single middle caste around which State politics could be organised. Probably, this peculiar situation led to sustained recourse to militant regional nationalism, particularly by the Dravid parties. However, as Washbrook observes, this Dravidianism 'neutralised many of the caste based issues of conflict that dominated Tamil Nadu politics in the first half of the twentieth century'. Perhaps, those contradictions, which Dravidianism sought to push under the carpet of regionalism, have resurfaced in Tamil Nadu with Dalit – OBC conflicts and Hinduisation of some backward castes. In the absence of any particular caste group as central to politics, Tamil politics took on an exclusionary character: exclusion of Brahmans, Aryans, North Indians and less explicitly, exclusion of even Adi Dravids.

Issues and Concerns

Demography, agrarian relations, political economy of post-independence period combined to produce the strong linkages between region and caste. In particular, the different patterns of caste relations gave substance to region as a political category in States like Andhra Pradesh, Tamil Nadu and Karnataka. These developments established the feature of region specific dominant castes in most parts of India. Both these ruptures in the established pattern of caste-region equation came as opposition to upper as well as newly dominant castes in various regions. In the interplay of caste and region, Dalits and OBCs were / are often excluded or marginalised.

At the intellectual level, Ambedkar was the first to grasp the implications of 'linguistic States' in terms of the consequent marginalisation of Dalits. But even before the issue of linguistic States came up, Ambedkar had realised the need to mobilise Dalits at an all-India level if they were to stake claims to political power. Thus, in the 1940s, abandoning the Independent labor party, he formed the Scheduled Castes Federation. On the one hand, through SCF, he sought to intervene in the negotiations for India's freedom and wrest minimum share in power. On the other hand, the SCF was also visualised as a major opposition to the upper caste dominated Congress in the period immediately after independence. The failure of the SCF notwithstanding, it is important to note that Ambedkar saw the unfolding of a process of conflict between SCs and upper castes and also believed that a united all-India instrument of SCs can alone take on the task of contesting upper caste claims. Although he once again veered to a more broad based party in the form of Republican party of India this party came to be identified as Dalit party and could not sustain the all-India claims which Ambedkar had always insisted upon. In the mid-eighties, Kanshi Ram formed the Bahujan Samaj Party. This party is seen primarily as the party of Dalits. In this sense, BSP manifests an all-India ambition and an awareness that upper caste domination has to be fought at the all-India level. Thus, initial lead by Ambedkar and more contemporarily the formation of BSP, challenge the caste-region nexus. They seek to problematise the caste question at the national level and force a solution through intervention in national politics. The former believes that only in a period of instability can Dalits force their entry into the network that controls national state apparatus. Therefore, unity of Dalits at all-India level and unity between Dalits and other disadvantaged castes are seen as strategies for shifting power away from Brahmanical sections of society towards the Bahujan Samaj.

In the mid-sixties, Lohia argued that 'backward castes' constitute a majority and they should be given a fair share in power. This was reminiscent of the arguments of non-Brahman movement in the south and in Maharashtra. Although backward caste politics gradually emerged in UP and Bihar, it was only in the nineties that it became an issue at an all-India level. After the agitations against reservations in Gujarat and Bihar in the late seventies and early eighties, the agitation in many north Indian States on the issue of reservations for backward castes underlined the simmering conflict between what Lohia had described as forwards and backwards. This resulted into large-scale mobilisation of backward castes dramatically catapulting protagonists of backward castes into positions of power.

These developments had two effects. Firstly, the political discourse in the country as a whole, changed considerably. 'Social justice' became the central term around which this discourse was constructed. Such a construction facilitated the entry of caste question onto the all-India political scene rather than remaining State-specific. Backwardness of certain castes and consequent political disadvantage was no more seen in State-specific contexts; instead it was conceived as a phenomenon following from Brahmanical Hindutva and domination of national politics by upper castes. As such, taking over power at Delhi was seen as the remedy. Secondly, 'OBC' claims were quickly recognised by the various political parties. In particular, the BJP exhibited remarkable adaptability by introducing changes in the social composition of its key workers in Maharashtra, Madhya Pradesh and UP. Most other parties, too, underwent the process of 'Mandalisation', the Congress probably being the slowest and most reluctant, However, even the Congress manifested awareness of this factor in Rajasthan, Gujarat, Madhya Pradesh, etc. In other words, OBC politics did not throw up any all-India instrument instead; it forced certain changes in political parties and in politics in general. Social composition of many legislatures changed during the decade of 1990 to 2000. At least at the formal level, parties conceded the claims of OBCs in terms of share in power. Politics of backward castes became an all-India phenomenon.

In the case of Dalit politics, one can witness a steady fragmentation in the post-Ambedkar period. This fragmentation takes place at three levels: party factionalism, State-specific distinction and intra-Dalit fragmentation. The RPI could never project itself as a united party of Dalits. Various rival RPI parties emerged competing with each other. The absence of a single effective political instrument resulted into the fragmentation of Dalit votes also. On the other hand, concrete political issues faced by Dalits took a State specific turn. In Maharashtra, for instance, the issue of 'renaming' a university after Dr. Ambedkar remained an emotive issue for Dalits for over a decade. In States like Bihar, atrocities by various middle castes became the main concern of Dalits. In Tamil Nadu, frustration with Dravid politics, non-accommodation in the regional identity and conflicts with lower OBC has been shaping Dalit politics at State level. Such State-specific situations are inevitable because of differences of levels of Dalit consciousness and differences in the political economy at State level. This means that the arena of conflict and the response by Dalits varies from State to State. The main adversaries of Dalits are also not necessarily common across States. The voting preferences of Dalits are also likewise shaped at State level. Dalits of Rajasthan, Gujarat, MP, Maharashtra tend to vote in favour of Congress Dalits of W. Bengal and Kerala prefer the left fronts in those States. In UP, the BSP has established itself as the main party of Dalits. In Bihar the BJP led alliance gets more Dalit votes than RJD of Laloo Yadav, probably because of the JD faction led by Ramvilas Paswan who allied with BJP. Similarly, in Karnataka also, the BJP alliance gets more Dalit votes than the Congress.

A further complication regarding the Dalit situation needs to be noted. While ideologues of Dalit politics prefer to project 'Dalit' as one social force, even at State level, Dalits do not constitute a unified social force. For various reasons, the State-specific reasons not the least, internal stratification among Dalits of different States in a reality. In Maharashtra, the Mahar Dalits are seen as politically advanced, the Matang and Chamar Dalits resist the 'Mahar domination'. The Mala-Madiga dispute in Andhra Pradesh reached such a proportion that the State government decided to divide reservation between these two communities. The Dalits of Bihar other than the Paswans do not look upon Ramvilas Paswan as their leader. In Karnataka, the large group of Madigas demand that the reservations for Dalits should be split; giving a fixed quota to Holeyas and other Dalits which will allow Madigas to enjoy 90 percent of the reservations. Further, in one instance of violent conflict between Holeyas and the dominant land owing groups, other Dalits did not come forward in support of the Holeyas. In UP, Jatavs are seen as politically powerful and getting all advantages. The Balmikis and Pasis feel deprived. In West Bengal, the Namsudras and Rajbanshis have their 'pockets' in Faridpur, Khulna, Jessore and in north Bengal districts of Cooch Behar, Jalpaiguri, Dinajpur, respectively. These two communities are seen as taking advantage of the reservations. All these details suggest the difficulty in organising an all India Dalit politics, Only by intervening in the State level political process; Dalits stand any chance of affecting politics.

The case of OBCs is not very different. To begin with, the 'OBC' category, though a convenient short hand for a large mass, is not very definitive. It includes, formally, castes included by governments in the State lists of other backward classes. As such, the question, 'Who are the OBCs?' is itself a controversial one. Inclusion or exclusion in the OBC list is often a matter of politics for those castes who have attained enough political skills. It is a common experience that castes would press for inclusion in the list of OBCs – Jats in Rajasthan, Vokkaligas and Lingayats in Karnataka are two famous examples. Needless to say, all these factors develop in the backdrop of State specific situations. Except on general issue of reservations all OBCs cannot be mobilised on an all-India level. Therefore, in the nineties, on the heels of Mandal controversy, many OBC organisations rallied round the issues of reservations. However, when it came to organising the nuts and bolts of OBC politics, the State specific situations asserted themselves. Thus, Janata Dal, which sought to bask in the glory of its pro-Mandal stand, witnessed internal bickering: the Orissa unit under Biju Patnaik distanced itself from the Mandal platform while the Karnataka unit under Hegde made its displeasure about 'Mandalisation' known to national leadership. Both State units felt it unnecessary to have V.P. Singh as a campaigner.

Much mobilisation on the Mandal platform took place in UP and Bihar. The politics of backward castes did not articulate in a substantial manner in Orissa and Andhra Pradesh. It did not have much relevance to Tamil Nadu since that State has had a long history of non-Brahman politics. In Karnataka, Congress under Devraj Urs had earlier mobilised the OBCs. Therefore, in the nineties, the Mandal platform did not evoke much enthusiasm there. This leaves the States of Uttar Pradesh and Bihar as the main theatre of OBC politics. In a sense, the so-called all-India claims on behalf of OBC politics are based on politics in north India where the caste issue has emerged onto the political scene rather late. Thus the phenomenon of OBC politics is much more relevant to UP and Bihar than to other States.

The internal stratification among 'OBCs' is another matter where State specific issues come to the forefront. As noted above, identification of certain castes as OBCs, is itself State specific. This is borne out by the case of Jats and more effectively, by the case of Lingayats of Karnataka. The State government went on appointing commission after commission in order to resolve the issue of whether Lingayats are backward or not. Even when the issue of identification is resolved, the question of share of different castes / caste groups continues to pose a challenge. In the field of reservations, most States seem to be veering to the strategy of classifying OBCs into two or three groups and assuring them separate 'quotas' of reserved seats. Besides reservations, the question of 'share' involves claims over power. Various backward castes not only want to be 'included' in the apparatus of power, they hope to use power to their advantage and if possible, gain controlling share in power. Negatively put, backward castes push for exclusion of the upper castes so that complexion and content of power would change substantively. These claims bring a double conflict into focus. On the one hand there is a conflict between the already established dominant caste and the aspiring caste / caste group. The constellations of these conflicts are again State specific because the ideological battle line of upper vs.

backward translates differently in each state. In Maharashtra, for example, when Maratha domination is sought to be challenged, Kunbis, who are included in the list of OBCs, would pose a problem. The 'Maratha' caste cluster includes Kunbis. Thus, the battle is between the dominant caste and a section of OBCs vs. other OBCs. In Karnataka, the OBCs compete with Lingayats who themselves have been claiming inclusion in the list of OBCs. Political economy of each State produces patterns of dominance in accordance to which these battle lines get defined. The other conflict involves the aspiring castes themselves. When the Brahmanical castes were displaced, on the whole, only one caste sought to replace them at the State level. With democratisation penetrating larger sections in the contemporary period, a peculiar development has taken place. Just as the established dominant caste is about to be displaced, more than one claimants emerge to stake claims over power. This does not allow any single caste to stabilise in power. The Yadavs of UP and Bihar, who claimed in the nineties that they were leading the OBC revolution, have been challenged by non-Yadavs in both the States. Both these conflicts are reflected in the party preferences of OBCs. Backward castes in different States vote differently and within a State, they are often divided among different parties. These claims and counterclaims have, in fact, further regionalised politics during the nineties. The unprecedented rise of regional parties in the nineties has been singularly unassociated with 'regionalism.'

State as a socio-linguistic region is a very convenient unit for caste to operate. Although many instances can be shown where small castes intervene in local political process, effective role of caste can be detected at the State level only. At the same time, castes cannot assume all-India identities and caste alliances cannot be easily forged at the all-India level. The political salience of caste increased only after castes transcended the 'local' identities and by forging new 'mega' caste identities became significant players at 'regional' level. However, this process probably stops at the regional level. Efforts of Kurmis to forge an alliance with Kanbis and Kunbis did not succeed. Even in the case of Jats, though the Jat Mahasabha exists, Jat politics in Punjab, Rajasthan, Haryana and western UP cannot be clubbed together. Thus, patterns of caste politics cannot be replicated in different regions nor can they become all-India in their reach or spread. In this sense, caste as a factor in modern politics, has become well entrenched or rooted at the regional / State level.

The relevance of caste at the regional level flows from the following four factors:

a) Social relations of hierarchy are identifiable at the regional level, some times even sub-regional level. The fact that somebody is a Brahman simply places that person in an ambiguous position of superiority outside the region where that person belongs; but in the region where s/he belongs, a fine tuning will be made depending upon whether that person is a Chitpavan or not. To take a concrete example, being a 'Maratha' carries meaning only in the context of Maharashtrian society. The Marathas will be simultaneously seen as farmers, warriors, ex-land lords, etc. Rather than their ritual status either as Kshatriyas or shudras, the historically constructed and materially experienced identity as 'powerful' will be quickly brought into focus. Regional associations also allow myths and prejudices / stereotypes operate as markers of ranking. These do not make sense outside of that region. Therefore for most castes, a hierarchical ranking is relevant only in specific region. Social relations based on these assumptions of hierarchy shape social attitudes about claims of power by different castes, giving way to competition or caste conflict. All the same, Brahmans accepted—though unwillingly—Maratha entry into the political arena. In contrast, the claims of Dalits are not so silently accepted.

b) Historically, many middle castes and some times even lower castes seek upward mobility in their ritual / social status. Studies of caste point out that this happens when a caste achieves material strength. It must be noted that the process of gaining upward mobility is strictly region-based. It is not so merely because one particular caste in one region attains material strength. It is also because, the claims are made regionally and accepted / legitimised regionally. Such 'mobile' castes even change their caste names and this is accepted in the given region. Transformations from Kunbi to Maratha or Kanabi to Patidar are of course famous. Similarly, the mobility of

Nadars of Tamil Nadu has been well documented. Other examples include the awadhias, mahatos, jhanuks taking up Kurmi identity, gwalas, gopes, becoming Yadavs, Padayachis of Tamil Nadu becoming Vanniyar Kshatriyas, etc. Such mobility facilitates horizontal unity among castes.

c) In the course of competition among castes, regionalism or sub-regionalism can be very easily invoked. Regionalism servers either of the two purposes. It can project one caste/ caste group as inheritor, protector or representative of regional identity and pride. This way, an assault on that caste or caste group is easily seen / shown as assault on regional pride and self-respect. Implicitly, this also means that advancement of the interests of that caste constitutes regional advancement and therefore, the demands of the caste group can be transformed into demands for regional development. To be sure, regionalist politics is shaped by many factors. What we are suggesting here is that once caste and region are identified, the interests of caste can be projected as regional interests.

d) Apart from the ideology of Regionalism, region can provide yet another advantage to the 'dominant' castes. Every dominant caste seeks to legitimise its dominant position on the basis of some ideological argument. Region as the social unit having a common cultural-linguistic context automatically forms a basis from which justification of domination can be adduced. Alternatively, arguments by the dominant caste make sense within the region. Thus, Jats' claim of being Kisans or Haryana Jats' claims for a martial tradition appeal the people in those respective regions rather than outside the regions. Similarly, Lingayats' claims of reformism in the orthodox Brahmanical Hinduism become relevant only in the Kannada speaking region. The ideology of 'Maharashtra Dharma' justifying the Brahman-Maratha leadership or the Bhadralok ideology of elite domination also has similar region-specific appeals. In the 'dominant caste thesis', the emphasis on numerical strength has deflected attention from both the contents of domination and the ways of attaining domination. Mere numerical strength would not lead to domination; claims of 'high' status usually

> accompany numerical strength. But a high ritual status is not the only 'ideological' component. 'Dominant' castes employ a more complex set of ideological arguments in order to win the 'dominant' position and we argue that region provides a helpful playground for working out these arguments.

It follows from this that any counter hegemonic assaults on the dominant caste would emanate from a similarly regionally situated arguments. In Tamil Nadu, the non-Brahman movement sought to delegitimise the Brahmans by suggesting that Brahmans are not true Dravids. But more forcefully, Phuley brings in the imagery of non-Brahmans as 'natives' by virtue of their association with agricultural activity. If both, the claims of domination and challenges to them, are regionally situated, region becomes a theatre of caste conflicts and configuring caste with political and economic dimensions.

Given the mutually reinforcing relationship of caste and region in contemporary Indian politics, it is argued here that challenges to concrete instances of caste domination can meaningfully rise at the regional level. This would further strengthen the links between caste and region. These links produce region/State-specific configurations of caste, which fit the region's political economy. In the light of this argument certain trends may be noticed. These trends indicate the possible ways in which caste is likely to be constructed in Indian politics.

In his introduction to 'Caste in Indian Politics', Rajni Kothari, long ago, pointed out the process of caste polarisation. He further said, '.... as one polarisation is resolved in favour of one caste or caste category, new polarisations emerge...'. In many parts of the country, instead of neat polarisation, 'more complicated and fragmented constellations of power' emerged. Thus, in the arena of caste politics, on the one hand new 'dominant castes' have emerged on the scene; at least many new 'ascendant' castes have come to the forefront. On the other hand new equations have emerged. The most noted one is the BJP led equation of upper castes and lower OBCs in Uttar Pradesh. In Maharashtra, the Charmakars and Matangs have been veering away from Congress and RPI, preferring the Shiv Sena and BJP. The Bahujan Mahasangh in Maharashtra has been trying to forge an alliance of Dalits and OBCs. These new equations do not necessarily follow a similar pattern across the States. But one common factor needs to be noted. In the emerging alliances traditional boundaries of ritual status are seldom followed. Alliances would be formed depending upon the perceptions about which caste / caste group monopolises resources. Beside, the choice of allies is often ad hoc, contingent upon who are perceived as adversaries. Underneath this contingent nature of alliances, there seems to be a consideration of two factors. One is consideration of material factors. Castes/caste groups tend to ally when their material interests do not clash—or in fact compliment—each other. When an alliance is likely to obtain some power for the caste such an alliance becomes acceptable. Both these considerations go beyond simple alliances based on ritual status—alliances are not made simply because castes occupy a common status as Shudras or Dalits.

Secondly, and partly following from the above, there is a disintegration of caste 'blocs' of Dalits and OBCs. Not only such blocs do not materialise at all-India level, they seem to be disintegrating even at the level of States. The trend seems to be moving in the direction of 'ethnicisation' of caste. One factor contributing to this process seems to be the pressure of modern reformist discourse delegitimising vertical structure of caste hierarchy. In this background, caste survives, if not as upper-lower then, as 'different' groups having different culture, ritual, 'histories', etc. Thus, caste becomes a 'community'. But ethnicisation of caste has other reasons as well. One is that small castes still find no place in calculations for electoral purposes. They may be relevant in constructing caste 'blocs' but do not receive the benefits either politically or materially. It is not necessary for us here to accept this logic but that seems to be a factor influencing the process of formation of single caste organisations. Such organisations function simultaneously as socio-cultural associations, pressure groups pursuing immediate material concerns of the caste and vehicles of caste elites for riding into the power structure. Although it is tempting to look at such caste organisations as a political resource, they imply localisation of caste. Such localised ethnicisation is bound to entrap castes both into local boundaries and issues of culture, identity, history rather than of material advance and structures of domination.

Thirdly, after reaching a high point through 'Mandlisation', caste appears to be reaching a dead end in terms of its mobilisational potential. At one stage caste interests were advanced through regional mobilisation. In the next phase, mobilisation took place on the issues of reservations for OBCs (in Bihar, Gujarat) followed up by the Mandal issues and claims of the leaders of OBCs for power sharing. The nineties have witnessed acceptance of OBC reservations as State policy. These developments have meant that the space to be occupied by caste issue is bound to shrink except for further competition among OBCs for greater share in power. At the local level, provision enabling reservations to SCs, STs and OBCs in local government bodies, has ensured that no effective mobilisation can take place and no party will take interest in such mobilisation. This does not imply that caste has lost relevance but that as an organising principle of politics, caste may have reached its limits. Like region earlier, caste may have to search for catalysts that will revitalise the emotive and mobilisation capacity of caste as a sphere of politics.

References

Assadi Muzaffar and S. Rajendran Karnataka. 'Changing Shape of Caste Conflicts'. *Economic and Political Weekly*. May 6-12. 2000.

Bashiruddin Ahmed. *Caste and Electoral Politics*. Asian Survey. Vol. 10, No. 11, Elections and Party Politics in India: A Symposium. Nov., 1970. pp. 979–992.

Bayly, Susan. *Caste, Society and Politics in India from the Eighteenth Century to the Modern Age*. Cambridge University Press. 1999.

Betteile Andre. *Society and Politics in India*. Delhi, OUP. 1992.

Hasan Zoya. *Quest for Power : Oppositional Movements and Post-Congress politics in Uttar Pradesh*. Delhi. OUP. 1998.

Kothari, Rajni. *Caste in Indian Politics*. Orient Longman.2004.

Nayar Baldev Raj. *Minority Politics in the Punjab*. N.J., Princeton University Press. 1998.

Nigam Aditya. 'India After the 1996 Elections: Nation, Locality and Representation'. *Asian Survey*. September. 199.

6

CASTE PRACTICES IN MODERN INDIA

Caste-based discrimination maybe abolished by law in India but it remains a major cause why backward classes, especially the Dalits, remain confined to menial tasks like manual scavenging and removal of dead animals, a latest report by the International Labour Organisation (ILO) on discrimination in the job sector has said. Affirmative action has been able to assist only a small number of Dalits in finding formal jobs but has failed to provide even and equal opportunities to all, the report added.

"Violence, discrimination and segregation are a daily experience for millions of men and women in several regions of the world. But the practice (of discrimination that is rooted in caste or similar systems) is most widespread in South Asia, particularly in India and Nepal," the report, titled *'Equality at Work: Tackling the Challenges'* a follow-up to the ILO Declaration on Fundamental Principles and Rights at Work, remarked.

The report added that Dalits are generally not accepted for any work involving contact for water and food for non-Dalits or entering a non-Dalit residence. "Thus, they are excluded from a wide-range of work opportunities in the area of production, processing or sale of food items, domestic work and the provision of certain services in the private and public sectors," the report said, adding their situation is further impaired by limited access to education, training and resources.

UNTOUCHABILITY

India's caste system is perhaps the world's longest surviving social hierarchy. A defining feature of Hinduism, caste encompasses a complex ordering of social groups on the basis of ritual purity. A person is considered a member of the caste into which he or she is born and remains within that caste until death, although the particular ranking of that caste may vary among regions and over time. Differences in status are traditionally justified by the religious doctrine of karma, a belief that one's place in life is determined by one's deeds in previous lifetimes.

Traditional scholarship has described this more than 2,000-year-old system within the context of the four principal varnas, or large caste categories. In order of precedence these are the *Brahmins* (priests and teachers), the *Ksyatriyas* (rulers and soldiers), the *Vaisyas* (merchants and traders), and the *Shudras* (labourers and artisans). A fifth category falls outside the varna system and consists of those known as "untouchables" or Dalits; they are often assigned tasks too ritually polluting to merit inclusion within the traditional varna system. Almost identical structures are also visible in *Nepal*. Despite its constitutional abolition in 1950, the practice of "untouchability"—the imposition of social disabilities on persons by reason of birth into a particular caste—remains very much a part of rural *India*. Representing over one-sixth of India's population-or some 160 million people-Dalits endure near complete social ostracisation. "Untouchables" may not cross the line dividing their part of the village from that occupied by higher castes. They may not use the same wells, visit the same temples, or drink from the same cups in tea stalls. Dalit children are frequently made to sit at the back of classrooms. In what has been called India's "hidden apartheid," entire villages in many Indian states remain completely segregated by caste.

"Untouchability" is reinforced by state allocation of resources and facilities; separate facilities are provided for separate caste-based neighbourhoods. Dalits often receive the poorer of the two, if they receive any at all. In many villages, the state administration installs electricity, sanitation facilities, and water pumps in the upper-caste section, but neglects to do the same in the neighbouring, segregated Dalit area. Basic amenities such as water taps and wells are also segregated, and medical facilities and the better, thatched-roof houses exist exclusively in the upper-caste colony. As revealed by the case study below on the earthquake in Gujarat, these same practices hold true even in times of great natural disaster.

Earthquake in Gujarat: Caste and its Fault-Lines

On January 26, 2001, a devastating earthquake rocked the northwest Indian state of Gujarat. Within days of the country's worst natural disaster in recent history at least 30,000 were declared dead and over one million were left homeless. In the months since the earthquake, residents of the state of Gujarat have been besieged by a man-made disaster: caste and communal discrimination in the distribution of relief and rehabilitation, corruption in the handling of aid, and political squabbling that has done little to help the earthquake's neediest victims.

Six weeks after the earthquake, The UN Human Rights Watch visited the towns of Bhuj, Bhijouri, Khawda, Anjar, and Bhachau in Kutch, the state's most devastated district. In all areas visited by Human Rights Watch, Dalits and Muslims lived separately from upper-caste Hindus. Several residents and survivors told us, "we are surviving the way we lived, that's why we are in separate camps." While the government has allocated equal amounts of monetary compensation and food supplies to members of all communities, Dalit and Muslim populations did not have the same access to adequate shelter, electricity, running water, and other supplies available to others. This was apparent in several cities near Bhuj, including Anjar and Bhachchau, where the government had provided far superior shelter and basic amenities to upper-caste populations. The attention is now shifting to the process of rehabilitation and reconstruction of homes.

Caste-based Discrimination in Tsunami-affected Areas

The tsunami that hit countries around the Indian Ocean on 26 December 2004 brought misery to all living along their coasts. India was no exception. However, in India, the suffering of Dalit—so-called 'untouchable'—communities affected by the disaster has been exacerbated due to caste-based discrimination in the provision of relief supplies and other assistance. The world is unaware and the Government of India has not acknowledged that relief operations are being carried out with caste as a determining factor.

Places such as Kadapakuppam and Pattipulam of the Kachipuram district in Tamil Nadu have received no relief whatsoever. This is despite 175 families in Kadapakuppam and

280 families in Pattipulam having felt the brunt of the disaster. Despite complaints by villagers in these two places, no government officials or aid agencies have gone to the assistance of these people. Likewise, in Pannanthittu village of Tamil Nadu's Chidambaram Thaluka, all 150 families affected by the tsunami have been denied aid and. Villagers in MGR Thattu, meanwhile, protest that they are being discriminated against, as little relief has been provided to them.

Caste-based discrimination has also been evident in relief operations elsewhere. When burying the dead, Dalits have been brought in to handle the bodies, as 'traditionally' they have been obligated to do. Community kitchens, established to distribute food to victims, were divided into two: one for caste Indians and one for Dalits, as upper castes would not consume food prepared by Dalits. It is a sad reality that even in times of extreme necessity caste prejudices dominate social exchanges.

The tsunami relief operations in South India are indicative of persistent caste discrimination throughout the country. In the state of Maharastra massive evictions from tribal lands in Nasik District have been witnessed in the recent past. If the claim for land by the Maharastra State Farming Cooperation deprived the basic right of the tribal community in Maharastra, in West Bengal, the eviction from Bellilious Park was because of the apprehension that the presence of Dalits would pollute the shrine atmosphere of the upper caste in the locality. In West Bengal even the High Court affixed its seal of approval for the eviction ignoring the basic legal virtue of fare hearing of *audi alteram partum*. However evictions do not remain as the one and only form of discrimination. The forced labour of manual scavenging and carrying of night soil, slave practices in granite quarries in Karnataka and Tamil Nadu, denial of education in Orrisa, starvation deaths in Maharastra, Bihar and Kerala are all shocking realities for the Dalits in India, and their position in the caste societal structure.

The caste system is a powerful tool for social segregation. It runs deep in the minds of Indians and has implications in everyday life. It weakens the human urge to excel and liberate since there is little chance of rising above one's status at birth. Despite caste being a violation of international human rights standards and domestic law prohibiting caste-based discrimination it continues to exercise a debilitating influence on the lives of millions in India daily.

The Constitution of India provides certain safeguards against caste discrimination. However, the constitutional remedy is often inaccessible to Dalits and lower castes, therefore literally taking away the equality quotient of human rights in terms of implementation. Considering India's vastness and its limited resources and poverty, the possibility of a victim, who is otherwise deprived of basic standards of living, approaching a constitutional court is most unlikely. Compounded by the burden of expenses in litigation and the immense time it takes for reaching a final verdict, such legal attempts are rarely taken by victims.

The Scheduled Castes and Scheduled Tribes (Prevention of Atrocities) Act 1989 criminalises atrocities committed against members of the Dalit community and other lower castes. The rules formulated in accordance with the legislation also provide for protection to the lower castes and are more preventive in nature. However, the law and rules are limited. They do not address the root cause: the caste system itself. In cases where compensation is awarded, the amount of damages is far below international standards.

Section 153A of the Indian Penal Code, which provides for punishment for instigating acts of enmity between groups based on religion, race, place of birth, residence and language all but unenforceable since the burden of proof in criminal trials is so high. The chances of a probable conviction are low.

The national and state-level human rights commissions do not have any authority to take affirmative action when receiving a complaint, be it of caste-based discrimination or otherwise. The powers of these institutions are not legally enforceable. Sections 12 and 13 of the Scheduled Castes and Scheduled Tribes (Prevention of Atrocities) Act limit the authority of the rights commissions to receipt of complaints, inquiries and inspection. They can then chose to either refer the matter to the appropriate authority for further action or provide advice to the government. This limitation makes the institutions incapable of protecting human rights. Their orders are limited to recommending the government collect a fine from a perpetrator and disburse an amount to the victim. If the perpetrator is not an employee of the government, the possibility that the order will be implemented is low. Even when the perpetrator is a government employee the order is often not executed. This makes a mockery of the system and discourages victims from approaching these institutions.

Caste and Marriage

Often, rigid social norms of purity and pollution are socially enforced through strict prohibitions on marriage or other social interaction between castes. While economic and social indicators other than caste have gained in significance, allowing intermarriage among upper castes, in many countries strong social barriers remain in place against marriage between lower and higher castes.

In India the condemnation can be quite severe, ranging from social ostracism to punitive violence. On August 6, 2001, in the north Indian state of Uttar Pradesh, an upper-caste Brahmin boy and a lower-caste Jat girl were dragged to the roof of a house and publicly hanged by members of their own families as hundreds of spectators looked on. The public lynching was punishment for refusing to end an inter-caste relationship. Inter-caste marriages can also lead to large-scale attacks on lower-caste communities. In May 2000 in Hardoi district in Uttar Pradesh, a police constable enraged by his daughter's marriage to a Dalit was joined by other relatives in shooting and killing four members of his son-in-law's family.

Dalits who marry high-caste persons in Nepal in some cases reportedly have been imprisoned by local authorities because of false cases filed against them by members of the upper-caste families. Dalits are often forbidden from performing marriage or funeral rites in public areas or, in some areas, from speaking to members of upper castes. In both the Tamil and Sinhala communities of Sri Lanka, intermarriage between upper-caste and lower-caste persons is still socially discouraged.

Caste and Labour

Allocation of labor on the basis of caste is one of the fundamental tenets of many caste systems, with lower-castes typically restricted to tasks and occupations that are deemed too "filthy" or "polluting" for higher-caste communities. Sanitation jobs—including street cleaning and the handling of human waste and animal carcasses—are functions almost exclusively performed by Dalits in India, Sri Lanka, Bangladesh, and Nepal.

Indian-origin Tamils in Sri Lanka continue to face severe social discrimination. For many of the country's minority Tamils, little has changed occupationally since the eighteenth century when members of lower-castes from southern India were brought to Sri Lanka as captive labor to work on plantations and as city cleaners. To this day, the traditional division of labor continues to be perpetuated. At the bottom of the caste hierarchy in the Indian Tamil community are three untouchable castes. While *Pallas* and *Nalavas* can work on upper-caste land for wages, *Paraiyars* are predominantly engaged in "unclean" sanitation work. Plantation laborers also remain marginalised from economic, educational, and social opportunities, and suffer from poor health care and an inability to participate in political life.

A recent allegation of discrimination based on descent is that made by Tamils of Indian origin employed mainly as tea estate workers in the hill country. With regard to wages, housing, sanitation, health and educational facilities, they were an oppressed group. Improvements have slowly been made as a result of government policies and powerful trade union action. Integration with the rest of society is more difficult owing to prejudice, but this is breaking down. There are signs of upward mobility through education and non-discriminatory laws. Caste distinctions exist among themselves and complaints have been made that workers (mostly Dalits) are kept out of trade union office by high caste supervisors.

Most Dalits in India continue to live in extreme poverty, without land or opportunities for better employment or education. With the exception of a minority who have benefited from India's policy of quotas in education and government jobs, Dalits are relegated to the most menial of tasks as removers of human waste and dead animals, leather workers, street sweepers, and cobblers. Dalit children make up the majority of children sold into bondage to pay off debts to upper-caste creditors.

According to government statistics, an estimated one million Dalits in India are "manual scavengers" (a majority of them women) who clear feces from public and private latrines and dispose of dead animals; unofficial estimates are much higher. Handling of human waste is a caste-based occupation, deemed too "polluting and filthy" for anyone but Dalits. Manual scavengers exist under different caste names throughout the country, such as the Bhangis in Gujarat, the Pakhis in Andhra Pradesh, and the Sikkaliars in Tamil Nadu. Members of these communities are invariably placed at the very bottom of the caste hierarchy, and even the hierarchy of Dalit sub-castes. Using little more than a broom, a tin plate, and a basket, they are made to clear feces from public and private latrines and carry waste to dumping grounds and disposal sites. Though long outlawed, the practice of manual scavenging continues in most states.

In November 1999, after a cyclone slammed into India's eastern state of Orissa, killing thousands and rendering millions homeless, the government brought in two hundred Dalit manual scavengers from New Delhi, and planned to bring five hundred more from other parts of Orissa, to load animal carcasses onto hand-drawn carts and take them away to be burned. Government officials had reportedly offered local upper-caste residents more than the daily minimum wage for each animal burned but they refused, citing the decayed conditions of the carcasses and the fact that the task was beneath them: they had "some self-respect left." As witnessed with the earthquake in Gujarat, even in times of natural disaster, the laws of "purity and pollution" prevail and the government's actions often reinforce the prejudice.

Debt Bondage and Slavery

The poor remuneration of manual scavenging, agricultural labor, and other forms of low-caste employment often force families of lower castes or caste-like groups into bondage. A lack of enforcement of relevant legislation prohibiting debt bondage in most of the countries concerned allows for the practice to continue unabated. An estimated forty million people in India, among them some fifteen million children, are working in slave-like conditions in order to pay off debts as bonded laborers. Due to the high interest rates charged, the employers' control over records, and the abysmally low wages paid, the debts are seldom settled. Bonded laborers are frequently low-caste, illiterate, and extremely poor, while the creditors/employers are usually higher-caste, literate, comparatively wealthy, and relatively more powerful members of the community. The Bonded Labour System (Abolition) Act, 1976 abolishes all agreements and obligations arising out of the bonded labor system. It aims to release all laborers from bondage, cancel any outstanding debt, prohibit the creation of new bondage agreements, and order the economic rehabilitation of freed bonded laborers by the state. It also punishes attempts to compel persons into bondage with a maximum of three years in prison and a Rs. 2,000 fine. However, relatively few bonded laborers have been identified, released, and rehabilitated in the country.

In Pakistan the debt bondage system is most prevalent in the agricultural provinces of southern Punjab and Sindh. Most laborers in these areas are minority Hindus from lower castes. In a pattern similar to that practiced in India, the charging of exorbitantly high interest rates ensure that loans from landowners never get repaid. While the loan agreement is often made between the landowner and the male head of the peasant household, the work to pay off the loan is performed by the entire family, including women and children. Women have also been held in custody by landowners when bonded male members of the family leave the land or area, and have even been sold into marriage or prostitution should the male family member fail to return. As in India, children often inherit their families' debts and remain trapped in a cycle of debt bondage.

A disturbing reflection of the slavery of centuries past is the well-documented practice of tying up or chaining bonded laborers to hinder their escape. Of the 7,500 bonded laborers reported to have escaped or been released since 1995 in the southern Sindh province, human rights organisations report that "several hundred" of them were found "tied up or in chains." Similarly, in 1991 the Pakistani army reportedly conducted a raid that unearthed the illegal detention of 295 laborers, including 132 children, all of whom were shackled each night. Most were only given flour and chili peppers as food and had no access to plumbing facilities or medical care. National legislation in Pakistan prohibiting these practices reportedly has done little to eradicate them. Provincial governments responsible for their enforcement have yet to establish mechanisms to put them into practice.

Caste and Socio-Economic Disparities

Lower-caste communities are often plagued by low literacy levels and a lack of access to health care and education. A lack of formal education or training, as well as discrimination that effectively bars them from many forms of employment, and the nonenforcement of protective legislation, perpetuates caste-based employment and keeps its hereditary nature alive. Children face a higher incidence of malnutrition and the general population lacks access to clean drinking water or proper health services.

Access to Education

High drop-out and lower literacy rates among lower-caste populations have rather simplistically been characterised as the natural consequences of poverty and underdevelopment. Though these rates are partly attributable to the need for low-caste children to supplement their family wages through labor, more insidious and less well-documented is the discriminatory and abusive treatment faced by low-caste children who attempt to attend school, at the hands of their teachers and fellow students. Over fifty years since India's constitutional promise of free, compulsory, primary education for all children up to the age of fourteen-with special care and consideration to be given to promote the educational progress of scheduled castes-illiteracy still plagues almost two-thirds of the Dalit population as compared to about one-half of the general population. The literacy gap between Dalits and the rest of the population fell a scant 0.39 percent between 1961 and 1991.

Most of the government schools in which Dalit students are enrolled are deficient in basic infrastructure, classrooms, teachers, and teaching aids. A majority of Dalit students are also enrolled in vernacular schools whose students suffer serious disadvantages in the job market as compared to those who learn in English-speaking schools.

Despite state assistance in primary education, Dalits also suffer from an alarming drop-out rate. According to the *National Commission for Scheduled Castes and Scheduled Tribes' 1996-1997 and 1997-1998 Report*, the national drop-out rate for Dalit children-who often sit in the back of classrooms-was a staggering 49.35 percent at the primary level, 67.77 percent for middle school, and

77.65 percent for secondary school. Rodiya children in Sri Lanka rarely study past elementary levels, if at all. Instead, their parents require them to realise their income-earning potential even as young children, and often prematurely take them out of school. Lower-caste Tamil plantation workers of Indian origin in Sri Lanka also have low literacy levels. According to a Sri Lankan activist only 65 percent of plantation workers can read or write, compared to a high 90 percent national average. Higher drop out rates among children of plantation workers stems partly from the employment of these children as domestic workers, hotel workers, or sanitation cleaners.

The Buraku of Japan also suffer from lower levels of higher education than the national average, and higher dropout rates than the broader society. In particular, Buraku women report lower levels of literacy, high school and university enrolment, and employment. Special scholarship programmes that bolstered national averages of Buraku education are expected to be phased out by March 2002, despite the considerable success they had in bridging the education gap between Buraku and non-Buraku. In Nepal the literacy rate for Dalits is low at 10 percent for men and 3.2 percent for women, compared to a national literacy rate that exceeds 50 percent. According to the government's own fourteenth periodic report under ICERD, "The lowest literacy is among the occupational castes. Women constitute more than two thirds of the illiterates."

Access to Land

Most Dalit victims of abuse in India are landless agricultural laborers who form the backbone of the nation's agrarian economy. Despite decades of land reform legislation, over 86 percent of Dalit households today are landless or near landless. Those who own land often own very little. Land is the prime asset in rural areas that determines an individual's standard of living and social status. As with many other low-caste populations, lack of access to land makes Dalits economically vulnerable; their dependency is exploited by upper- and middle-caste landlords and allows for many abuses to go unpunished. Landless agricultural laborers throughout the country work for a few kilograms of rice or Rs. 15 to Rs. 35 a day, well below the minimum wage prescribed in their state. Many laborers owe debts to their employers or other moneylenders. Indian laws and regulations that prohibit alienation of Dalit lands, set ceilings on a single landowner's holdings, or allocate surplus government lands to scheduled castes and scheduled tribes have been largely ignored, or worse, manipulated by upper castes with the help of district administrations.

Political Representation and Political Rights

India's policy of "reservations" or caste-based quotas is an attempt by the central government to remedy past injustices related to low-caste status. To allow for proportional representation in certain state and federal institutions, the constitution reserves 22.5 percent of federal government jobs, seats in state legislatures, the lower house of parliament, and educational institutions for scheduled castes and scheduled tribes.

The reservation policy, however, has not been fully implemented. The National Commission for Scheduled Castes and Scheduled Tribes' (1996-1997 and 1997-1998) report indicates that of the total scheduled caste reservation quota in the Central Government, 54 percent remains unfilled. More than 88 percent of posts reserved in the public sector remain unfilled as do 45 percent in state banks. A closer examination of the caste composition of government services, institutions of education and other services, however, reveals what Dalit activists call an "unacknowledged reservation policy" for upper-castes, particularly Brahmins, built into the system. Though they represented only 5 percent of the population in 1989, Brahmins comprised 70 percent of the Class I officers in governmental services. At universities, upper-castes occupy 90 percent of the teaching posts in the social sciences and 94 percent in the sciences, while Dalit representation is only 1.2 and 0.5 percent, respectively.

Dalits throughout India also suffer in many instances from de facto disenfranchisement. While India remains the world's largest democracy, for many of its Dalit citizens democracy has been a sham. During elections, many are routinely threatened and beaten by political party strongmen in order to compel them to vote for certain candidates. Already under the thumb of local landlords and police officials, Dalit villagers who do not comply have been harassed, beaten, and murdered.

Police and upper-caste militias, operating at the behest of powerful political leaders in India's states, have also punished Dalit voters. In February 1998, police raided a Dalit village in Tamil Nadu that had boycotted the national parliamentary elections. Women were kicked and beaten, their clothing was torn, and police forced sticks and iron pipes into their mouths. Kerosene was poured into stored food grains and grocery items and police reportedly urinated in cooking vessels.

In Bihar, political candidates ensure their majority vote with the help of *senas*, civilian militias, whose members intimidate and kill. The Ranvir Sena, a private militia of upper-caste landlords, was responsible for killing more than fifty people during Bihar's 1995 state election campaign. The sena was again used to intimidate voters in Ara district, Bihar, during the February 1998 national parliamentary elections. Dalits who have contested political office in village councils and municipalities through seats that have been constitutionally "reserved" for them have been threatened with physical abuse and even death in order to get them to withdraw from the campaign. In the village of Melavalavu, in Tamil Nadu's Madurai district, following the election of a Dalit to the village council presidency, members of a higher-caste group murdered six Dalits in June 1997, including the elected council president, whom they beheaded.

Unlike India, Nepal does not provide for reservations of posts or quotas in political bodies, civil sector jobs, and institutions of higher learning. Though they comprise over 20 percent of the population, lower castes are dramatically under-represented in government. Since 1958, only fourteen Dalits in Nepal have become members of parliament (upper house) through a system of nomination, all of them men.

Only one Dalit has been elected to the House of Representatives. Furthermore, there has been a dearth of Dalits in Nepal's administrative and judicial system; and discrimination continues to persist in the Nepal Royal Army. Conversely, according to an NGO study on discrimination against Dalits in Nepal, while Brahmins constitute only 16 percent of the population, they represent 57 percent of parliament and a staggering 89 percent of the judiciary. The result is that a full one-fifth of Nepal's population is effectively excluded.

Physical and Economic Retaliation

A principal weapon in sustaining the low status of Dalits in India is the use of social and economic boycotts and acts of retaliatory violence. Dalits are physically abused and threatened with economic and social ostracism from the community for refusing to carry out various caste-based tasks. Any attempt to alter village customs, defy the social order, or to demand land, increased wages, or political rights leads to violence and economic retaliation on the part of those most threatened by changes in the status quo. Dalit communities as a whole are summarily punished for individual transgressions; Dalits are cut off from community land and employment during social boycotts, Dalit women bear the brunt of physical attacks, and the law is rarely enforced.

Since the early 1990s, violence against Dalits has escalated dramatically in response to growing Dalit rights movements. Between 1995 and 1997, a total of 90,925 cases were registered with the police nationwide as crimes and "atrocities" against scheduled castes. Of these 1,617 were for murder, 12,591 for hurt, 2,824 for rape, and 31,376 for offenses listed under the Prevention of Atrocities Act. Given that Dalits are often both reluctant and unable (for lack of police cooperation) to report crimes against themselves, the actual number of abuses is presumably much higher.

India's National Commission for Scheduled Castes and Scheduled Tribes has reported that these cases typically fall into one of three categories: cases relating to the practice of "untouchability" and attempts to defy the social order; cases relating to land disputes and demands for minimum wages; and cases of atrocities by police and forest officials. Most of the conflicts take place within very narrow segments of the caste hierarchy, between the poor and the not so poor, the landless labourer and the marginal landowner. The differences lie in the considerable amount of leverage that the higher-caste Hindus or non-Dalits are able to wield over local police, district administrations, and even state governments. On the night of December 1, 1997, an upper-caste landlord militia called the Ranvir Sena shot dead sixteen children, twenty-seven women, and eighteen men in the village of Laxmanpur-Bathe, Jehanabad district Bihar. Five teenage girls were raped and mutilated before being shot in the chest. The villagers were alleged to have been sympathetic to a guerilla group known as Naxalites that had been demanding more equitable land redistribution in the area.

On April 10, 1997, in the village of Ekwari, located in the Bhojpur district of Bihar, police stationed in the area to protect lower-caste villagers instead pried open the doors of their residences as members of the sena entered and killed eight residents. In other cases, police raids have followed attacks by the senas. Sena leaders are rarely prosecuted for such killings, and the villagers are rarely or inadequately compensated for their losses. Even in cases where police are not hostile to Dalits, they are generally not accessible to call upon: most police camps are located in the upper-caste section of the village and Dalits are simply unable to approach them for protection.

Caste and Gender

Lower-caste women are singularly positioned at the bottom of caste, class, and gender hierarchies. Largely uneducated and consistently paid less than their male counterparts worldwide they invariably bear the brunt of exploitation, discrimination, and physical attacks. Sexual abuse and other forms of violence against women are often used by landlords and the police to inflict political "lessons" and crush dissent within the community. Lower-caste women also suffer disproportionately in terms of access to health care, education, and subsistence wages as compared to women of higher castes. Dalit women in *India* and *Nepal* make up the majority of landless laborers and scavengers, as well as a significant percentage of the women forced into prostitution in rural areas or sold into urban brothels. As such, they come into greater contact with landlords and enforcement agencies than their upper-caste counterparts. Their subordinate position is exploited by those in power who carry out their attacks with impunity. Incidents of gang-rape, stripping, and parading women naked through the streets, and making them eat excrement are all crimes specific to Dalit women in India. Sexual violence is also linked to debt bondage in India, Pakistan, and Nepal.

According to a Tamil Nadu state government official, the rape of Dalit women exposes the hypocrisy of the caste system as "no one practices untouchability when it comes to sex." Like other Indian women whose relatives are sought by the police, Dalit women have also been arrested and tortured in custody as a means of punishing their male relatives who are hiding from the authorities.

Failure of Laws

The practice of "untouchability," other caste-based discrimination, violence against lower-caste men, women, and children, and other abuses violate numerous domestic and international laws. International human rights law imposes on governments a duty to guarantee the rights of all people without discrimination and to punish those who engage in caste-based exploitation, violence, and discrimination. In its August 2000 resolution, the U.N. Subcommission on the Promotion and Protection of Human Rights urged governments to ensure that "appropriate legal penalties and sanctions, including criminal sanctions, are prescribed for *and applied to* all persons or entities within the jurisdiction of the Governments concerned who may be found to have engaged in practices of discrimination on the basis of work and descent." The subcommission's working paper on work and descent-based discrimination noted a year later, "The laws are there, but there is a clear lack of will on the part of law enforcement officers to take action owing to caste prejudice on their part or deference shown to higher-caste perpetrators."

Though constitutional guarantees and other national legislation banning caste discrimination suggest that various governments have successfully tackled caste-related violations, much of the legislation remains unenforced. Official condemnation alone has proven insufficient in many countries in abolishing caste-based abuses.

In India, for example, laws are openly flouted while state complicity in attacks on Dalit communities continues to reflect a well-documented pattern. India's own constitutional and statutory bodies, including the National Human Rights Commission and the National Commission for Scheduled Castes and Scheduled Tribes, have repeatedly confirmed and decried the prevalence of the abuses. Other government authorities, however, have facilitated continued discrimination. Indeed it would be difficult to convince Dalits that, over fifty-four years after independence, the government had done anything to end the violence and discrimination that has ruled their lives.

The message sent from the judiciary on caste discrimination is equally disturbing: in July 1998 in the state of Uttar Pradesh, an Allahabad High Court judge reportedly had his chambers "purified with Ganga jal," water from the River Ganges, because it had earlier been occupied by a Dalit judge. The state's failure to prosecute atrocities against Dalits is well illustrated by its manipulation of the Scheduled Castes and Scheduled Tribes (Prevention of Atrocities) Act. Enacted in 1989, the act provides for certain stiffer punishments for abuses against members of scheduled castes and scheduled tribes when committed by non-scheduled caste or tribe members.

Its enactment represented an acknowledgment on the part of the government that abuses, in their most degrading and violent forms, were still perpetrated against Dalits despite the constitutional abolition of "untouchability" four decades earlier. The potential of the Scheduled Castes and Scheduled Tribes (Prevention of Atrocities) Act, 1989, to bring about social change, however, has been hampered by police corruption and caste bias, with the result that many allegations of caste crimes are not entered in police records. Ignorance of procedures and a lack of knowledge of the act have also affected its implementation. Even when cases are registered, the absence of special courts to try them can delay prosecutions for up to three to four years. Some state governments dominated by higher castes have attempted to repeal the legislation altogether.

In 1957 the government of Sri Lanka passed the Prevention of Social Disabilities Act making it an offence to deny access to various public places to persons by reason of their caste. A 1971 amendment imposed stiffer punishments for the commission of offenses under the 1957 act. According to the U.N. Subcommission's working paper: "Initially there were some prosecutions in the North but there was a tendency for the police not to take action against violations. In a celebrated temple-entry case, the Act was challenged as interfering with customs and ancient usages that prohibited defilement of a Hindu temple by the entry of low-caste persons. This argument was rejected by the

Supreme Court and Privy Council." Unlike India's constitution, Sri Lanka's 1978 Constitution does not provide for community-based affirmative action. It does however prohibit discrimination on the grounds of caste, including caste-based restrictions on access to shops, public restaurants, hotels, places of public entertainment, and places of worship of one's own religion. Despite these constitutional prohibitions, serious problems remain.

References

Pauline Kolenda. *Caste in Contemporary India: Beyond Organic Solidarity* Menlo Park. Benjamin/Cumming Publishing Co. 1978.

Srinivas, M. N. (ed.). *Caste: Its Twentieth Century Avatar*. New Delhi: Viking, 1996.

Human Rights Watch, *Broken People: Caste Violence Against India's "Untouchables"*. New York: Human Rights Watch. 1999.

Pieter H. Streefland, *The Sweepers of the Slaughterhouse: Conflict and Survival in a Karachi Neighborhood*. Assen, the Netherlands: Van Gorcum. 1979.

Rajendra Kalidas Wimala Goonesekere, "Prevention of Discrimination and Protection of Indigenous Peoples and Minorities". New York: United Nations. 2001.

Nireka Weeratunge, *Aspects of Ethnicity and Gender Among the Rodi of Sri Lanka*. Sri Lanka: International Centre for Ethnic Studies. 1988.

National Commission for Scheduled Castes and Scheduled Tribes. *Highlights of the Report for the Years 1996-97 and 1997-98*. New Delhi. Government of India, 1999.

7
RESERVATION POLITICS

India was a country with highly rigid caste-based hierarchal structure, with ascending order of privileges and descending order of disabilities, which operated for about 3000 years. There was an overwhelming majority in the nation that was still backward – socially, economically, educationally, and politically. These victims of entrenched backwardness comprise the present scheduled castes (SC), scheduled tribes (ST) and other backward classes (OBC). Even though, these classes are generically the "Backward Classes," the nature and magnitude of their backwardness are not the same. After achieving independence from the British in the late 1940s, it became a democratic and egalitarian nation. It was imperative at that point to establish a code for the political, economic, and social structure. The Constitution, established in 1950, strove to do the same.

The STs were the tribes that had not confirmed to Hinduism in the historical perspective and lived animistic lifestyles. SCs were the lower castes in the caste-hierarchy of the Hindu culture. The Constitution directs in its Article 46 that the state shall promote with special care the educational and economic interests of the weaker sections of the people, in particular, of the SCs and STs, and shall protect them from social injustice and all forms of exploitation. Central to this directive, and other related provisions is reservation, which is a package of constitutional provisions and their intended follow-up programmes for the social advancement of the weaker sections.

In the Indian context, reservations were introduced during the last decades of the 19th century at a time when the subcontinent could be broadly divided according to two main forms of governance – British India and the 600 princely states. Some of these states were progressive and eager to modernise through the promotion of education and industry and by maintaining unity among their own people. Mysore in south India and Baroda and Kolhapur in western India took considerable interest in awakening and advancement of the minorities and deprived sections of the society. It should not surprise us then that the very first records of implementing reservations policies are from these princely states.

When English was introduced as the official language, the upper and monetarily well off classes decided to go into law or civil service. The untouchables, or the repressed classes had joined the presidency armies and fought battles under the command of British officers. They had contributed a great deal towards the creation of the British Empire. The untouchables were asking for concessions and facilities for their upliftment and had not organised themselves as a political force. It was with the arrival of Ambedkar that they acquired a leader of stature and education who could make a political difference.

Framing of Reservation Policy

On May 16, 1946, the British government released the Cabinet Mission Statement, a set of proposals to guide the framing of a new Indian constitution. By this time, the wheels for India's independence had already been set in motion by Clement Atlee's Labor Party government in London. Among other recommendations, the Cabinet Mission laid out a detailed plan for the Constituent Assembly's composition, such that the body be "as broad-based and accurate a representation of the whole population as possible." Three categories from which to draw delegates were proposed. In addition to divisions for Muslims and Sikhs, the Cabinet Mission suggested a "general" category which would include all others groups—Hindus, Anglo-Indians, Parsis, Indian Christians, the Scheduled Castes and Tribes, and women, among others. Delegates were appointed on the basis of indirect elections in the provincial legislative assemblies.

In March 1947, Britain sent Lord Louis Mountbatten, war hero and royal relative, to New Delhi as the King-Emperor's last

Viceroy. His mission was to transfer power to an independent Indian government. In the end, power was transferred to two successor entities, Pakistan on August 14, 1947, and India on August 15, 1947.

Under the Cabinet Mission plan the Constituent Assembly was to consist of 389 seats, 296 of which were filled by delegates elected from the directly-administered provinces of British India and 93 of which were allotted to the princely states. The total number of seats was based on an undivided India, and, overall, represented a cross-section of the population of the country. Given the Muslim League's boycott of the Assembly, the impact of partition and subsequent migration, and the lengthy process of integrating the princely states, the number and distribution of seats continually fluctuated from the time of the first meeting on December 9, 1946. With the 1947 partition, many Muslim delegates left for Pakistan, terminating their membership in the Assembly. As a result, the body was reorganised. By November 26, 1949, it consisted of 324 seats, divided among the provinces and the princely states and representative of all major minority groups.

The make-up of the Constituent Assembly reflected the reality of what groups wield power in India, then and now. An analysis of membership in the most important advisory committees of the Constituent Assembly found that 6.5 percent were SCs. Brahmins made up 45.7 percent. Minority and Scheduled Caste delegates did have some influence during the Assembly proceedings, with several holding significant positions. Dr. H.C. Mookherjee, an Indian Christian, was Vice-President of the Constituent Assembly as well as Chairman of the Sub-Committee on Minorities. However, by far the most important was Dr. Ambedkar.

Jawaharlal Nehru (1889-1964), India's first Prime Minister and dominant political figure until his death, had already selected Ambedkar, an accomplished lawyer, as his Law Minister. A Brahmin himself, Nehru sought to build a secular India free from caste discrimination. He was among the "many educated Hindus" opposed to the caste system as noted by Gandhi in his 1933 *Harijan* exchange with Ambedkar. Given Nehru's views and Ambedkar's talents, it is not surprising that Ambedkar became chairman of the drafting committee for India's new constitution.

From the outset, the Constituent Assembly laid out clearly its objectives and philosophy for the new constitution. Several of the framers' main goals, articulated in the "Objectives Resolution," included guarantees of equality, basic freedoms of expression, as well as "adequate safeguards...for minorities, backward and tribal areas, and depressed and other backward classes." These principles guided the delegates throughout the Constitution-making process.

The Assembly set up a special Advisory Committee to tackle minority rights issues. This committee was further divided into several subcommittees. The Subcommittee on Minorities focused on representation in legislatures (joint versus separate electorates and weightings), reservation of seats for minorities in cabinets, reservation for minorities in the public services, and administrative machinery to ensure the protection of minority rights. After extensive research and debate, the Subcommittee on Minorities drafted a report of its findings for submission to the Advisory Committee. The latter supported most of the Subcommittee's recommendations.

Vallabhbhai Patel (1875-1950), Chairman of the Advisory Committee and the most powerful member of the governing Congress party after Nehru, submitted the Report on Minority Rights to Rajendra Prasad, President of the Assembly, and on August 27, 1947, the Assembly convened to discuss the Report. Patel opened the debate by presenting the Advisory Committee's main recommendations. Rejecting separate electorates—Congress wanted no repeat of the separate electorates granted to the Muslims by the British—and a "weightage" system, the Report endorsed the creation of joint electorates and proportional representation. Reservations were approved for minorities, as long as the reservations were in proportion to the population of the targeted groups. Some minorities, like the Parsis, voluntarily gave up this right.

Treatment of the Scheduled Castes was extensively debated. Efforts by Ambedkar and his allies to craft a provision requiring a "tripwire" 35 percent of Scheduled Caste votes in a constituency reserved for the Scheduled Castes failed. The principle of common voting and reserved seats in legislative bodies throughout the country was retained despite strong opposition from influential

Constituent Assembly members like Nehru. However, the colonial-era system of having the Scheduled Castes choose candidates for reserved seats through local "electoral colleges" was dropped. Throughout the debate, caste Hindus permitted nothing that would suggest splitting off the Scheduled Castes in an electoral sense from the Hindu community.

Reservations Under the Constitution

On January 26, 1950, India ended its "Dominion" status, became a republic, and put in effect its new constitution. With an entire section dedicated to "Fundamental Rights," the Indian Constitution prohibits any discrimination based on religion, race, caste, sex, and place of birth (Article 15[1]). This law extends to all public institutions, such as government-run educational facilities, to access to hotels and restaurants, public employment and public wells, tanks (manmade ponds for water supply and bathing), and roads. The practice of untouchability is declared illegal (Article 17).

Significantly, Article 15, which prohibits discrimination, also contains a clause allowing the union and state governments to make "any special provision for the advancement of any socially and educationally backward classes of citizens or for the Scheduled Castes and Scheduled Tribes." This language was added in 1951 within weeks of a Supreme Court decision outlawing quotas in school admissions. The speed of the amendment is indicative of the strong political support for reservations, Nehru's personal views notwithstanding.

Similarly, Article 16, calling for "equality of opportunity in matters of public employment," contains clauses permitting the "reservation of appointments or posts in favour of any backward class of citizens which, in the opinion of the State, is not adequately represented in the services under the State" and another allowing "reservation in matters of promotion" for Scheduled Castes and Scheduled Tribes.

A separate section of the Constitution, "Special Provisions Relating to Certain Classes," requires the reservation of seats in the "House of the People," or Lok Sabha, and the Legislative Assemblies of the states for the Scheduled Castes and Scheduled Tribes. The numbers of reserved seats are determined by the proportion Scheduled Caste and Scheduled Tribe members to the general population, based on population estimates from the most recent decennial census. The President of India and the Parliament, in consultation with the state governments, determine the list of groups qualifying as Scheduled Castes, Scheduled Tribes, and "backward classes."

Several safeguards accompany these provisions for reservation. First, the Constitution originally required the reservation of seats in the Lokh Sabha and state legislatures to end after ten years. After five amendments, the policy is now set to expire on January 25, 2010. Secondly, regarding the reservation of jobs, Article 335 of the Constitution mandates that the "claims of the members of the Scheduled Castes and Scheduled Tribes shall be taken into consideration, consistently with the maintenance of efficiency of administration." Finally, a National Commission for Scheduled Castes and Scheduled Tribes was created to investigate, monitor, advise, and evaluate the progress of the Scheduled Castes and Scheduled Tribes under the schemes aimed at the socio-economic development of these groups. Another Commission was also created to investigate the conditions of the socially and educationally backward classes.

It is interesting to note that the Constitution's reservations construct, which explicitly singles out certain castes for special preferential treatment, contradicts the document's prohibition on discrimination based on caste, race, and other such criteria. Furthermore, India's caste system itself, with its strict hierarchy dictated by birth, is at odds with the ideals of equality and social justice.

Despite the creation of centrally based commissions to monitor reservations and other schemes, the Constitution gives great liberties to the individual states to determine the quantity and limits of reservation and what, for example, qualifies as the "maintenance of the efficiency of administration." The clause giving states the authority to formulate and implement policy to facilitate "the advancement of any socially and educationally backward classes of citizens," is also decidedly vague. No concrete definition of "backward" is provided either. In addition, though a specific—if, in practice, flexible—time limit is placed on the reservation of seats in the Lok Sabha and state legislative assemblies, there is no such clause regarding the future termination of reservations of jobs and promotions.

The reservations for the backward classes are of three broad categories: political, educational and employment. For the first, the Constitution provides for reservation of seats in proportion to their numbers for the SCs and the STs in the Lok Sabha (The Lower House) in its Article 330, and in the Vidhan Sabha (The Upper House) in Article 332. These provisions do not exist for the OBCs, which indicate that the principal categories for the affirmative action are the SCs and STs according to the Constitution.

For the second, an implication exists in the constitutional provision—Article 15(4), which allows the state to make any special provision for the advancement of any socially and educationally backward classes of citizens or for the SCs and STs.

For the third, the constitutional provisions as modified and simplified from time to time are the Article 16(4), Article 16(4A), Article 16(4B), Article 335, and Article 320(4). These articles provide explicitly for reservation in educational institutions for the backward classes and the authority of the state to make any required changes with time, as required.

Other Legal Protections

To give teeth to the protections for the Scheduled Castes and Tribes mandated by the Constitution, India's Parliament has passed two major laws. The Untouchability (Offenses) Act of 1955 (renamed the Protection of Civil Rights Act in 1976) was intended to provide enforcement of Article 17 of the Constitution, outlawing untouchability. It fell short of expectations. In the words of India's National Commission for Scheduled Castes and Scheduled Tribes, "All the measures taken were not found to be effective enough in curbing the incidents of atrocities on Scheduled Castes and Scheduled Tribes." In 1989 a new law, the Scheduled Castes and Scheduled Tribes (Prevention of Atrocities) Act, came into force. Similar to an American hate crimes statute, it provides heavier penalties than under ordinary law for eighteen specified crimes including forcing the eating of obnoxious substances, bonded labor, and sexual exploitation.

AIMS OF RESERVATION POLICY OF INDIA

Reservation in Indian law provides for a quota system whereby a percentage of posts are reserved in employment in Government and in the public sector units, and in all public and private educational institutions, except in the religious/ linguistic minority educational institutions, in order to mitigate backwardness of the socially and educationally backward communities and the Scheduled Castes and Tribes who do not have adequate representation in these services and institutions. The reservation policy is also extended to the Scheduled Castes and Scheduled Tribes for representation in the Parliament of India. The central government of India reserves 27 per cent of higher education, and individual states may legislate further reservations. Reservation cannot be exceeded 50 per cent, as per the rulings given by the supreme court, but certain Indian states like Rajasthan have proposed a 68 per cent reservation which includes a 14 per cent reservation for forward castes.

Reservations are intended to increase the social diversity in campuses and workplaces by lowering the entry criteria for certain identifiable groups that are grossly under-represented in proportion to their numbers in the general population. Caste is the most used criteria to identify under-represented groups. However there are other identifiable criteria for under-representation—gender (women are under represented), state of domicile (North Eastern States, as Bihar and Uttar Pradesh are under-represented), rural people, etc.—as revealed by the Government of India sponsored National Family Health and National Sample surveys.

The underlying theory is that the under-representation of the identifiable groups is a legacy of the Indian caste system. After India gained independence, the Constitution of India listed some erstwhile groups as Scheduled Castes (SC) and Scheduled Tribes (ST). The framers of the Constitution believed that, due to the caste system, SCs and the STs were historically oppressed and denied respect and equal opportunity in Indian society and were thus under-represented in nation-building activities. The Constitution laid down 15 per cent and 7.5 per cent of vacancies to government aided educational institutes and for jobs in the government/public sector, as reserved quota for the SC and ST candidates respectively for a period of five years, after which the situation was to be reviewed. This period was routinely extended by the succeeding governments.

Later, reservations were introduced for other sections as well. The Supreme Court ruling that reservations cannot exceed 50 per cent (which it judged would violate equal access guaranteed by the Constitution) has put a cap on reservations. However, there are state laws that exceed this 50 per cent limit and these are under litigation in the Supreme Court. For example, the caste-based reservation fraction stands at 69 per cent and is applicable to about 87 per cent of the population in the state of Tamil Nadu.

Politics of Reservation

Reservation has become a political gimmick rather than a tool of equality. There is a dire need to review the policy that has let caste system exist perpetually in India. There is a need of social awareness rather than legal provisions.

The principle of equality is one of the basic features of the Indian Constitution. It has also been enshrined as a fundamental right to all the citizens of India, irrespective of their caste, sex, colour, religion or region. India, is however, a vastly diverse country and some strata have been consistently unequal than some others. Owing to numerous factors like their regional isolation, financial deprivation, social bias, administrative apathy, they have been more backward than their fellow countrymen. For their sake, our constitution provided for certain enabling provisions for ensuring their due uplift.

Article (15) prohibits discrimination of any sort among Indian nationals, but its amended sub clause four also entitles the state to take special measures for the socially and economically backward sections. Also the directive principle under article 46 also binds the state for their special care. They may be given entitlements as reservation in jobs and education or other special benefits till they catch up with the mainstream. It implies that the provision is meant for bringing the unequal at par with others and should remain in existence till equality is attained. Unfortunately, our self-seeking politicians would never let that happen. They have turned the sensitive issue into a popular political strategy. The political parties tend to appease the minorities and fill up their vote banks by including quota provision in their election manifesto. It has become an extremely handy tool in their hands to sway the gullible electorate.

The verdict in Mandal Case in 1993, sent ripples across the country and unleashed violent protests by anti-reservation sections. Presently, there is 13 per cent quota for scheduled castes, three per cent for denotified tribes, eight per cent for nomadic tribes and seven per cent for scheduled tribes, and 19 per cent for OBC in public employment, leaving just half seats for the general category. Worse, many states don't even follow that direction of Supreme Court and reserve more than 50 per cent. A few years back, the announcement of 27 per cent OBC quota in higher educational institutions made the students come to streets in two distinct groups—forward and backward. They probably would not have been aware of such distinctions any time before. The pro and anti agitations have divided our youth to the detriment to nation's integrity.

The abusive language and sense of contempt against the reserved category is but a natural fall out, as many of the deserving candidates fail to receive their due just because they are not reserved. We, not very long back, saw Gujjars of Rajasthan lobbying for their inclusion in reserved category. This brings home the strange race of being declared backward than others because being 'backward' eventually 'pays' in terms of reservation.

It is an undeniable fact that certain weak communities do require special protection and entitlements for their advancement. But this needs to be achieved by a rational policy. There are several considerations to be taken care of for striking a balance between equality and positive discrimination. Firstly, there has to be adequate criteria for identifying the backward. It has to be an individual status rather than group identity to decide whether one deserves extra support or not. A scheduled caste boy of a rich bureaucrat needs no reservation but surely a meritorious child of a poor general category farmer does need it.

Today, there is another controversy of extending reservation benefits of SC/ST to the backward groups of other minorities as well. Here pitches in religious distinction and there seems to be no end to fragmenting the single identity-Indian. Secondly, any reservation policy should be a time bound initiative. One needs to ask the pro elements that why the backward people are still backward despite the quotas being prevalent for almost six decades. There have been some successful men who could flourish just because of the protective discrimination, but that is a very small number. Therefore, we do need to revisit our reservation provisions as they have failed to deliver much per se.

Reservation as an Electoral Tool

Today the question of reservation has plunged the whole country into an atmosphere of madness. Unfortunately instead of appreciating the spirit of reservation in a right way as envisaged in the Constitution and consistent with its leasie [sic] spirit and creating a suitable atmosphere therefore it is being used the arithmatics [sic] of votes as an unerring weapon for strengthening the party base in the context of all prevailing real politics prevalent all over the country. The reservation is not only turning into a partnership in the gains of exploitation but also an instrument of permanent division, prejudices, inequality and distress created thereby in the society. Thus today the foremost question is how far and how much the interests of the country and society will continue to be sacrificed for the immediate political gains.

Thus, part of the explanation for the reservations policy's problems stems from the system having become a political tool for political parties looking to expand their vote banks. Though they may jump to support reservations and even seek the policy's extension, such parties lack the political will to follow through with their promises once they have achieved election.

A survey of the manifestos of the major political parties in the late 1990s indicates that nearly all groups address the issue of reservations. Furthermore, adopting a pro-reservations stance is often the course of action, since, as the policy expands, opposing the reservations is considered "electoral suicide." In 1996, for example, four major parties— Congress I, BJP, Janata Dal, and CPI(M)—endorsed reservations. While the BJP, Janata Dal, and CPI(M) supported reservations for backward classes, the Congress party even proposed to extend reservation to women in the Lok Sabha.

This is not a new development on the Indian political scene. As Christophe Jaffrelot argues in his book *India's Silent Revolution: The Rise of the Low Castes in North Indian Politics,* the Congress party had long been aware of the significance of the SC vote as well as of the electoral potential of the reservations system:

Congress succeeded in projecting itself as the natural representative of the Scheduled Castes because of its skill in promoting or co-opting Untouchable leaders—including cadres of the parties established by Ambedkar—and getting them elected in the framework of the reservation system. Even if they had propogated revolutionary views in their early career, they often forgot them, once integrated to the political elite.

The Changing Face of the BJP Since the waning of Congress' dominance, the BJP has emerged as India's leading party. In addition to being characterised as a Hindu nationalist party fiercely opposed to Muslim culture, the BJP has also been described as perpetuating a "Brahminical Social Order" in which upper caste Hindus dominate and oppress the lower castes in Indian society. Since its political troubles after the 1996 elections, when the party could not find any coalition partners and was unsuccessful in forming a government, the BJP has attempted to alter its image to widen its appeal.

One major change has been the BJP's effort to tone down its traditionally militant Hindu nationalist rhetoric. Its manifesto features sections on "Commitment to the Welfare of the Scheduled Castes and Scheduled Tribes" and "Untouchability: A Crime Against Humanity." Among its promises are those for a law to back up the reservations policy, special tribunals to deal with complaints of non-implementation of the policy, and efforts to see that preferential opportunities benefit the largest and widest cross-section of SCs. The BJP has even invoked the name of Ambedkar, announcing in its 1998 manifesto that "a befitting National Memorial in honour of Dr. Babasaheb Ambedkar, who dedicated his life to the cause of social justice, will be erected at Chaityabhoomi in Mumbai on the lines of national memorials like Raj Ghat, Shanti Van and Vijay Ghat." The most recent manifesto from 1999 for the BJP-led National Democratic Alliance contains pledges to protect existing reservations policy for SCs. Such statements are no doubt aimed at wooing SC voters.

Moderating its position has also facilitated the BJP's attempt to forge more widespread alliances with regional parties. In 1997, the BJP formed a coalition with the BSP in the Uttar Pradesh government. Most recently, with its success in the 1999 elections, it heads the National Democratic Alliance. The Alliance, which includes leftist parties like SC-politician Ram Vilas Paswan's Lok Jan Shakti Party, controls the Lok Sabha.

Within its party ranks, the BJP has also tried to advance members with non-traditional backgrounds, such as SCs. For example, it made Bangaru Laxman, an SC, its president. However, he was forced to resign when the Tehelka scandal involving bribery and defense contracts surfaced in 2001.

Obstacles to the Success of Reservations Policy

As a perusal of any report from the National Commission for SCs and STs will reveal, the Indian government, from central to local levels, has often displayed a lackadaisical attitude in administering reservations policy. At the same time, SC interests often take a back seat on the political agenda. The reservations system has evolved into a bureaucratic structure with major inefficiencies.

There are two major reasons for these realities. First, with the fading of the Congress party's dominance, the Indian political scene has witnessed the flowering of many new parties and the intensification of party competition. As the population of SCs increases, faster than the rate of growth of the general population, political parties have realised the electoral potential of this group and have sought to use reservations as a way of garnering votes. Christophe Jaffrelot has argued that the Congress party in its heyday used such a strategy, "bargaining and extending its patronage in exchange for electoral support." However, once in office, politicians lose their incentive to see that reservations are implemented effectively.

A second reason is the fact that Dalits have failed to unite as an All-India political force. Though there have been Dalit political success stories, such as the rise to power of the Bahujan Samaj Party in Uttar Pradesh, these achievements have been restricted to certain regions. Dalits have been plagued by internal rivalries, including their own caste hierarchy.

A politically influential national Dalit movement has yet to emerge. Consequently, they have not been able to lobby effectively for the efficient implementation of the reservations policy. Dalit politicians who are elected to reserved seats in legislative bodies like the Lok Sabha have also been known to be servants of the party rather than representatives of their SC constituents. Furthermore, the general politicisation of reservations has contributed to Dalit disunity, sparking disputes over the distribution of benefits.

This section will examine obstacles to the success of the reservations policy. It begins with an example of the administrative difficulties and inefficiencies of the system.

Administrative Deficiencies

Any consideration of reservations as a form of social engineering to redress the grievances of a minority must touch on the mechanics of the system. It is a system that has grown enormously since its origins in the 1930s and reaches into all levels of Indian politics, education, and government employment, including the substantial number of public sector "undertakings," as government-owned industries are known.

The cornerstone of the system is the official list, or schedule, that gave the "Scheduled Castes" (SCs) their name. Originally compiled by civil servants in the 1930s, the current version shows 1,091 Scheduled Castes. States with the greatest numbers of SCs are Karnataka (101), Orissa (93), and Tamil Nadu (76). A Scheduled Caste in one state may not be so in another state or even in another part of the same state.

Over time, a large body of administrative regulations, forms, and case law has come into being to guide the reservation process. There are, for example, a "Pro forma for sending proposals for dereservation of vacancies," an instruction for the "Grouping of isolated posts for purposes of orders regarding reservation," and "Descheduling of Caste of Scheduled Caste person after his initial appointment." However, the most important form is the certificate every Scheduled Caste member must have to apply for reserved employment, educational benefits, holding reserved legislative seats at any level, or receiving "benefits under various developmental programmes meant for members of Scheduled Castes & Scheduled Tribes."

Any of eighteen specified local officials can issue a certificate, but the rules for issuing a certificate are complex. An applicant who moves to an area of his state in which his group is not "scheduled" can still get a certificate, but if he moves to another state where his group is not "scheduled" he will not. Should he convert to other than Hinduism, Sikhism, or Buddhism, he may not receive a certificate. If he converts while holding a "reserved" job, he will be stripped of his SC promotion advantage. Should he reconvert, he can get a certificate only if he can show he is accepted back by his former group.

Inevitably, the issuing of certificates has become a source of corruption. Jobs, schooling, grant money, and even some share of political power—perhaps a seat on a village or municipal council—are at stake. On the receiving end, there is often a lack of Scheduled Caste candidates for mid- or higher-level positions. Given employer or school interest in filling SC positions, a "don't ask, don't tell" attitude may prevail. At all levels above traditional untouchable occupations like sweeper, the possibility exists that caste Hindus with bogus SC certificates are squeezing out real members of the Scheduled Castes.

The problem of false certificates is of long standing. Earlier mentions are often couched in bureaucratic language, like this example from 1976:

> . . . Complaints continued to be received in this Organisation about false certificates obtained by non-Scheduled Caste/ Scheduled Tribe persons to get the facilities admissible to members of Scheduled Caste/Tribe communities. At times, it was observed that the authorities empowered to issue caste certificates did not satisfy themselves adequately about the genuineness of the castes to which the applicants claimed to belong. Sometimes, certificates were issued without necessary inquiries/verifications. This matter was also highlighted in the last report. . . The [Home] Ministry has further suggested that the officials concerned may also be informed that action would be taken against them under the relevant provisions of the Indian Penal Code if any of them is found to have issued the certificates carelessly and without making proper verifications. . ."

Although the possibility that officials were selling certificates is not mentioned, it is implied by the threat to use the Indian Penal Code.

By the mid-1990s, the problem had worsened and "False Certificates" has its own chapter in the two most recent reports of the National Commission for Scheduled Castes and Scheduled Tribes. Concerned about the "widespread incidence" of false certificates, the Commission in 1996 carried out pilot field studies in several states. The studies confirmed the irregularities and the trend. A check on twelve Central Government organisations in Tamil Nadu found 338 holders of fraudulent ST certificates. In the end, only six were dismissed after what the Commission termed "enormous delays." Nearly a quarter of the individuals thwarted removal by getting stay orders from cooperative local courts.

The Commission has repeatedly called on the government to crack down on fraudulent certifications. It has made detailed proposals for corrective measures, but none have been forthcoming. The appearance is that few in government really care.

Reservations Watchdogs

As mandated by Article 338 of the Constitution, a special officer was appointed in 1950 to monitor safeguards for the SCs. The post has since been altered several times. At one point, two government organisations existed concurrently—a Commissioner's office and the Directorate General of Backward Classes. A constitutional amendment in 1978 merged the two bodies to create the National Commission for Scheduled Castes and Scheduled Tribes. Despite this apparent improvement, understaffing continues to be a chronic problem. In 1992, six of seventeen field-office directors posts were abolished. Offices in Patna, Bihar and Hyderabad, Andhra Pradesh, two states where atrocities against SCs are particularly prevalent, were among the posts sustaining cutbacks. At times even the central head post has been left vacant, as one outgoing commissioner related:

> No successor has been appointed creating a Constitutional vaccum [sic]. I do not know how long this will continue. This is another incident of constitutional violation concerning the safeguards of the SCs and STs which I have been repeatedly asserting. But this is how the current of arowed [sic]equity and social justice for the weakest sections of our society flows in our country.

Another problem the Commission has encountered consistently is the difficulty of obtaining data from state and local governments in a timely and complete manner. In 1953, the Commissioner for Scheduled Castes and Scheduled Tribes, L.M. Shrikant, lamented:

> Experience has...shown that in spite of repeated and urgent reminders, it has not been possible for the State Governments to furnish me with the required and sufficient data in time for inclusion in the Report. Moreover, it is found that at times the information furnished by the State Governments is very sketchy and incomplete and, it being already too *late, no time is left to obtain further details from them.*

This is still an issue. The Tamil Nadu government, for example, which has been conducting censuses of its employees since 1978, did not collect any data on reservations until 1992. Such evidence is illustrative of the general lack of priority given to issues involving the welfare of SCs.

The story at the central level is no better. Frequently, Commission reports are not reviewed by Parliament for months or even years after they are completed. In 1964, Commissioner Anil Chanda politely noted the "long gap between presentation of [the annual] Report to the President and its placing before Parliament." He attributed this to a delay in printing and in translating the text into Hindi. Commenting on the same problem thirty years later, B.D. Sharma, then holding the Commissioner's post, was not as forgiving:

> Even if a report is presented it remains shelved for months and years together without any action being taken on it. Even when the Parliament finds time...there is hardly any discussion on the contents of the report and the formality is over in no time. Of what use is such an arrangement?

Success of reservations policy will be measured by results—how Dalits fare in Indian society. A precursor example was the selection in 1997 of K.R. Naryanan, a Dalit, as India's President. His distinguished career has included time as a journalist, heading a university, and service as Ambassador to the United States. Dalit political activism is another indicator of change. Well orchestrated protests at the 2001 United Nations Conference on Racism in Durban, lively Internet sites of Dalit advocacy groups, and, most of all, growing involvement in political life show that increasing numbers of Dalits are making their presence felt.

The emergence of well-educated, articulate, and middle class Dalits raises the question of what was responsible for such progress. In the case of Dr. Ambedkar, a maharaja stepped in to help at a critical juncture in his education. For those following in his footsteps, the "maharaja" may be the reservations system.

Criticised, with justification, for inefficiency (or worse), the network of reservations in its half century of existence has contributed to Dalit opportunity. On a nationwide scale, it has meant more educational and better government job opportunities for Dalits. Statistical evidence (Tables 3 and 8, above) shows decidedly positive trends for Dalits entering into senior civil service ranks, an eight-fold increase from 1959 to 1995, and receiving higher education, a near-doubling over 17 years ending in 1996.

Literacy rates through 1991 are less compelling and showed that Dalits were not closing the gap with the general population. However, the 2001 Census reports a ten-year jump of 27 percent in national literacy (to 65 percent). Census data on Dalit literacy are not yet available, but an independent 1997-1998 study found that Dalit educational achievement for younger age groups in villages in Rajasthan and Madhya Pradesh had surged to the point that it was virtually the same as for upper castes.

What is harder to pinpoint is how much improvement can be credited to reservations and how much might have occurred without them as a result of general government development policies and economic growth. Dalit groups are in no mood to find out.

Realistically, the system has become such a mainstay in India, involving a significant portion of the population, that it is doubtful that the dismantling of the system is even feasible. No politician will risk trying to roll back these "temporary" measures.

Reservations will continue to play a useful role but will likely be a diminishing part of the solution of Dalit problems. There are major flaws. Reservations apply to the public sector but not the private sector, the probable growth area of the Indian economy. Then there are tens of millions of Dalits living in rural areas and not part of the "organised" economy. It is often a difficult life. In

1976, Shankarrao Mane, the then Commissioner for Scheduled Castes and Scheduled Tribes, wrote the following appraisal:

> The hard fact of our social life is that the Scheduled Castes are fighting alone. Houses in Caste Hindus localities are not available to them on rent even in urban areas; drinking water wells are generally not open to them, the services of priests, barbers and washermen are still denied to them in several parts of the country and they are paid nominal wages for hard labour in the fields. And, when they try to assert their rights to use common services or demand proper wages, they are subjected to inhuman atrocities, abuses, assaults, social boycott, loot, arson, murder and what not. They are branded with red hot iron. Even their women are not spared. Still they struggle.

Let the Scheduled Castes be assured that in their struggle they are not alone. That the enlightened among the Indians are with them not only with words of sympathy but with concrete action.

Reporting by Indian and foreign human rights groups and governments indicates that problems of this kind remain in many parts of India despite the Constitution, laws, and the desire of a great many Indians for an end to mistreatment of Dalits.

The reservations system would benefit markedly from an administrative face-lift. As recommended by the Commission for Scheduled Castes and Scheduled Tribes, a comprehensive act, articulating the policy, is needed. The revision and streamlining of procedures, such as SC certification, might help curb abuse. In addition, social programmes such as those directed at improving the education system, especially at the primary level and in rural areas, should be given more emphasis.

References

Chalam, K.S. "Caste Reservation and Equality of Opportunity in Education" *Economic and Political Weekly*. Vol. 25, No. 41. October 13. 1990.

Das, Bhagwan. "Moments in a History of Reservations." *Economic and Political Weekly*. Vol. 35, No.43 and 44. October 28. 2000.

Kundu, Amitabh. "Reservation, Anti-reservation and Democracy." *Economic and Political Weekly*. Vol. 25, No. 45. November 10, 1990.

Nigam, Aditya. "Mandal Commission and the Left". *Economic and Political Weekly*. Vol. 25, No. 48,49. December 1-8, 1990.

Omvedt, Gail. "Hinduism and Politics." *Economic and Political Weekly*. Vol. 25, No, 14, April 7, 1990.

Pandian M.S.S. "One Step Outside Modernity." *Economic and Political Weekly*. Vol. 37, No. 18, May 4, 2002.

Pinto, Amrose. "U.N. Conference Against Racism – Is Caste Race?" *Economic and Political Weekly*. Vol.36, No. 30, July 28, 2001.

Radhakrishnan P. "Sensitising Officials on Dalits and Reservations." *Economic and Political Weekly*. Vol. 37, No. 7, Feb. 16, 2002.

Virginius. "Protective Discrimination : Why Scheduled Tribes Lay Behind Scheduled Castes." *Economic and Political Weekly*. Vol.36, No.29, July 21, 2001.

8
BACKWARD COMMUNITIES AND DEVELOPMENTAL ISSUES

Inclusive growth demands that all social groups have equal access to the services provided by the State and equal opportunity for upward economic and social mobility. It is also necessary to ensure that there is no discrimination against any section of our society. In India, certain social groups such as the SCs, STs, OBCs and Minorities have historically been disadvantaged and vulnerable. Then there are certain other groups which may be discriminated against and which suffer from handicaps. These include persons with disabilities, older persons, street children, beggars and victims of substance abuse. Our Constitution contains various provisions for the development of such marginalised groups, for instance, Article 341 for SCs, Article 342 for STs, Article 340 for OBCs, Article 30 which provides the right to minorities to establish and administer educational institutions, and so on. Their individual and collective growth, however, cannot be ensured without improving their surroundings and providing clean drinking water, toilets and educational opportunities.

The present chapter deals with the efforts made for the socio-economic development of these groups and the new initiatives that will be taken during the Eleventh Plan.

Scheduled Castes (SCs)

The SCs constitute 16.23 per cent of India's population. In the past, they have been socially ostracised, economically exploited and denied human dignity and a sense of self-worth. The socio-economic development and protection of SCs from discrimination and exploitation has been a high priority from the very start of the planning process.

People belonging to SC communities are spread all over the country, with 80 per cent of them living in the rural areas. They constitute more than a fifth of the population of Uttar Pradesh, Punjab, Himachal Pradesh and West Bengal. Punjab has the highest proportion of SCs to the State population. More than half of the SC population is concentrated in the five States of Uttar Pradesh (35.1 million), West Bengal (18.4 million), Tamil Nadu (11.8 million), Andhra Pradesh (12.3 million) and Bihar (13.0 million).

Constitutional Safeguards

The Constitution of India guarantees protection from social injustice and all forms of exploitation (Art. 46). It guarantees equality before law (Art. 14), and enjoins upon the State not to discriminate against any citizen on grounds of caste (Art. 15 (1)). Untouchability is abolished and its practice in any form is forbidden (Art. 17). The Constitution mandates that no citizen shall, on grounds only of caste or race, be subjected to any disability and restriction (Art. 15 (2)). It empowers the State to make provisions for reservation in educational institutions (Art. 15 (4) and (5)), and in appointments for posts in favour of SCs (Art. 16 (4), 16(4A), 16(4B) and Art. 335). Reservation of seats for SCs in the Lok Sabha is provided under Article 330, in the State Assemblies under Article 332 and in the Local Self-Governments bodies under Articles 243D and 340T. In addition to the above, the Parliament has enacted the Untouchability (Offences) Act, 1955, renamed as Protection of Civil Rights Act, in 1976. To check and deter atrocities against SCs, the Scheduled Castes and the Scheduled Tribes (Prevention of Atrocities) Act, 1989 has also been enacted.

Scheduled Castes Development

The Tenth Five Year Plan (2002–07) adopted a multi-pronged approach for the socio-economic development of the SCs: social empowerment through educational development; economic empowerment through income and employment enhancing avenues; protection through effective implementation of protective legislations and eradication of occupations such as manual scavenging; and holistic development through earmarking of funds proportionate to the population. [Scheduled Caste Sub-Plan (SCSP) and Tribal Sub-Plan (TSP)].

Educational Development

With respect to the educational development of SCs, the Central Government has introduced major scholarship programmes. These are:

- *Post-Matric Scholarships (PMS)* implemented since 1944–45 to promote higher education among SCs by extending scholarships to pursue studies beyond matriculation. In the Tenth Plan, an amount of Rs 1822.25 crore was utilised to reach the coverage of 29.59 lakh students in 2006–07.
- *Pre-Matric Scholarships* are being awarded since 1977–78 with an objective to encourage children of scavengers and those engaged in menial works, to pursue education. 4.72 lakh children were awarded pre-matric scholarships for which Rs 56.41 crore was utilised in the Tenth Plan.
- *Upgradation of Merit for SC Students Scheme* in operation since 1987–88 to extend remedial and special coaching offered to students to remove their deficiencies in school subjects (class IX to XII) into professional and technical courses. An expenditure of Rs 14.68 crore was incurred to benefit 10625 students.
- *Rajiv Gandhi National Fellowships* launched in the Tenth Plan in 2005–06 as a special incentive to extend scholarships to SC students to pursue higher studies and research degrees such as M.Phil. and Ph.D. An amount of Rs 50.20 crore was earmarked for this scheme in the Tenth Plan to benefit 2666 SC students.

The other important schemes for the educational development of SCs: are (i) providing coaching facilities to students to prepare them for various competitive examinations being conducted by Union Public Service Comission (UPSC), State Public Service Commissions, banks, and so on; and (ii) hostel facilities to both boys and girls for pursuing education from middle level onwards.

Economic Development

The National Scheduled Castes Finance and Development Corporation (NSFDC) established in 1989, provides financial and other support to beneficiaries for taking up various income generating activities. An amount of Rs 388.80 crore was made available to the Corporation up to 31 March 2007 as equity share contribution against the authorised share capital of Rs 1000 crore. The number of SC persons who received assistance during the Tenth Five Year Plan (up to December 2006) is 257901.

The National Safai Karamcharis Finance and Development Corporation was established in 1997 to provide financial support to the *safai karamcharis* (scavengers) to take up various income-generating activities. During the Tenth Five Year Plan, the Corporation introduced the Micro Credit Finance Scheme and the Mahila Samridhi Yojana, benefitting 102187 persons. During 2006–07, it disbursed loans to 16545 beneficiaries (up to December 2006) for various income generating activities in 23 States and two UTs.

The scheme of grant-in aid to the Scheduled Castes Development Corporations (SCDCs) was introduced in 1978–79 as a CSS for participating in the equity share of the State corporations in a Centre–State ratio of 49:51. The SCDCs finance employment oriented schemes that cover: (i) agriculture and allied activities including minor irrigation; (ii) small-scale industry; (iii) transport; and (iv) trade and service sector. They also finance projects by dovetailing the loan component from NSFDC/Banks with margin money out of their own funds and subsidy out of the SCA. sectors in proportion to the population of SCs and STs, respectively for their overall development.

Protective Measures

Two important protective legislations in operation for people belonging to SCs are the Protection of Civil Rights Act, 1955 and the Scheduled Castes and Scheduled Tribes (Prevention of Atrocities) Act, 1989. However, despite these Constitutional provisions, atrocities and crimes on members of SCs, especially the women, continue to occur in all parts of the country in varying degrees. As per the National Crime Records Bureau Report 2005, the crimes against SCs in the last few years were mainly atrocities followed by hurt and rape. Data for the last five years are reproduced in Table 1.

Table 1.Comparative Incident of Crime against Scheduled Castes

Crime-Head	Years					per cent Variation in
	2001	2002	2003	2004	2005	2005 over 2004
Murder	763	739	581	654	669	2.3
Rape	1316	1331	1089	1157	1172	1.3
Kidnapping/ Abduction	400	319	232	253	258	2.0
Dacoity	41	29	24	26	26	0.0
Robbery	133	105	70	72	80	11.1
Arson	354	322	204	211	210	–0.5
Hurt	4547	4491	3969	3824	3847	0.6
Protection of Civil Rights Act	633	1018	634	364	291	–20.0
SC/ST (Prevention of Atrocities) Act	13113	10770	8048	8891	8497	–4.4
Others	12201	14383	11401	11435	11077	–3.1
Total	33501	33507	26252	26887	26127	–2.8

Implementation of the Scheduled Caste Sub-Plan (SCSP) and Tribal Sub-Plan (TSP)

In view of the persistent and wide-spread socio-economic backwardness of SCs and STs, a distinct need was felt for innovative policy intervention to enable these groups to share the benefits of growth in a more equitable manner. The government prepared a separate Development Plan called Tribal Sub Plan for STs in 1976. It was followed by the Special Component Plan for the SCs in 1978 (recently renamed the Scheduled Caste Sub Plan [SCSP]).

The SCSP and TSP aim at facilitating convergence and pooling of resources from all the other development sectors in proportion to the population of SCs and STs, respectively for their overall development.

At present, 27 States/UTs are implementing SCSP through different mechanisms. The State Governments generally divide their resources into 'divisible' and 'non-divisible' components and earmark funds for SCs only from the divisible pool. As a result, the actual funds flowing directly to SCSP from the total State Plan becomes much less than the proportion of SC population to the total population of the State.

The State Government of Maharashtra has pioneered a special mechanism to ensure effective operationalisation of SCSP and TSP. Other States could explore replication of this mechanism.

The Prime Minister has reiterated the need for effective implementation of SCSP and TSP during the 51st and 52nd NDC meetings held on 27 June 2005 and 9 December 2006. He emphasised that the SCSP and TSP strategies should become an integral part of the Annual Plans as well as the Five Year Plans so that full inclusion of SCs and STs in socio-economic development is achieved within a period of 10 years.

All Central Ministries/Departments are also expected to formulate SCSP and ensure that the flow of funds to SCSP in their plans is at least in proportion with the SC population of the country. At present,.17 Central Ministries/Departments have done so. These are the Ministries of Labour, Coal, Commerce and Industries, Textiles, Non-Conventional Energy Sources, Women and Child Development, Steel and Rural Development, and the Departments of Agriculture and Cooperation, Small-Scale Industries and Agro and Rural Industries, Biotechnology, Science and Technology, Health, Family Welfare, Elementary Education and Literacy and Secondary and Higher Education. Many Ministries/ Departments maintain that they are unable to provide funds for SCSP because their funds are devoted expenditure on large projects and are not divisible.

The implementation of SCSP and TSP leaves much to be desired. This applies equally to the Central as well as State governments. Though there may be several reasons for this lacklustre implementation, lack of statutory or clear-cut administrative sanction is an important one.

To look into the issues related to TSP and SCSP, a Central Standing Tripartite Committee (CSTC) which includes representatives of the Planning Commission, National

Commission for SCs and STs, the Ministries of Social Justice and Empowerment and States/UTs Ministries/Departments, was set up in May 1999. The CSTC was reconstituted in early 2006 to review the formulation, implementation and monitoring of SCSP and TSP and advise the Planning Commission and Prime Minister on measures which would serve the interests of the SCs and STs more effectively.

Present Status of the Scheduled Castes

Education

Although the literacy rate of SCs has increased considerably, from 10.3 per cent in 1961 to 54.7 per cent in 2001, till recently the gap between literacy rates of the general and SC population had not reduced. However, the Census in 2001 showed a distinct reduction in this literacy gap (Table 2).

The school dropout rate is a crucial indicator of lack of educational development. The dropout rates for SC children are still very high –32.7 per cent in Classes I to V; 55.2 per cent in Classes I to VIII; and 69.1 per cent in classes I to X in 2004–05 (Table 2). The gap between the SC population and the general category increases at higher levels of schooling. However, an encouraging sign is the reduction in the gap between the dropout rates of the total population vis-à-vis the SCs at all levels.

In the area of higher education, also, there is a gap between the SCs and the general population. The gross enrolment ratio for the country as a whole in 2000 was about 10 per cent. For the SCs, however, it was significantly lower at 6.4 per cent.

Table 2. Literacy Rate of General Population and SC Population, 1961–2001

Year	General			SC		
	Male	Female	Total	Male	Female	Total
1961	34.44	12.95	24.02	16.96	3.29	10.27
1971	39.45	18.70	29.45	22.36	6.44	14.67
1981	46.89	24.82	36.23	31.12	10.93	21.38
1991	64.1	39.3	52.2	49.91	23.76	37.41
2001	75.3	53.7	64.8	66.64	41.90	54.69

Occupational Status

45.61 per cent of SC workers at the all-India level and 52 per cent at the rural level were agricultural labourers, compared to 26.55 and 33.05 per cent among all workers at the national and rural levels, respectively. The position is reversed when we come to the share of SCs among cultivators, which is 19.99 per cent and 23.47 per cent for rural workers compared to 31.65 and 40.24 per cent, respectively for all workers.

Availability of Basic Amenities

Another important dimension of discrimination is the wide gap between the SCs and the rest of the population with respect to the availability of basic civic amenities such as electricity, banking services, *pucca* houses, water supply, toilet facilities, drainage and telephone facilities.

In 2000, about two-thirds of rural SC households were landless and near landless, compared to one-third among others. Less than one-third of SC households had acquired access to capital assets, compared to 60 per cent among the others. About 60 per cent of SC households still have to depend on wage labour, compared to one-fourth for the others. Employment rates and wage earnings among SCs have also tended to be low. Similar disparities exist in the status of health of SCs. The incidence of anaemia among women and mortality rate among children are higher than in other groups. Studies also show evidence of discrimination in various market and non-market transactions, including access to social services like education, health and housing, and in political participation.

The cumulative impact of all these disparities, therefore, is reflected in the high levels of poverty, about 36 per cent among SCs as compared to only 21 per cent among others.

Access to Agricultural Land and Capital Assets

About 80 per cent of the SCs live in rural areas. In 2000, only 16.8 per cent of them pursued cultivation as an independent self-employed occupation, whereas among the non-SC/ ST this percentage was more than double (41.11 per cent). The percentage of those employed in some kind of non-farm self-employment activities (read business) was about 12 per cent and 15 per cent, respectively for SCs and others. In rural areas, about 28 per cent of SC households had acquired some access to fixed capital assets compared to 56 per cent for other households (non SC/ST). In urban areas, also, the access to capital assets for SCs was low (27 per cent) as compared to other households (35.5 per cent). In rural as well as urban areas, due to inadequate access to fixed capital assets, an exceptionally high percentage of all SC households, more than 62 per cent, was dependent on wage employment.

Unemployment

In 2000, the CDS employment rate in rural areas was 46 per cent for SC male workers, compared with 48.40 per cent for other male workers. Similarly, the CDS employment rate for SC workers in urban area was 45.8 per cent, compared to 49.9 per cent for other households. Disparities between the SC and others are also reflected in the unemployment rate. Unemployment rate based on CDS for SCs was about 5.0 per cent as compared to about 3.5 per cent for other workers in rural and urban areas. The NSSO data on wage earning revealed disparities in labour wages for SCs and others. For instance, in 1999–2000, the average weekly wage earning of an SC worker (at 1993–94 price) was Rs 174.50 compared to Rs 197.05 for other workers.

Economic Status

Available empirical evidence suggests discrimination against SCs in employment, wages, credit, and so on. These factors have acted as constraints to their occupational mobility. In urban areas, too, there is prevalence of discrimination by caste; particularly discrimination in employment, which operates at least in part through traditional mechanisms; SCs are disproportionately represented in poorly paid, dead-end jobs. Further, there is a flawed, preconceived notion that they lack merit and are unsuitable for formal employment.

Due to the lack of access to fixed sources of income and high incidence of wage labour associated with high rate of under-employment and low wages, SC households are often faced with low incomes and high incidence of poverty. In 2004–05, about 36.80 per cent of SC persons were BPL in rural areas as compared to only 28.30 per cent for others (non-SC/ST). In urban areas the gap was slightly larger; 39.20 per cent of SC households were BPL compared to 25.70 per cent among other households. The variation in poverty ratio across household types or occupational groups is striking. In 1993–94, the incidence of poverty was about 60 per cent among agricultural labour followed by 41.44 per cent among non-agricultural labour. The level was relatively low for persons engaged in self-employed activities in agriculture (37.71 per cent) and in the non-agricultural sector (38.19 per cent). In urban areas the incidence was astonishingly high among the casual labour (69.48 per cent). Poverty was also high among the self-employed households (54 per cent).

Human Development Index

According to the UNDP India Report (2007) on Human Poverty and Socially Disadvantaged Groups in India, the HDI at all India level for SCs is estimated to be 0.303, which is lower than the HDI for non-SC/ST at 0.393 for the period 1980–2000. The variation across States is very large, ranging from 0.661 for Kerala to 0.195 for Bihar. There are ten States with HDI value higher than the all-India average for SCs and six States with HDI value lower than this average.

HPI is a measure to assess the level of deprivation among a given social group with reference to Infant Mortality Rate, Illiteracy Rate, Poverty Ratio (Head Count Ratio), Health Status and Nutritional Status. The value of HPI was estimated at 33.63 per cent for all social groups taken together at the all-India level. The HPI for SCs was estimated to be 41.47 per cent for all India, which was much higher compared to non-SC/STs (31.34 per cent). The HPI revealed significant variation across the States with values ranging from 18.62 to 59.36 per cent. The level of deprivation was greatest in Bihar (59.36 per cent) followed by Uttar Pradesh (50.03 per cent), Orissa (47.66 per cent), Rajasthan (43.78 per cent) and Madhya Pradesh (43.68 per cent), as compared to the all-India level (41.47 per cent). In the remaining 11 States, the rate of deprivation was lower than the all-India value. Deprivation was found to be least in Kerala (18.62 per cent).

Representation in Government Services

Table 3 shows a marginal improvement in the percentage of overall SC representation in the Group A, B and C categories of

Central Government services from 1994 to 2004, while there was a substantial decline in the Group D category.

Table 3. SC Representation in Central Government Services in 1994, 1999, and 2004 (as on 1.1.2004)

	1999			2004		
Group	Total	SCs	% of total	Total	SCs	% of total
A	93520	10558	11.29	80011	9744	12.2
B	104963	13306	12.68	135409	19602	14.5
C	2396426	378115	15.78	2040970	344865	16.9
D	949353	189761	19.99	802116	147212	18.4
Total	3544262	591740	16.7	3058506	521423	17.05

Approach in the Eleventh Five Year Plan

The efforts made in the previous Five Year Plans have brought about some empowerment of SCs. However, gaps still exist in almost all social and economic dimensions between SCs and the general population. The Eleventh Plan provides an opportunity to restructure policies for faster, more broad-based and inclusive growth. In the following paragraphs, the steps that will be taken for the socio economic development of SCs are discussed.

Educational Development

With respect to elementary education, various incentives in the form of abolition of tuition fee, free supply of books, mid-day meals, scholarships, and so on, shall be provided to SC children. Among the SCs, children of scavengers are educationally the most backward. The existing Pre-Matric scholarship for them needs to be revised in its funding pattern from 50:50 to 100 per cent so that more target families send their children to schools. Special attention needs be paid to retention in schools of SC students and the quality of teaching for them.

The scheme of Post-Matric Scholarships for SCs provides scholarships to SC students for pursuing higher education in various courses beyond matriculation. Under this scheme, States are required to bear the committed liability over and above the expenditure incurred in the last year of the Five Year Plan which becomes the committed liability of the States in the first year of the next Plan. The issue of the committed liability to be borne by the states always prevents the States from coming forward to access this Central assistance. Ultimately, it is the SC students who are deprived of higher education. This needs to be addressed. In order to maximise their capabilities, SC students should have the opportunity to study in quality institutions. Today, the high cost of private education turns them away. Thus, there is need for extending financial assistance so that they can access top class educational institutions, including those in the private sector.

SC students also need to be encouraged to prepare for various competitive examinations. Reputed institutions charge very high fees for coaching students for competitive examinations. The existing scheme of coaching for SCs does not cover the fees charged by such reputed coaching institutes. There is a need to modify the scheme to ensure such coverage.

Over the last few years, higher technical and professional education is increasingly being provided by private unaided institutions. In the absence of explicit government aid, they charge high fees which SC/ST students simply cannot afford to pay. Therefore, the government may reimburse the total fee charged by such institutions.

The Rajiv Gandhi National Fellowship for SC students was introduced in 2005–06 to provide fellowship to 1333 SC students for pursuing higher studies leading to M.Phil. and Ph.D. degrees. The response under this scheme has been very encouraging in the last two years and this will necessitate increasing the number of fellowships. Those who cannot continue their education after schooling, or who wish to diversify, should be provided with vocational training/skill training programmes in ITIs, polytechnics, or other institutes. These institutes should have adequate seats on population basis and should be located closer to the SC dominated communities. The stress should be not merely on subject learning but also on personality development and entrepreneurship skills.

Economic Development

In the Eleventh Plan, a Commission on Land Reforms will be set up which will specifically look into issues of: (i) continued possession and effective uses of land distributed earlier to SCs under various programmes/ legislative interventions; and (ii) availability of land for distribution to SCs/STs/landless families. In all these, care will be taken to ensure preferential/joint ownership by women. The unemployment rate of SCs in rural and urban areas is about 5.5 per cent as against 3.5 per cent for others. Special programmes of employment are necessary to reduce this by increasing employment among SCs. Priority needs to be given to SCs in the Employment Guarantee Scheme with proper monitoring of coverage.

The National Sample Survey Organisation (NSSO) on Employment and Unemployment Situation among Social Groups in India in its report (61st Round, July 2004– June 2005) brought out that the proportion of persons in the labour force was the highest among STs followed by SCs, OBCs and others. The labour force participation rate for these groups were 51 per cent, 44 per cent and 40 per cent, respectively. Those belonging to the SC communities suffer from very high incidence of poverty and need to be provided with job-oriented training to enable them to have better opportunities. Large numbers of SCs and STs depend on agricultural wages to sustain themselves and the State Governments thus needs to revise agricultural wages every five years.

Various financial institutions such as Public Sector Banks and National Finance and Development Corporations for SCs and safai karmcharis and State-level SCDCs providing credit to SCs have been facing the problem of low recovery rate of loans from the beneficiaries through SCAs. This puts a question mark on the economics of the schemes as well as on the capability of the loanees. There is a need to restructure the schemes so that they become more 'sustainable'. The corporations need to be thoroughly professionalised so that programmes financed by them help develop entrepreneurial skills of the loanees. Based upon the effective performance of the Finance and Development Corporations, the capital available at their disposal may be increased substantially to provide support to SC/ST businesses.

Among the SCs, persons engaged as manual scavengers need special attention to put an end to the degraded practice of manual scavenging. In the Eighth Five Year Plan, the National Scheme for Liberation of Scavengers was launched with the aim to train manual scavengers and rehabilitate them in alternative occupations. Despite commitments made to the eradication of the obnoxious and dehumanising practice of handling night soil manually, it still continues. Only 19 States and all UTs have adopted the Employment of Manual Scavengers and Construction of Dry Latrines (Prohibition Act, 1993). Nine States are yet to adopt the Act. A new scheme, namely the, Self Employment Scheme for Rehabilitation of Manual Scavengers, has been formulated to rehabilitate the remaining 3.42 lakh of 7.73 lakh scavengers in a time-bound manner by March 2009 through training, and extension of loans and subsidies. This has to be done in a missionary mode with commitment and zeal.

Protective Measures

There is a need to complement protective legislations, that is, the Protection of Civil Rights Act, 1955 and Scheduled Castes and Scheduled Tribes (Prevention of Atrocities) Act, 1989 with a promotive legislation which should cover the rights of SCs with respect to education, vocational training, higher education and employment. Such a legislation may be drafted along the lines of the Persons with Disabilities (Equal Opportunities, Protection of Rights and Full Participation)

Act, 1995 which clearly spells out what is to be done, and who should do it. The implementation of the PCR Act, 1955 and SC and ST (POA) Act, 1989 has to be enforced in letter and spirit to bring about speedy justice to the aggrieved.

The Department of Justice in the GoI may establish a Special Law facility to deal with the legal issues of educating judicial officers, public prosecutors and police officials to carry out the necessary research for effective implementation of these two Acts. The Department should also review the judicial aspects and take appropriate steps towards sensitising the Judiciary, especially at the level of lower courts, to ensure more and speedier convictions. It should also be ensured that Revenue, Health and other concerned Departments in the States become more sensitised on the issue so that procedural delays in the investigation of offences under the Act are reduced.

Elimination of caste-based discrimination and harassment in educational institutions should be ensured by institutions by establishing 'Equal Opportunity Offices'.

Reservation for SCs

The government is committed to providing reservations for SCs in education and employment. Action needs to be taken to clear the backlog in filling up SC reserved posts of various categories in the government. However, the government alone cannot accomplish the task of providing job opportunities to SCs. The private corporate sector will have to play a proactive role in providing sufficient job opportunities to the especially marginalised and discriminated sections of Indian society. The government shall explore all possibilities of introducing, in one form or the other, affirmative action including reservations, in the private sector.

There is a need to monitor implementation of the programmes under the SCSP and Tribal Sub Plan. A Committee meant for this purpose will be set up which will ensure that each Ministry's allocation of SCSP is indicated well in advance. Further, if any particular Ministry is not able to utilise the earmarked allocation, action should be initiated to transfer the unused fund available to those Ministries/Departments which have implemented the SCSP/TSP more effectively.

Scheduled Tribes

The population of STs in India stood at 84.33 million as per the Census of 2001. STs constitute 8.2 per cent of the total population of the country with 91.7 per cent of them living in rural areas and 8.3 per cent in urban areas. The sex-ratio of ST population in 2001 was 978, which was much higher than the national average of 933. The proportion of ST population to the total population had also increased from 6.9 per cent in 1971 to 8.2 per cent in 2001.

The proportion of STs to the total population in States/UT was highest in Mizoram (94.5 per cent) and Lakshadweep (94.5 per cent) followed by Nagaland (89.1 per cent) and Meghalaya (85.9 per cent). Within major States, Chhattisgarh (31.8 per cent) had the highest percentage followed by Jharkhand (26.3 per cent) and Orissa (22.1 per cent). Of the total ST population in the country, Madhya Pradesh accounted for the highest proportion of ST population (14.5 per cent) followed by Maharashtra (10.2 per cent), Orissa (9.7 per cent), Gujarat (8.9 per cent), Rajasthan (8.4 per cent), Jharkhand (8.4 per cent) and Chhattisgarh (7.8 per cent).

In fact, 68 per cent of the country's ST population lives in these seven States only.

Constitutional Safeguards

The Constitution of India has made several provisions to safeguard the interests of the STs in Articles 15(4), 16(4), 46, 243M, 243 ZC, 244, the first and second provisos to 275(1), Articles 334, 335, 338A, 339(1), and the Fifth and the Sixth Schedules. Besides these, several laws have been enacted by the Central Government like the Protection of Civil Rights Act, 1955; the Scheduled Castes and Scheduled Tribes (Prevention of Atrocities) Act, 1989; the Provisions of the Panchayats (Extension to Scheduled Areas) Act, 1996; the Scheduled Tribes and Other Traditional Forest Dwellers (Recognition of Forest Rights) Act, 2006 as well as by the State Governments (relating to the prevention of alienation and restoration of tribal land, money-lending, reservations, and so on). The Centre has been given the authority of giving directions to the State Governments (cf. Article 339(2), Para 3 of the Fifth Schedule) in the interest of tribal people. Further, a National Tribal Policy is on the Central anvil.

Development of Scheduled Tribes

The Tenth Five Year Plan continued with the schemes and programmes directed at the socio-economic development of the tribal population through an area based approach. Initiatives to arrest the incidence of land alienation through legislative mechanisms were also explored during the Tenth Plan.

Educational Development

The Departments of Elementary Education and Literacy and of Higher Education in States have provided special incentives to ST students which include textbooks, uniform, abolition of tuition fee, and so on. Special focus is also accorded to ST students under the District Primary Education Programme, Kasturba Gandhi Balika Vidyalaya, Mid-day Meal Programme, Navodaya Vidyalaya, National Talent Search Scheme, and the like. The Post-Matric Scholarship scheme is in operation since 1944–45, and open to all ST students whose parents' annual income is up to Rs 1 lakh, to facilitate students to pursue professional courses. An amount of Rs 58.9 crore was utilised to benefit seven lakh ST students in the Tenth Plan. The scheme of establishing Ashram schools in TSP areas provides funds for construction of school buildings as well as hostels and staff quarters. Seventy-eight Ashram schools with a capacity of 9610 seats were supported at a cost of Rs 22.34 crore. The scheme of construction of hostels for ST boys and girls provides for the construction of new hostel buildings as well as extension of the existing hostel buildings. An amount of Rs 57.84 crore was utilised for the construction of 120 hostels for 9884 students. The scheme of setting up educational complexes is being implemented for promotion of education among tribal girls in 136 identified low literacy districts of the country. In the Tenth Plan, an amount of Rs 62 crore was allotted under the scheme to set up 76 complexes. A scheme for vocational training in tribal areas for developing the skills of tribal youth for a variety of jobs as well as self-employment, is also in operation.

However, the problem of adequacy of the school buildings, both in number and in facilities, still remains. The lack of education in the mother language or dialect in primary classes, ignorance of non-tribal teachers about tribal languages and ethos, delay in distribution of scholarships, textbooks and uniforms, continue to be sources of worry.

Economic Development

The National Scheduled Tribes Finance and Development Corporation (NSTFDC) was set up in 2001 with an authorised share capital of Rs 500 crore. The Corporation supports various income and employment generating activities though loans, marketing support, training, and so on. Special focus is accorded to ST women beneficiaries under programmes such as the Adivasi Mahila Shashaktikaran Yojana, which facilitate income generating activities through women's self-help groups (SHGs). Under NSTFDC, 14.53 lakh STs were benefited during the Tenth Plan. The State ST Development Corporations (STDCs) which function as channellising agencies in identifying eligible beneficiaries and extending financial and other assistance to them, are also supported by NSTFDC. The STDCs were provided with funds to the tune of Rs 48.76 crore in the Tenth Plan. The Tribal Cooperative Marketing Development Federation of India Ltd (TRIFED) provides marketing assistance and remunerative prices to STs for collection of minor forest produce (MFP), and surplus agricultural produce to protect them from exploitative private traders and middlemen. In the Tenth Plan, States were provided SCA of Rs 2518.07 crore to strengthen their Tribal Sub Plans.

Though the majority of the tribals are settled cultivators, their farming activity is generally uneconomical and non-viable due to the lack of access to necessary agricultural inputs, specially assured irrigation. Therefore, a special provision of funds under grant-in-aid under Article 275 (1) of the Constitution has been made for financing minor irrigation works.

Restoration of Traditional Rights

The government took a major initiative in enacting the Scheduled Tribes and Other Traditional Forest Dwellers (Recognition of Forest Rights) Act, 2006 which was notified in the Gazette of India, extraordinarily, dated 2 January 2007. The Ministry has also framed the draft Rules for implementation of the provisions of the Act. The major rights that are granted under the Act inter alia are the right to cultivate forest land to the extent under occupation, (subject to a ceiling of 4 hectares); the right to own, collect, use and dispose of MFP; rights inside forests which are traditional and customary, for example, grazing.

Self Governance

Despite some protective measures and developmental efforts, the emerging tribal scenario characteristically continues to manifest:

- increasing tribal alienation on account of slipping economic resources like land, forest, common property resources;
- displacement and dispossession of life-support systems;
- general apathy of official machinery;
- escalating atrocities, at times related to assertion of rights;
- growing clout of market forces; and,
- meagre advancement through planned development efforts.

The scenario calls for a major shift towards entrusting, enabling and empowering the tribal people to look after their own welfare and address issues of development through their own initiative.

The extant constitutional-cum-legal-cum-policy framework has been enormously strengthened by the enactment of the Provisions of the Panchayats (Extension to the Scheduled Areas) Act, 1996 (PESA), a charter of autonomous tribal governance, embodying rights in favour of tribal communities coupled with respect for their ethos.

Protective Measures

Despite protective legislation, incidents of atrocities on members of STs, including gang rape and murder, continue to take place in almost all parts of the country. During the period 2001 to 2005, the total recorded incidents of atrocities against STs were 30128.

Five States—Madhya Pradesh, Orissa, Rajasthan, Andhra Pradesh, and Chhattisgarh—contributed 72 per cent of the total incidents of crimes against STs.

Primitive Tribal Groups (PTGs)

There are 75 identified Primitive Tribal Groups (PTGs) spread across 17 States/UTs living in utmost destitute conditions. Some of them, in dire straits, also face the threat of extinction. In order to provide focused attention to the survival, protection and development of these PTGs, a special scheme launched in 1998–99 was implemented during the Tenth Plan to provide tribe-specific services and support including, inter-alia, housing, land, agricultural inputs, cattle rearing, health, nutritional services and income generating programmes.

Displacement, Rehabilitation, and Resettlement

Ancestral land, villages, habitations and environs belonging to the tribal people have been made available for various development projects as tribal areas possess 60–70 per cent of the natural resources of the country. In such cases, though primary displacement appears small due to low population density, secondary displacement has been extensive, encompassing common property resources that provided supplemental livelihoods, particularly to those with low or no dependence on farming. Estimates of STs displaced on account of acquisition over the past six decades vary between 8.5 and 10 million (roughly about 40 per cent of all oustees). The widespread secondary displacement in the zone of influence has neither been measured nor was provided for, calling for an accurate verification of actual displacement both in terms of persons and resource loss. Cash compensation for land having been the practice as per the provisions of the Land Acquisition Act, 1894, oustees owning little land, such as wage-labour artisans, have hardly figured in the relief and rehabilitation packages. As a result, some groups have continued to suffer successive, multiple displacement.

Land (both owned by community and individuals) is the most important source of livelihood for the tribal people for agriculture (settled and shifting cultivation), horticulture, floriculture, forestry and animal husbandry. Several laws and regulations have been in place to prevent the alienation of tribal land and private grabbing of such land. A Report of the Ministry of Rural Development reveals in March 2005:

- 3.75 lakh cases of tribal land alienation have been registered covering 8.55 lakh acres of land;
- Out of the above, 1.62 lakh cases have been disposed of in favour of tribals covering a total area of 4.47 lakh acres;
- 1.55 lakh cases covering an area of 3.63 lakh acres have been rejected by the courts on various grounds; and
- 57521 cases involving 0.44 lakh acres of land are pending in various courts of the country.

Despite the fair rate of disposal, the other related issues are: (i) the time taken in disposal, (ii) the number of alienations for which STs found access to courts difficult, if not impossible and (iii) the physical possession of the land needs to be addressed comprehensibly.

Present Status of Scheduled Tribes (STs)

Educational Status

Between 1961 and 2001, the literacy rate of STs increased 5.32 times, while that of total population increased 2.69 times. However, the gap between the literacy rates of STs and of the general population continued during the three decades between 1971 and 2001 almost at the same level of 17.70 per cent and above, but with marginal variations (Table 4).

Table 4. Literacy Rate of General Population and ST Population during 1961–2001

Year	General			SC		
	Male	Female	Total	Male	Female	Total
1961	34.44	12.95	24.02	13.83	3.16	8.53
1971	39.45	18.70	29.45	17.63	4.85	11.30
1981	46.89	24.82	36.23	24.52	8.04	16.35
1991	64.1	39.3	52.2	40.65	18.19	29.60
2001	75.3	53.7	64.8	59.17	34.76	47.10

The dropout rate is a critical indicator reflecting lack of educational development and inability of a given social group to complete a specific level of education. In the case of tribals, dropout rates are still very high –42.3 per cent in Classes I to V; 65.9 per cent in Classes I to VIII; and 79.0 per cent in Classes I to X in 2004–05. Ab out 4.34 lakh ST students were studying at different levels of higher education as on 30 September 2004.

Occupational Status

81.56 per cent of the total ST workers, both rural and urban taken together, are engaged in the primary sector, of whom 44.71 per cent are cultivators and 36.85 per cent are agricultural labourers. The corresponding figures for all workers are 31.65 per cent (cultivators) and 26.55 per cent (agricultural labourers). This indicates that STs are essentially dependent on agriculture.

Availability of Basic Amenities

. Since most of the tribal habitations are located in isolated villages and hamlets in undulating plateau lands coinciding with forest areas, they have limited access to critical infrastructure facilities such as roads, communication, health, education, electricity, drinking water, and so on. This widens the gap between the quality of their life and the people in the country.

Access to Agricultural Land and Capital Assets

The STs are mainly landless poor forest dwellers and shifting cultivators, small farmers and pastoral and nomadic herders. The livelihood strategy would thus have to take into account the land structure, level of skills, socio-economic conditions, low level of HDI along with the physical infrastructure and natural resource base in the tribal areas.

Extent of Poverty

The incidence of poverty amongst STs still continues to be very high at 47.30 per cent in rural areas and 33.30 per cent in urban areas, compared to 28.30 per cent and 25.70 per cent, respectively in respect of total population in 2004–05. A large number of STs who are living below the poverty line are landless, with no productive assets and with no access to sustainable employment and minimum wages. The women belonging to these groups suffer even more because of the added disadvantage of being denied equal and minimum wages.

Human Development Index

As per the UNDP India Report 2007 on Human Poverty and Socially Disadvantaged Groups in India the HDI for STs at the all-India level is estimated at 0.270, which is lower than the HDI of SCs and non-SC/ST for the period 1980–2000. The HPI for STs is estimated at 47.79, which was higher than SCs and non-SC/ST for the period 1990–2000.

Representation in General Services

Table 5 shows a marked improvement in the representation of STs in various categories of services during 1994 and 2004, though they are yet not adequately represented in any of the four categories. The situation is especially unsatisfactory with respect to the A and B categories.

Table 5. Percentage of ST Representation in Central Government Services in 1994, 1999, and 2004 (as on 1.1.2004)

	1999			2004		
Group	All	STs	% of All	All	STs	% of All
A	93520	3172	3.39	80011	3311	4.1
B	104963	3512	2.35	135409	6,274	4.6
C	2396426	145482	6.07	2040970	136630	6.7
D	949353	66487	7.00	802116	53776	6.7
Total	3544262	218653	6.17	3058506	199991	6.54

Approach in Eleventh Plan

The Eleventh Plan will attempt a paradigm shift with respect to the overall empowerment of the tribal people, keeping the issues related to governance at the Centre. The operational imperatives of the Fifth Schedule, TSP 1976, PESA 1996, RFRA 2006; the desirability of a tribal-centric, tribal-participative and tribal-managed development process; and the need for a conscious departure from dependence on a largely under-effective official delivery system will be kept in view during this shift.

Self Governance

Article 243G of the constitution and PESA Act make it incumbent that State legislations endow power and authority on Panchayats in Scheduled Areas enabling them to function as institutions of self-governance, preparing and implementing schemes of economic development and social justice. The Act confers abundant powers on the four tiers—Gram Sabha, Gram Panchayat (extant since decades), Intermediate Panchayat (development block tier) and Zilla Panchayat (ZP, district tier)—which need to be given effect in real operational terms. The vision of self-governance should be made functional forthwith in keeping with the spirit of PESA.

The Gram Sabha and the three other hierarchical Panchayats would require infrastructure, personnel, and financial resources to carry out their tasks. Apart from other sources, the State Finance Commissions need to provide the necessary devolutions for Scheduled and Tribal Areas, as per Article 243(I) of the Constitution. The Ministry of Tribal Affairs should ensure direct flow of funds to the ZPs of the districts in these areas, which should apportion them on an equitable basis to the three lower Panchayat bodies for various programmes.

The Fifth Schedule needs to be urgently operationalised. The Tribes Advisory Council (TAC) needs to be made proactive, functioning as an advisory body to the State Government in matters relating to STs. Second, it should function as a tier in between the ZPs in Scheduled Areas and the State Government. Its jurisdiction should be expanded to cover all matters relating to tribes people, and not limited, as of now, to those which are referred to it by the Governor. The Ministry of Tribal Affairs is required to ensure regular and meaningful annual reports for the Governor as per para 3 of the Schedule. The Ministry should also examine the feasibility of insertion in the Fifth Schedule of a suitable provision to the effect that discretionary power may be exercised by the Governor on the advice of TAC. Lastly, the Scheduled Areas and Tribal Sub Plan areas should be made co-terminus, enabling protective and legal measures to be available in all TSP areas. To the extent possible, demarcation of Scheduled Areas should be notified down to the village level and other settlements.

Educational Development

The following measures should be taken to accelerate the educational progress among the tribal population during the Eleventh Plan:

- In the deficit areas, the requisite number of primary schools needs to be established. Specific norms for middle schools and high schools for tribal areas will be evolved and deficiencies made up. All schools should have proper school buildings, hostels, water, toilet facilities (particularly for the girls' schools).
- Residential high schools for ST boys and girls will be set up at suitable places. At the Gram Panchayat level, ensuring girls' hostels will be attached to the existing primary/elementary schools that do not have hostels, wherever it is feasible to do so.
- Textbooks in tribal languages, especially at the primary level, will be produced to enable better comprehension by ST students in classes up to III. Side by side, adequate attention will be paid to the regional language so that children do not feel handicapped in higher classes.
- Efforts will be made to set up Industrial Training Institutes (ITIs) in the TSP areas. Other training centres will include community polytechnics, and undertaking rural/ community development activities in their proximity, through application of science and technology.
- Timely distribution of fellowships, scholarships, textbooks, uniforms and school bags to students.

— The ICDS/Anganwadi schemes for tribal areas will be evaluated and shortcomings eliminated.
— A larger number of special coaching classes will be organised and the concerned institutions will be suitably aided to enable ST students to compete in entry-level competitive examinations for professional courses.
— Adult education will be paid adequate attention.
— Steps will be taken to promote tribal languages, culture and heritage through adaptation of pedagogical methods, community participation in school management, and so on.
— There is a need to constitute a special committee composed of eminent sociologists, anthropologists, educationists, administrators, representatives of ST communities, and so on, to comprehensively assess the problems of ST education and make recommendations for implme-ntation.

Health

Efforts will be made to make available affordable and accountable primary health care facilities to STs and bridge the yawning gap in rural health care services through a cadre of ASHA and sectoral convergence of all the related sectors. Periodic reviews will be conducted on the delivery system and functioning of the health care institutions under three broad heads to optimise service in the tribal areas: (i) health infrastructure, (ii) manpower and (iii) facilities like medicines and equipment. Action will be taken to make up the shortfall in the different categories of health institutions, liberalisation of norms, addressing infrastructural deficiencies, application of quality standards and revitalisation of Health Care Systems, PHCs and CHCs.

Economic Sectors and Livelihood Opportunities

An overwhelming proportion of STs depend on MFP, cottage and small industries, and horticulture for their livelihood. Towards making the existing tribal livelihoods more productive, intensive efforts will be mounted to restitute, vitalise and expand the agricultural sector. Use of irrigation in agriculture with a preference for organic farming, will be a major step. Training centres will be opened to impart skills for diverse occupations to the tribals. Efforts will be made to promote horticulture, animal husbandry, dairy farming, sericulture, sylviculture and cottage and small industry by extending the necessary technology and credit, marketing and entrepreneurial information, and training. TRIFED has to shoulder the task of marketing to ensure remunerative prices to STs.

Lending by agencies like the State Governments, NSTFDC and TRIFED will be streamlined by better coordination at higher levels and efficient delivery at the field level. Large-Scale Multi Purpose Corporate Societies and such like cooperative institutions in tribal areas will be revived to make them representative, autonomous and professional.

Tribal–Forest Interface

To enable the tribal primary producers, collectors and consumers to enter into transactions with primary cooperatives, the monopoly of corporations in certain items procured by them through contractors and middlemen will be replaced by alternative market mechanisms like minimum price support with institutional backing. It will be incumbent on the national-level organisations like TRIFED and NAFED to play their due role in marketing of the tribal MFP. Technological support for value addition will be extended to the corporations as well as other institutional and private processors. Skills like culling, barking, tapping of gums, storage of sal seeds and preparation of tamarind extracts, need to be upgraded through ITIs, TRIFED, NSTDFC and other training organisations.

As visualised under the National Forest Policy (NFP) Resolution (1988), tribal association with forestry will be maximised through tribal cooperatives and SHGs of tribal women. Specific schemes for quality improvement, higher productivity and regeneration of MFP species will be implemented to facilitate sustainability of this source of tribal livelihood. No outside labour will be engaged where tribal labour is available. Inter-disciplinary scientific studies to develop feasible agronomic strategies to make shifting cultivation ecologically compatible and economically viable will be undertaken. Special protection will be extended to Jhumias. Rules under the Forest Rights Act, 2006 and PESA need to be framed expeditiously.

ST women will be recruited to the posts of forest guards, foresters and forest rangers, by suitably lowering the educational qualifications, if required. Such forest guards and foresters will ensure safety of the women venturing in the forest areas for their livelihood needs.

Tribal Sub-Plan and Tribal Policy

As has been explained in the earlier section on SCs, the TSP will be reformed to restore its dynamic character and make it an effective instrument for tribal development. Once the National Tribal Policy is finalised, action will be taken to follow up on it.

Tribal Unrest and Socio-Political Movements

Lack of socio-economic development, physical and economic exploitation, land alienation and other problems have led to a situation in which 75 predominantly tribal districts are affected by violence. The situation could be remedied by taking the following steps.

- Prevention of exploitation of tribals through strict penal action against errant moneylenders, businessmen, traders, middlemen, government servants and other exploiters. Effective implementation of the SC and ST (Prevention of Atrocities) Act, 1989.
- The practice of employment of contractors and middlemen by public sector organisations should be replaced by tribes-benefitting procedures.
- Amendment of instruments the like Land Acquisition Act, 1894; Forest Act, 1927; Forest (Conservation) Act, 1980; Coal Bearing Areas (Acquisition and Development) Act, 1957; and National Mineral Policy, 1993 to eliminate iniquitous provisions ensuring protection of the interest of tribals.
- Displacement should be avoided in the first place. If inescapable, it should be the minimum possible; land for land will be the general rule.
- Land reforms should be implemented stringently.
- The Scheduled Tribes and Other Traditional Forest Dwellers (Recognition of Forest Rights) Act, 2006 should be implemented by the States in letter and spirit.

- Rigorous implementation of the provisions of laws combating land alienation and simultaneous stringent steps to restore the alienated land back to the people.

Prevention of Land Alienation

Apart from rigorous implementation of laws for preventing alienation of tribal land and plugging loopholes in such laws, the following measures also need to be taken.

- Updating and computerisation of land records in tribal areas
- Separate fast-track courts in the Scheduled Areas to deal with cases of tribal land alienation.
- Translation of anti-alienation laws into regional languages and, possibly, in tribal languages, for wide dissemination in tribal areas.
- A law for urban agglomerates in Scheduled Areas on the analogy of PESA Act, 1996 needs to be considered for enactment.

Rehabilitation and Resettlement

The government has recently approved the National Rehabilitation and Resettlement Policy 2007, with the following objectives:

- Minimise displacement and promote non-displacing or least-displacement alternatives
- Ensure adequate and expeditious rehabilitation with participation of the Project Affected Families (PAFs)—through an independent authority
- Create obligations on the State to protect the rights of weaker sections, particularly SCs and STs
- Provide a better standard of living with sustainable income
- Integrate rehabilitation concerns into development planning and implementation.

Effective follow-up action will be taken to operationalise the policy.

Infrastructure

Both the Fifth and Sixth Schedule Areas are considered backward, with poor infrastructure being a major handicap in improving the quality of life. The first proviso to Article 275(1) of the Constitution directs building infrastructure in such areas on par with that of the rest of the areas in the country by providing monies from the Consolidated Fund of India. Focused strategies for infrastructure development in sectors like education, drinking water, PDS, health, minor irrigation, roads, housing, telecommunications and electrification will be pursued.

Primitive Tribal Groups (PTGs)

The strategy will be different for the two distinct groups of PTGs. The approach for heritage groups will place emphasis on conservation of the ecosystem, lifestyle and traditional skills along with an economic component. In the case of peripheral communities, the approach will be conservation of the ecosystem, along with stress on economic programmes. For the purpose, the unique attributes of each group will determine specific treatment in planning and implementation.

A National Plan of Action for tribe-specific comprehensive conservation-cum-development needs to be formulated and executed. Periodic reviews need to be conducted on the functioning of health care institutions in the tribal areas under three broad heads: (i) health infrastructure, (ii) manpower and (iii) facilities like medicines and equipment. The NRHM seeks to strengthen the public health delivery system at all levels.

The Department of Drinking Water Supply needs to cover all uncovered tribal areas before the end of the Plan period. Urban tribal pockets and other tribal habitations need to be covered with sanitary latrines equipped with minimum basic facilities. Many tribal areas receive adequate rainfall. Rain-water harvesting structures will be installed appropriately, particularly in schools and colleges. TPDS will be revamped to ensure its outreach actually extends to tribal areas. The system should convey to them foodstuffs of their choice like coarse cereals, pulses, edible oils, and so on. There is a need to ensure that the tribal villages are automatically electrified, taking recourse also to non-conventional sources of energy. Universal telecom voice coverage will be ensured in the tribal areas during the Plan period.

In 1975, guidelines to States/UTs were issued by the Centre for taking steps for discontinuation of commercial vending of liquor in tribal areas in pursuance of the Excise Policy, 1974. Although the States/UTs have accepted the guidelines, commercial vending of intoxicants continues in tribal areas and stringent measures are needed for its prevention.

Data-based Planning

The issues in tribal development are complex and often not understood very well. Each of the nearly 300 main tribal groups differ from each other in customs, practices, traditions, faith, and language. As such, uniformity in socio-economic development plans for all tribal groups and programmes is not appropriate. Vast quantities of data, generated at various geographical sites across the country, lie scattered, unanalysed and unused. They need to be processed and stored meaningfully in a tribal data bank. The programmes and schedules of the 18 State Tribal Research Institutes (TRIs) in the country demand coordination and synergy. The issues of scheduling and de-scheduling of communities have assumed national importance and need to be appraised rationally and dispassionately. All these point to the need at the Central level for a National Institute of Tribal Affairs (NITA) to deliberate on these matters as also on a whole range of other issues. NITA will serve as a think tank to the Ministry of Tribal Affairs. Expeditious steps will be taken to set up NITA.

OTHER BACKWARD CLASSES (OBCs)

The Second Backward Classes Commission headed by B.P. Mandal (1980), basing its calculation on the Census of 1931, estimated that OBCs constituted 52 per cent of the population. Recently, the NSSO 61st Round (July 2004 to June 2005) report on 'Employment and Unemployment Situation among Social Groups in India' gave an estimate of OBCs constituting 41 per cent of the population. State-wise, OBC-wise data on population as well as vital and demographic variables are not available, which is the main hurdle in the formulation of policies and programmes for the development of the Other Backward Classes.

Constitutional Safeguards

Though the Constitution does not make specific provisions for OBCs, it empowers the State to make provisions for reservation in appointments or posts in favour of any backward class of citizens which, in the opinion of the State, is not adequately represented in the Services under the State [Article 16(4)]. It also empowers the State to appoint a commission to investigate into the conditions of socially and educationally backward classes (Article 340). In pursuance of the Supreme Court judgment, *Indira Sawhney and Others* vs *Union of India* (1992), the National Commission for Backward Classes was set up on 14 August 1993 under the National Commission for Backward Classes Act, 1993. Thus, after 46 years of independence of the country, the backward classes or OBCs got recognition as a separate group of people for the purpose of 27 per cent reservation in services in the GoI and public sector undertakings. The States/UTs were free to decide the quantum of reservation based on the OBC population in their State/UT. All State Governments/UT Administrations were also directed by the Supreme Court of India in the same case to set up a permanent body and to draw up their own list and decide the quantum of reservation as per their demography.

Development of Other Backward Classes

Specific programmes for the development of OBCs were initiated from the Eighth Plan. The National Backward Classes Finance and Development Corporation (NBCFDC) was set up in 1992 with an authorised share capital of Rs 200 crore. This was augmented to Rs 700 crore in the Ninth Plan. The objective of NBCFDC is to promote self-employment projects among the OBCs living below the poverty line.

During the Ninth Five Year Plan period, programmes such as Pre-Matric and Post-Matric scholarship schemes, construction of hostels and pre-examination coaching centres for OBCs were introduced. The Pre-examination Coaching Scheme for OBCs was merged with the umbrella Coaching and Allied Scheme for Weaker Sections including SCs, OBCs, and minorities from September 2001.

Economic Development

The NBCFDC provides financial assistance through SCAs nominated by the State Governments/ UTs. NBCFDC assists a wide range of income generating activities which include agricultural and allied activities, artisan and traditional occupations, technical trades, small-scale and tiny industry, small business, transport services. Entrepreneurs with annual income less than double the poverty line are eligible for concessional finance. The GoI has made available Rs 448.35 crore to the Corporation as paid-up capital towards the authorised share capital of Rs 700.00 crore. The Corporation has disbursed Rs 1150.89 crore, covering 750432 beneficiaries.

Reservation in Higher Educational Institutions

In the last year of the Tenth Plan, the GoI decided on another way to introduce reservation for OBC students in institutes imparting higher education. The Oversight Committee under the Chairmanship of Veerapa Moily was constituted in 2006 to prepare a policy roadmap for implementation of reservation for OBCs in higher educational institutions. The matter, however, is sub-judice.

Reservation in Services

Despite 27 per cent posts being reserved for OBCs from 1993, Table 6 shows that the overall representation of OBCs in government service is abysmally low, just 4.53 per cent. Only 3.9, 2.3 and 5.2 per cent, respectively of Group A, B, and C posts are occupied by OBC persons. This is indeed a matter of concern.

Table 6. Percentage of OBC Representation in Central Government Services (as on 1.1.2004)

Group	Total	OBCs	% of total
A	80011	3090	3.9
B	135409	3123	2.3
C	2040970	106309	5.2
D	802116	26158	3.3
Total	3058506	138680	4.53

Eleventh Plan Approach

The Eleventh Plan will address the issues for development of OBCs through a three-pronged strategy: of (i) educational development, (ii) economic development and (iii) social development.

Educational Development

While the universalisation of primary education through the SSA is poised to take care of OBC children, their continued education through the secondary and higher education stages must be ensured. The Eleventh Five Year Plan shall give priority to designing and implementing of schemes to provide the necessary facilities to OBC students to get better education at all levels. Reservation for OBC students in all the Central and Centrally aided schools/ colleges/professional institutes needs to be ensured.

Both Pre-Matric and Post-Matric Scholarship schemes should be revised by enhancing the income ceiling for eligibility and rate of scholarship and maintenance allowance, as these have not been revised since 1998.

The performance of the existing coaching scheme for SCs and OBCs is not good and the scheme needs to be revised to attract good, professionally reputed coaching institutions.

Hostels for OBC boys and girls are constructed by the State Governments and UT Administrations. However, where hostel facilities are not available for them, they should be provided facilities in general hostels by earmarking a certain percentage of seats for them.

National Overseas Scholarship Scheme for OBCs should also be formulated similar to those for SCs and STs so that OBC students can also go abroad for better educational and professional courses which are generally not available in the country

Economic Development

In economic and occupational terms, the backward classes comprise of peasants, landless labourers, artisanal communities such as handloom weavers, carpenters, metal workers, stone cutters and fishermen, and those who provide various traditional services. The plight of these categories of the backward classes has worsened in recent years due to extensive mechanisation and market competition. There is a need to ensure upgradation of skills of such categories so that they can compete better in the market. Credit flow must be unhampered and easy to access, especially in occupations which have been the traditional forte of OBCs, for example, weaving, pottery, quarrying, cultivation of fruits and vegetable, and so on.

A suitable marketing strategy needs to be worked out on the lines of TRIFED to market the products manufactured by small artisans. The strength and capability of NBCFDC should be augmented.

Social Development

Like SCs, STs, Minorities, and Persons with Disabilities, there is an imperative need to carry out a census of OBCs now or in the next census in 2011. In the absence of exact assessment of their population size; literacy rate; employment status in government, private and unorganised sectors; basic civic amenities; health status; poverty status; and human development and HPIs; it is very difficult to formulate realistic policies and programmes for the development of OBCs.

Since some backward class people are also working in occupations which are hazardous, the government should identify occupational diseases prevalent among them and take steps to prevent and treat such diseases. The *Report on Conditions of Work and Promotion of Livelihood in the Unorganised Sector* by Arjun K. Sengupta et al., National Commission of Enterprises in the Unorganised Sectors, New Delhi (August 2007) deals with the issue of workers in the unorganised sector.

The income ceiling of Rs 2.5 lakh per annum for purposes of obtaining OBC certificates may be periodically reviewed to make it more realistic.

De-notified, Nomadic, and Semi-nomadic Tribes

De-notified, Nomadic and Semi-Nomadic Tribes and Banjara communities constitute the most vulnerable and disadvantaged sections of the Indian society. Some of these communities were identified as 'Criminal Tribes' (which included both castes as well as tribes) in pre-Independence India. Although the Criminal Tribes Act, 1871 was repealed soon after Independence, persons belonging to these communities are still viewed by society as habitual criminals.

After the repeal of the Criminal Tribes Act, 1924 in 1952, the government was keen to undertake schemes that would accelerate the process of integration of the de-notified tribes into mainstream society. A small beginning was made in the First Five Year Plan in this direction. In the Fifth Five Year Plan, all welfare schemes for de-notified tribes were transferred to the State Plans. Unfortunately, these groups still continued to be marginalised and their specific needs even today are neither adequately understood nor catered to. In order to acquire a comprehensive picture of the situation of these communities and to suggest action for their socio-economic development, a National Commission for De-notified Tribes, Nomadic Tribes and Semi-Nomadic Tribes was set up in 2005. In the Eleventh Plan, special attention will be accorded to the well-being of these groups through steps in pursuance of the recommendations of the Commission.

One particular area where attention must be paid is towards elementary education of the children of Nomadic, and Semi-Nomadic and De-notified tribes. Due to their family's mobility from one place to another, children in such tribes remain deprived educationally.

Mobile schools of high quality should be set up to meet their specific needs. Nomadic, Semi-Nomadic and De-notified tribes reside in secluded places. Arrangement should be made to extend the benefit of the flagship programmes to these areas on a priority basis.

Minorities

In pursuance of the Constitutional provisions, the government is committed to the well being of the minorities. Such measures are not limited to protecting and promoting their language, religion and culture, but also in making special efforts for their socio-economic development and mainstreaming. As per the provisions under the National Commission of Minorities Act, 1992, five religious communities including Muslims, Christians, Sikhs, Buddhists, and Zoroastrians (Parsis) have been notified as minorities. Among the minorities, Muslims, especially Muslim women, need special attention since relative to other communities they have remained socially, educationally and economically backward.

According to the Census of 2001, 18.4 per cent of our population belongs to Minority communities. Muslims constitute 13.4 per cent, Christians 2.3 per cent, Sikhs 1.9 per cent, Buddhists 0.8 per cent and Parsis 0.07 per cent of the country's total population. In absolute numbers, Muslims (nearly 140 million) account for 72.8 per cent of the total minority population of 189.5 million.

The distribution of minority population indicates that Muslims are in majority in the Union Territory of Lakshadweep and in the State of Jammu and Kashmir. In six States the proportion of Muslims to total population is above the national percentage of 13.4 per cent—Assam (30.9 per cent), West Bengal (25.2 per cent), Kerala (24.6 per cent), Uttar Pradesh (18.55 per cent), Bihar (16.5 per cent) and Jharkhand (13.8 per cent). In absolute numbers, Uttar Pradesh (30.7 million), West Bengal (20.2 million), Bihar (13.7 million), and Maharashtra (10.70 million) have the largest Muslim population. The highest percentages of Christians to total population are in Nagaland (90 per cent), Mizoram (87 per cent), and Meghalaya (70.03 per cent). There are also substantial numbers of Christians in Kerala, Tamil Nadu, Andhra Pradesh, Jharkhand, Orissa, Maharashtra, and Karnataka. Sikhs constitute 60 per cent of the population of Punjab. Buddhists are categorised into traditional and neo-Buddhists.

Traditional Buddhists are, by and large, from tribal communities inhabiting the hilly areas of Ladhakh, Himachal Pradesh, West Bengal, Sikkim, Assam and the North Eastern States. The highest percentage of Buddhists is in Sikkim (28.1 per cent) followed by Arunachal Pradesh (13 per cent). In absolute numbers, Maharashtra reported 58.38 lakh Buddhists, the highest in the country. Parsis number just 69000, and reside mostly in Maharashtra.

Constitutional Safeguards

Following are some of the special constitutional safeguards for minorities:

- *Article 15*: Prohibition of discrimination on grounds of religion
- *Article 16*: Equality of opportunity in matters of public employment

- *Article 25*: Freedom of conscience and free profession, practice and propagation of religion.
- *Article 26* Freedom to manage religious affairs
- *Articles 29*: Right to conserve language, script, and culture
- *Article 30*: Right to establish and administer educational institutions
- *Article 347:* Recognition of language
- *Article 350*: Redressal of grievances to any authority in the government in any of the languages used in the States/ Union Territories
- *Article 350(A):* Instruction through mother tongue at the primary stage of education
- *Article 350(B):* Investigate all matters relating to linguistic minorities.

Development Of Minorities

As the well-being of minorities has been a deep concern of the government, a HLC to study their conditions was set up in 1980 under the chairmanship of Gopal Singh. The Committee, in its report, concluded that the poor among the Muslims could not avail opportunities in education, employment, and economic activities because of isolation and various historical factors. In view of this, in 1983, the Prime Minister's 15-Point Programme was launched to provide a sense of security to minority communities and ensure their rapid socio-economic development. This Programme was based on a three-pronged approach: (i) to tackle the situation arising out of communal riots; (ii) to ensure adequate representation of the minority communities in employment under the Central and State Governments as well as PSUs; and (iii) other measures, such as ensuring flow of benefits to the minority communities under various development programmes, maintenance and development of religious places, Wakf properties and redressal of grievances of the minorities.

Till the Seventh Five Year Plan, however, minorities continued to get the developmental benefits along with OBCs. In 1989, an autonomous, non-political, non-profit organisation—the Maulana Azad Education Foundation (MAEF)—was set up to promote education among educationally backward Muslims in general, and Muslim girls in particular. With a corpus of Rs 100 crore, it undertook activities like establishing and expanding schools/residential schools/ colleges/hostels; purchasing laboratory equipment and furniture; setting up/strengthening vocational/technical training centre/ institutes; providing scholarships to meritorious girl students; opening Maulana Azad Sadbhawana Kendras; (since discontinued) and announcing Maulana Abul Kalam Azad Literacy Awards. In the final year of the Tenth Plan the corpus of Rs 100 crore with the Foundation was doubled. The interest accrued on the corpus was used for implementation of its educational schemes. It sanctioned a total grant-in-aid of Rs 91.81 crore to 702 NGOs/local bodies located in 20 States and two UTs for construction/expansion of schools/ colleges/girls hostels/ polytechnics/ and purchase of equipments/ machinery/ furniture up to December 2006. The Foundation also distributed scholarships amounting to Rs 6.98 crore to 6986 girl students in 29 States/UTs between 2003–04 and 2005–06.

During the Eighth Plan (1992–97), two exclusive schemes were introduced for their educational and economic development. In 1994, the National Minorities Development and Finance Corporation (NMDFC) was set up with an authorised share capital of Rs 500 crore.

Scheme for Pre-examination Coaching for Weaker Sections based on economic criteria. It assisted voluntary organisations to run coaching centres to prepare minorities for various competitive and professional examinations. As few organisations came forward, this scheme, along with the Pre-examination Coaching Scheme for OBCs, was merged with the existing Centrally Sponsored Coaching Scheme for Scheduled Castes in 2001. It was renamed Coaching and Allied Scheme for Weaker Sections including SCs, OBCs, and minorities. During the Tenth Five Year Plan, the authorised share capital for NMDFC was raised to Rs 650 crore. Of this, the share of the GoI is Rs 422.50 crore (65 per cent) and that of the State Governments is Rs 169 crore (26 per cent). The remaining Rs 58.50 crore (9 per cent) is to be contributed by institutions/individuals interested in the well being and empowerment of minorities. The task of NMDFC is to extend loans at concessional rates to enable economically weak minorities to take up income generating activities. Since its inception,

NMDFC has given financial assistance of Rs 827 crore to 2.16 lakh beneficiaries spread over 25 States and three UTs.

Despite these schemes, till the end of 2005–06, the Ministry of Social Justice and Empowerment continued to be the implementing agency for programmes for educational development and economic empowerment of minorities. Then, on 29 January 2006, a separate Ministry of Minority Affairs (MMA) was created. Meanwhile, the GoI also constituted a HLC under the Chairmanship of Justice (Retd.) Rajinder Sachar to prepare a report on the social, economic and educational status of the Muslim community. In its comprehensive Report, the Committee observed that Muslims have been left behind the growth and development process. It recommended setting up of an autonomous Assessment Monitoring Authority, creation of a National Data Bank and constitution of an Equal Opportunity Commission (EOC). It also suggested provision of hostel facilities at reasonable cost, inclusion of minority aspects in the general curriculum for teacher training, setting up and strengthening of State-run Urdu medium schools, linkage of madarsas to Higher Secondary Boards, recognition of degrees of madarsas for eligibility in competitive examinations, and provision of financial and other support to madarsas.

Prime Minister's New 15-Point Programme

The Prime Minister's New 15-Point Programme was launched in 2006 aimed at ensuring the well being, protection and development of minorities. While the 15-Point Programme of the 1983 centred on communal riots, representation of minorities in services and ensuring flow of benefits to individual beneficiaries, the focus of the new Programme is to make certain that benefits of various schemes/programmes flow equitably to the minorities. For this, it quantifies a certain portion of development projects to be established in areas with a concentration of minorities. It stipulates that wherever possible, 15 per cent of targets and outlays under various schemes will be earmarked for the minorities. All Central ministries/ departments, State Governments/UT Administrations have been advised to implement this new Programme. Five Central Ministries—HRD, Labour and Employment, Housing and Poverty Alleviation, RD and Women and Child Development—have been given responsibilities in their respective areas. The procedure for monitoring the outcomes of these multiple initiatives is clearly laid out. It will be done on a half-yearly basis by the Committee of Secretaries (COS) and the Cabinet. MMA is the nodal Ministry for coordinating and monitoring the implementation. The key elements of the monitoring will be: (i) focus on meeting financial targets; (ii) target oriented monitoring based on a plan of achievable outcomes under each programme and Ministry; (iii) outcome targets to be staggered and time-bound, and monitored accordingly; (iv) regular evaluation studies conducted by both MMA and by external expert evaluators; (v) space for concurrent evaluation through existing, identified institutions in key target States; (vi) focus on regular and accurate information flow from District to State to Centre; (vii) focus on smooth fiscal flow and regular identification of bottlenecks; and (viii) flexibility for review and revision of programme designs.

Present Status of Minorities

Education

Table 7 shows that literacy rates among Muslims, both men and women, have been the lowest among all the religious minorities.

Table 7. Literacy Rate among all Religious Communities in 2001

Communities	Male	Female	Total
All religious communities	75.38	53.7	64.8
Muslims	67.6	50.1	59.1
Christians	84.4	76.2	80.3
Sikhs	75.2	63.1	69.4
Buddhists	83.1	61.7	72.7

The Sachar Committee Report found that enrolment of children aged 6–14 years at the all-India level was 85.3 per cent for all communities. The enrolment figures for Muslims was lower (81.8 per cent) than the national average as well as relative to 'All others' (89.9 per cent), but higher than SCs/STs (79.3 per cent). The gap between Muslims and other SRCs increases as the level of education advances.

The literacy rate for Muslim girls is particularly low. This can be attributed to a number of reasons. Many parents do not send their girls to school as they feel unsafe, especially in view of the growing communalism. Further, as the dependency ratio for the young is high among Muslims, older siblings often have to stay home and provide care. Given the high levels of poverty and self-employment, children also provide much needed labour.

While it is a misconception that most Muslim children go to madarsas, a large proportion of parents do want their children to receive some form of religious education in addition to the general curriculum. For this, it is vital to ensure that the school timings do not clash with those of madarsas and *maktabs*. Kerala has successfully managed to do this and hence has a high literacy rate among Muslims.

Finally, many Muslim girls and boys are first-generation learners. Like the children belonging to SC/ ST communities, they need support and grooming. This, combined with the presence of women teachers who are non-partisan, will go a long way in checking dropout rates among Muslims.

Table 8. Prime Minister's New 15-Point Programme for the Welfare of Minorities

(A) Enhancing Opportunities for Education

- *Equitable availability of ICDS services:* A certain percentage of ICDS projects and Anganwadi Centres to be located in blocks/villages with a substantial population of minority communities; equitable availability of benefits to be ensured.
- *Improving access to school education*: A certain percentage of all schools under the Sarva Shiksha Abhiyan, the Kasturba Gandhi Balika Vidyalaya Scheme, and other similar government schemes will be located in villages/localities having a substantial minority population.
- *Greater resources for teaching Urdu:* Recruitment and posting of Urdu language teachers in primary and upper primary schools.
- *Modernising Madarsa Education:* Strengthening the Central Plan Scheme of Area-Intensive and Madarsa Modernisation Programme to provide basic educational infrastructure in areas of concentration of educationally backward minorities.
- *Scholarships for meritorious students from minority communities:* Formulation of schemes for pre-matric and post-matric scholarships for students from minority communities.

– *Improving educational infrastructure through the Maulana Azad Education Foundation (MAEF):* To expand the activities of MAEF more effectively.

(B) Equitable Share in Economic Activities and Employment

– *Self-employment and wage employment for the poor:* A certain percentage of the physical and financial targets under some schemes, for example, the SGSY, SJSRY, Sampurna Grameen Rozgar Yojana SGRY), will be earmarked for beneficiaries belonging to the minority communities and living below the poverty line in rural areas. Simultaneously, a certain percentage of the allocation will be earmarked for the creation of infrastructure in such villages which have a substantial population of minorities.

– *Upgradation of skills through technical training*: A certain proportion of all new ITIs will be located in areas predominantly inhabited by minority communities and a proportion of existing ITIs for upgradation to 'Centres of Excellence' will be selected on the same basis.

– *Enhanced credit support for economic activities:* To strengthen the National Minorities Development and Finance Corporation (NMDFC) by providing it greater equity support to enable it to fully achieve its objectives. An appropriate percentage of the priority sector lending in all categories to be targeted for the minority communities.

– *Recruitment to State and Central services*: In the recruitment of police personnel, Central and State Governments will be advised to give special consideration to minorities. The composition of selection should have Minorities' repres-entation. Employment opportunities to be provided in the Railways, nationalised banks and PSEs. An exclusive scheme is to be launched to provide coaching to minority candidates.

(C) Improving the Conditions of Living of Minorities

– *Equitable share in rural housing scheme:* This is sought to be achieved through the Indira Awaas Yojana (IAY) for poor beneficiaries from minority communities in rural areas.

– *Improvement in condition of slums inhabited by minority communities:* Ensuring provision of physical amenities and basic services to be equitably extended under the schemes of the Integrated Housing and Slum Development Programme and JNNURM to the minority communities and to cities/slums with minority concentrations.

(D) Prevention and Control of Communal Riots

– Prevention of communal incidents

– Prosecution for communal offences

– Rehabilitation of victims of communal riots

Economic Development

Work Participation Rate (Wpr)

The WPR for all religious communities was 39.1 per cent in the Census of 2001. Buddhists had 40.6 per cent WPR, Christians 39.7 per cent and Muslims 31.3 per cent (being the lowest).

Occupational Category

Table 9 shows that Muslims and Buddhists both comprise 20 per cent each of the cultivator category; Sikhs were highest at 32.4 per cent followed by the Christians with 29.2 per cent.

The Sachar Committee Report clearly shows that due to limited land ownership, most Muslims are engaged in non-agricultural occupations. They are usually merchants, shopkeepers, sales persons, shop assistants, tailors, dress makers, transport equipment operators, tobacco preparers, tobacco product makers, spinners, weavers, knitters, dyers, machinery fitters, assemblers and precision instrument makers. Being self-employed and often in the unorganised sector, they lack any kind of social security. Further, Muslims have traditionally been engaged in skilled occupations like weaving, spinning, artisanship and tailoring. A large proportion of them are also street vendors. As these are professions which have suffered maximum reversals due to globalisation, more and more Muslim families are being left without a source of livelihood. The self-employed, especially entrepreneurs, are unable to get credit to expand and run their micro and small enterprises. This is leading to increasing frustration and discontent.

Health

Census data indicates that Muslims have the highest sex-ratio of any social group in the country (950/ 1000).1 However, among other minorities like the Sikhs and Jains, who incidentally have better female literacy figures, the sex-ratio is alarming (786 and 870 for Sikhs and Jains, respectively).

Muslims have the second lowest infant and under-5 mortality rate of any SRC in India. Infant mortality is lower for Muslims than Hindus—59 against 77 for every 1,000 births in 1998–99 (NFHS-2). Muslims are, however, worse off than most other groups in terms of child undernutrition; for instance, Muslim children suffer from the highest rate of stunting and the second highest rate of under-weight children among all social groups. This can be primarily attributed to lack of access to PHCs and ICDS centres.

Table 9. Work Participation Rate by Male and Female Population in Minority Communities

Communities	Male	Female	Total
All religious communities	51.7	25.6	39.1
Muslims	47.5	14.1	31.3
Christians	50.7	28.7	39.7
Sikhs	53.3	20.2	37.7
Buddhists	49.2	31.7	40.6

Table 10. Distribution of Category of Workers

Category	All religious Communities	Muslims	Christians	Sikhs	Buddhists
Total	100.0	100.0	100.0	100.0	100.0
Cultivators	31.7	20.7	29.2	32.4	20.4
Agricultural labourers	26.5	22.0	15.3	16.8	37.6
Households Industry Workers	4.2	8.1	2.7	3.4	2.9
Other	37.6	49.1	52.8	47.3	39.2

Violence against minority communities is on the rise worldwide. India too has seen various instances of communal violence which has led to trauma and growing fear and suspicion in the minds of people. This—combined with economic and social backwardness—has resulted in the alienation of large segments of the population, many of whom belong to the minority communities. Provision of adequate social and physical infrastructure, economic opportunities, justice and counselling services are thus vital.

Eleventh Five Year Plan: A Way Ahead

Though previous Five Year Plans have attempted to focus on weaker sections of the society, they have failed to include many groups, especially Muslims, into the development net. The Eleventh Plan will therefore accord highest priority to the development of innovative programmes, expansion of existing schemes, implementation and monitoring of all initiatives for the minorities by making adequate budgetary allocations at every level of governance. The Eleventh Plan agenda for empowerment of the minorities will focus on:

- Access, retention and achievement in primary, elementary and higher education, with particular emphasis on the education of the minority, especially Muslim, girl child.
- Enhanced access to credit and subsidy for self-employment, export promotion of traditional crafts, upgradation of technical skills and provision of vocational training with forward linkages in terms of employment, that is, equal opportunity in public and private sector employment.
- Access to government schemes and programmes, including schemes aimed at poverty alleviation; provision of physical infrastructure such as housing; provision of civic amenities and health infrastructure in Muslim-dominated village clusters and urban neighbourhoods as envisaged under the PM's New 15-Point Programme Multi-sectoral Plan for Minority Concentration Districts and 338 towns with substantial Minority population.
- Create a national data bank to collect data on various aspects of socio-religious communities through comprehensive surveys on education, health, access to government, access to justice, situation of girls and women; conduct qualitative studies to understand the persisting bottlenecks in access to a wide range of government services and programmes, to understand patterns of discrimination and its socio-economic implications; to suggest long- and short-term remedies; and to understand regional variations in the condition of the minorities from the perspective of plan interventions.

- In-depth evaluation and performance reviews of a host of institutional mechanisms including the NMDFC and the MAEF to improve their efficacy and suggest other institutional innovations.
- Establish measurable, monitorable outcomes and set up national-level monitoring mechanisms for all aspects of plans, programmes and schemes intended to benefit the minorities, particularly poor Muslims.

In implementing this agenda, the Plan will recognise the heterogeneous nature of different minority groups and the need for common, as well as targeted, interventions based on differential situations.

Education and Social Security

The government is committed to mainstreaming minorities in the process of economic growth. The SSA will ensure universal coverage for the children of educationally backward sections, with special focus on Muslim girls. Specific SSA components like the centrally funded KBGVs will be set up for minority communities. At the same time, all State plans to access SSA funds will be reviewed to ensure that Minority children have equal space to participate in the State's school system. As SSA only covers children up to the elementary (Class VIII) level, measures will be undertaken to ensure that minority children have equal access to education up to senior secondary level (Class XII). The Eleventh Plan will also look at issues like recruitment of female teachers, provision of amenities and transportation to reach schools, and setting up of girls' hostels and girls' schools.

In pursuance of the guidelines issued under the Prime Minister's New 15-Point Programme, scholarship schemes, namely the Pre-Matric, Post-Matric, and Merit-and Means-based schemes for minority students will be formulated and implemented in the Eleventh Plan. The objective of Pre-Matric Scholarships will be to provide encouragement to students of the minority communities from Classes I to X for general and/or technical and vocational courses. Similarly, the Post-Matric Scholarship scheme will cover minority students studying in Classes XI and XII for general as well as technical and vocational courses. The major thrust will be on education of girls. Merit- and

Means-based scholarship scheme will provide scholarships to meritorious students from poor families to pursue technical and professional courses. In order to ensure effective implementation of the New 15-Point Programme in letter and spirit, rigorous and continuous monitoring will be ensured. All State Governments will be required to submit half-yearly reports on their plans and achievements in reaching minority populations for elementary, secondary and senior secondary education. These reports will be made available in the public domain. Besides, periodic reviews will also be undertaken by the CoS and the Cabinet.

Concerted efforts will be made to ensure that universally available services under ICDS, NHRM, and so on, reach the localities where the minority communities live. Minority leaders will be roped in to communicate public health messages and dispel existing myths. As Muslims are mostly self-employed and work in professions such as weaving, spinning and dyeing, which lead to occupational ailments, appropriate health services will be made available. State governments will be required to report their achievements in terms of minority access to these services to the Planning Commission.

Employment and Skill Development

A majority of the Muslim workforce is self-employed and engages in artisanal work. These occupations have been under stress due to the radical changes in the economy. Developmental projects have also led to loss of livelihoods for street vendors, most of whom are Muslims. As a result, deskilling is taking place and artisans and vendors are being forced to move to unskilled, informal work. The Eleventh Plan recognises the need to provide support to these artisanal groups not just for ensuring inclusive growth and development of the minorities, but for promotion of exports, employment and GDP as well. Consequently, schemes of the Ministries of T e xtiles; Micro, Small and Medium Enterprises; Agro and Rural Industries; and Food Processing Industries, among others, will be revised to accommodate the interests of minority community workers who are in distress. Provision of inputs including credit, design and marketing support will be undertaken. At the same time social security measures like health and life insurance will be provided.

Priority sector lending: Access of Muslims to bank credit, including priority sector advances, is low and inadequate. To empower Muslims economically it is necessary to support self-employed persons by ensuring smooth flow of credit to them. During the Eleventh Plan period, all public sector banks shall have targets for priority sector advances to members of the minorities, particularly Muslims. Steps shall be introduced to create awareness about various credit schemes, organise entrepreneurial development programmes, and bring transparency in reporting on credit availability.

New Scheme for Development of Minority Concentrated Areas

As many pockets with substantial minority populations continue to lack adequate physical and social infrastructure, the Eleventh Plan will adopt an area-based approach. According to the Census of 2001, 1228 community development blocks (out of a total of 6406 in the country), 338 Class I towns and 156 districts have minority populations of 25 per cent and above. Both infrastructure development (physical, electricity, roads, that is, development of amenities) and beneficiary-oriented programmes will be launched in these areas.

To ensure comprehensive development through a multi-sectoral approach, 90 Minority Concentration Districts (MCDs) covering 34 per cent of the minority population in the country, have been identified on the basis of either human development indicators or basic amenities indicators. The human indicators include: (i) literacy rate of minorities; (ii) female literacy rate; (iii) WPR; and (iv) female work participation. The basic amenities indicators include: (i) percentage of households with pucca walls; (ii) percentage of households with safe drinking water facilities; (iii) percentage of households with electricity; and (iv) percentage of households with W/C latrines. The identification of the MCDs was also based upon certain population norms:

- Districts where the minority population is at least 25 per cent of the total population were identified in 29 States/UTs.
- Districts having a minority population exceeding five lakh where the percentage of minority population is between 20 and 25 per cent were identified in 29 States/UTs.

- Six minority-concentrated States/UTs (Jammu and Kashmir, Meghalaya, Mizoram, Nagaland, Punjab, and Lakshadweep), and districts having 15 per cent minority population other than the minorities (for example, other than Muslims in Jammu and Kashmir; other than Christians in Meghalaya, Mizoram, and Nagaland, Punjab, and Lakshadweep).
- The preparation and implementation of area/ problem-specific special developmental plans for these MCDs are already in progress. The effort is to improve the socio-economic conditions through provision of better infrastructure for education, health, sanitation, pucca housing, safe drinking water, promotion of income generating opportunities, skill development and marketing support.

Furthermore, about 35.7 per cent Muslims live in urban areas and 36.92 per cent of them are below the poverty line. During the Tenth Plan, an Inter-Ministerial Task Force was constituted under the chairmanship of Bhalachandra Mungekar to identify towns/ cities that have substantial concentration of the minority population and require special attention, and to formulate the approach for a multi-sectoral plan for provision of basic civic amenities within those areas. The Task Force was also asked to suggest special schemes for funding specific projects which were not covered under existing schemes and programmes.

The Task Force reiterated the uneven distribution of minorities in the country and revealed that in six States/UTs—Jammu and Kashmir, Meghalaya, Mizoram, Nagaland, Punjab, and Lakshadweep—at least one of the minorities is in majority. Using socio-economic indicators similar to those used for MCDs, 338 towns/cities in which the minority communities constituted more than 25 per cent of the population or more, were identified. Of these 338 towns/cities, 251 have emerged as being relatively backward and in need of urgent attention. Programmes for the provision and development of amenities and infrastructure should immediately be taken up in these towns and cities.

The endeavour in the Eleventh Plan will be to ensure the availability of all essential amenities in not just the identified MCDs and towns/cities, but in all the other minority localities as well. The area-based approach is not an attempt at ghettoisation; it is a response to the existing ghettoisation and location of the minorities. It is an attempt to provide each and every citizen of the country access to all amenities, irrespective of their religion or location.

Security and Freedom from Suspicion

In keeping with the Common Minimum Programme's (CMP) commitment of security and justice for minorities, efforts will be made to carry out interventions which ensure prevention of communal violence. A comprehensive communal violence legislation will be enacted and justice and reparations will be ensured for survivors of communal crimes. Minorities, especially Muslims, are under-represented in Public Security and Defence institutions. This will be remedied. Workshops will be carried out to sensitise law enforcers and ensure that youth are not harassed simply because they profess a certain faith. The government will partner with CSOs to spread the message of communal harmony and dispel suspicions, fears and biases. The government will, through the Ministry of Information and Broadcasting, ensure that no community is depicted in a manner that creates, propagates or nurtures biases and suspicions.

Linguistic Minorities—Monitoring Mechanisms

Linguistic minorities living in relative social and economic backwardness and in need of preservation of their culture and language will be paid special attention. Protective and promotive measures will be undertaken to ensure their overall protection, well being and development in the Eleventh Plan.

If the Eleventh Plan agenda for inclusive growth has to succeed, then monitoring of all existing and new interventions is imperative. One important activity of the MMA in the Eleventh Plan will be to ensure that the minorities get their due share in the developmental schemes of various ministries and departments at the Central as well as State level. The Ministry will have to advise other concerned Ministries and Departments and monitor the implementation of the PM's 15-Point Programme. This will entail collection of information at regular intervals, its analysis, preparation of various reports and providing suitable directions. To assist the Ministry, the government will examine the feasibility of a separate committee comprising of government as well as civil society representatives, to undertake a six-monthly review of all programmes deemed to be targeting the minorities. The idea of setting up a National Resource Group for Minority Affairs to strengthen specific components of the Plan based upon responses from the field and design special inputs, programmes or projects for particular social sub-groups will also be considered. Finally, efforts will be made to establish a Grievance Redressal Cell in the MMA as part of monitoring efforts to allow complaints of non-compliance, interference and non-implementation to be addressed.

Role of Voluntary Organisations (Vos)

Recognising the complementary and supplementary role played by VOs, the government has been extending financial and other support to them, especially to organisations which have an all-India base, to undertake activities aimed at socio-economic development and empowerment of the disadvantaged and the under-privileged sections such as SCs, STs, OBCs, minorities, disabled, older people and other social defence groups. Such VOs, especially those managed by the target group itself, will continue particularly in areas/regions which have not yet been covered.

Non-governmental organisations of repute should be invited to play the role of designated agents/informants and identify cases of untouchability, atrocities and other forms of discrimination based on caste, creed, religion, and so on. They need to be encouraged to assist the implementing agency in investigation and trial and also safeguarding against various pressures aimed at nullifying the impact of legal proceedings.

Voluntary action acquires greater significance in the tribal context in view of the virtual absence of tribes peoples' own VOs, that is, VOs as we understand the term, though they have their own traditional organisations. Their inability to negotiate with the formal administrative system, limited worldview and low level of awareness and literacy add to the need for bridges with the other worlds. Vol untary groups will be encouraged to train tribal peoples' own organisations to make them capable of articulating their own needs and advocating their rights.

- While encouraging voluntary action, a system of accountability would have to be established for the NGOs so as to ensure effective delivery of services. The corporate sector and public sector undertakings could be encouraged for productive interventions for social welfare problems in their own industries.

Research, Monitoring, and Evaluation

Development programmes for the welfare of socially disadvantaged groups and marginalised sections of society have been in operation from the First Five Year Plan onwards. Whether the benefits of these programmes reach the targeted persons, needs to be monitored on a periodical basis at the district, State and national levels. Continuous monitoring and evaluation would justify the continuation of programmes. The Ministries of Social Justice and Empowerment, Tribal Affairs and Minorities have developed mechanisms of monitoring and evaluating their programmes. These Ministries also sponsor research studies by independent agencies such as university departments/reputed research bodies/VOs. Based on the findings of such studies, efforts are made to improve upon the strategy for implementation of schemes. During the Eleventh Five Year Plan, particular stress will be laid on ensuring that such evaluation does not become routine, and results in actual improvements in the schemes.

Need for Database

The Census of India and NSSO are the two agencies which make available data on various aspects of social groups. Data on SCs, STs, Minorities and Persons with Disabilities have been made available by these agencies. Census data are not available for OBCs and persons who are victims of drug addiction and alcoholism. The Eleventh Plan will address the need for survey of such category of persons for proper formulation of policies and programmes towards their welfare and rehabilitation. The Eleventh Plan will also address the issue for adopting a uniform definition for identification of disabled persons by both the agencies.

Affirmative Legislation Action

The prevailing gaps in socio-economic status between SCs, STs and other disadvantaged groups vis-à-vis the rest of the population need to be speedily bridged by taking innovative measures. As a first step, there is a need to assess the gaps between SCs and other social groups with respect to various parameters of growth and development and construct an index of development/ vulnerability/deprivation on the basis of which policy and programme interventions can be formulated and administered. State governments, Central ministries/ departments and public authorities are to be made accountable for purposeful and affirmative action within their jurisdiction to bring about overall development of the people belonging to SCs/STs and to bridge the gaps between their and other social groups. The proposed legislation should cover assessing the gaps between SCs/ STs and other social groups, constructing suitable indices and providing appropriate intervention in the areas of education, higher education including vocational training and employment for bridging the gaps on a lifetime capacity building basis. The legislation should also provide for appropriate penalty for non-performance of the obligations created by it. It should be adopted by all the States to implement it in its letter and spirit. Action may be taken on the lines of the Persons with Disabilities (Equal Opportunities, Protection of Rights and Full Participation) Act, 1995

Plan Outlay

In the Eleventh Plan, a tentative outlay of Rs 13043 crore has been earmarked for the Ministry of Social Justice and Empowerment for the development of SCs, OBCs and other vulnerable groups. Similarly, tentative allocation of Rs 3709 crore and Rs 7000 crore have been made to the Ministry of Tribal Affairs and MMA, respectively for the welfare and development of STs and minorities. The allocation indicated for the Ministry of Tribal Affairs does not include SCA to TSP and grant-in-aid under Article 275(1) of the Constitution. In addition to this, social welfare programmes receive Plan financial support from the State sector also.

References

Susan Bayly. *Caste, Society and Politics in India.* Cambridge. Cambridge University Press. 1999.

Beteille, Andre. *Caste, Class and Power: Changing Patterns of Stratification in a Tanjore Village.* New Delhi. Oxford University Press. 1996.

Gupta, S.K. *The Scheduled Castes in Modern Indian Politics: Their Emergence as a Political Power.* New Delhi. Munshiram Manoharlal Publishers Pvt. Ltd. 1985.

Mahar, J. Michael, (ed.) *The Untouchables in Contemporary India.* Tucson. The University of Arizona Press. 1972.

Michael, S.M., (ed.) *Untouchable: Dalits in Modern India.* Boulder. Lynne Rienner Publishers. 1999.

Parikh, Sunita. *The Politics of Preference: Democratic Institutions and Affirmative Action in the United States and India.* Ann Arbor: University of Michigan Press. 1997.

Report of the Commissioner for Scheduled Castes and Scheduled Tribes, 1974. New Delhi: Government of India Press. 1977.

Rudolph, Lloyd I. and Susanne Hoeber Rudolph. *In Pursuit of Lakshmi: The Political Economy of the Indian State.* Chicago: University of Chicago Press. 1987.

BIBLIOGRAPHY

Aggarwal, Patrap. *Caste and Social Stratification Among Muslims in India.* Manohar. 1978.

Ainapur, L. S. *Dynamics of Caste Relations in Rural India.* Rawat Publications. Jaipur. 1986.

Akerolof, George. "The Economics of Caste and of Rat Race and Other Woeful Tales", *Quarterly Journal of Economics,* XC.4, November. 1976.

Assadi Muzaffar and S. Rajendran Karnataka. 'Changing Shape of Caste Conflicts'. *Economic and Political Weekly.* May 6-12. 2000.

Bandyopadhyay, Sekhar. *Caste, Culture, and Hegemony: Social domination in Colonial Bengal.* Sage Publications. New Delhi. 2004.

Banerjee, Biswajit and J.B. Knight, "Caste Discrimination in Indian Urban Labour Market" *Journal of Developing Economics.* 1985.

Bashiruddin Ahmed. *Caste and Electoral Politics.* Asian Survey. Vol. 10, No. 11, Elections and Party Politics in India: A Symposium. Nov., 1970. pp. 979–992.

Bayly, Susan *Caste, Society and Politics in India from the Eighteenth Century to the Modern Age.* Cambridge University Press. 1999.

Benjamin, Joseph. *Scheduled Caste in Indian Politics and Society.* Ess Ess Publishers, New Delhi. 1989.

Beteille, Andre. *Caste, Class and Power: Changing Patterns of Stratification in a Tanjore Village.* New Delhi. Oxford University Press. 1996.

Betteile Andre. *Society and Politics in India.* Delhi, OUP. 1992.

Blunt. E.A.H. *The Caste System of North India.* S.Chand Publishers. 1969.

Chalam, K.S. "Caste Reservation and Equality of Opportunity in Education" *Economic and Political Weekly.* Vol. 25, No. 41. October 13. 1990.

Das, Bhagwan. "Moments in a History of Reservations." *Economic and Political Weekly*. Vol. 35, No.43 and 44. October 28. 2000.

Ghurye, G. S. *Caste, Class and Occupation*. Popular Book Depot, Bombay. 1961.

Gupta, S.K. *The Scheduled Castes in Modern Indian Politics: Their Emergence as a Political Power*. New Delhi. Munshiram Manoharlal Publishers Pvt. Ltd. 1985.

Gurr, T.D. *Minorities at Risk: A Global View of Ethnopolitical Conflicts*, Washington DC, Institute of Peace Press. 1993.

Hasan Zoya. *Quest for Power : Oppositional Movements and Post-Congress politics in Uttar Pradesh*. Delhi. OUP. 1998.

Human Rights Watch, *Broken People: Caste Violence Against India's "Untouchables"*. New York: Human Rights Watch. 1999.

Jaffrelot, Christophe. *India's Silent Revolution: The Rise of the Lower Castes*. C. Hurst & Co. 2003.

Jogendra Nath Bhattacharya, *Hindu Castes and Sects, Munshiram Manoharlal*, Delhi. 1896.

Kane, Pandurang Vaman. *History of Dharmasastra: (ancient and mediaeval, religious and civil law)*. Poona. Bhandarkar Oriental Research Institute. 1962.

Kothari, Rajni. *Caste in Indian Politics*. Orient Longman.2004.

Kundu, Amitabh. "Reservation, Anti-reservation and Democracy." *Economic and Political Weekly*. Vol. 25, No. 45. November 10, 1990.

Mahar, J. Michael, (ed.) *The Untouchables in Contemporary India*. Tucson. The University of Arizona Press. 1972.

Michael, S.M., (ed.) *Untouchable: Dalits in Modern India*. Boulder. Lynne Rienner Publishers. 1999.

Murray Milner, Jr. *Status and Sacredness: A General Theory of Status Relations and an Analysis of Indian Culture*, New York: Oxford University Press. 1994.

Murray Milner, Jr. *Status and Sacredness: A General Theory of Status Relations and an Analysis of Indian Culture*, New York: Oxford University Press. 1994.

National Commission for Scheduled Castes and Scheduled Tribes. Fourth Report 1996-97 & 1997-98, vols. I &II, Delhi. 1998.

National Commission for Scheduled Castes and Scheduled Tribes. *Highlights of the Report for the Years 1996-97 and 1997-98*. New Delhi. Government of India, 1999.

Nayar Baldev Raj. *Minority Politics in the Punjab*. N.J., Princeton University Press. 1998.

Nigam, Aditya. "Mandal Commission and the Left". *Economic and Political Weekly*. Vol. 25, No. 48,49. December 1-8, 1990.

Nireka Weeratunge, *Aspects of Ethnicity and Cender Among the Rodi of Sri Lanka*. Sri Lanka: International Centre for Ethnic Studies. 1988.

Omvedt, Gail. "Hinduism and Politics." *Economic and Political Weekly*. Vol. 25, No, 14, April 7, 1990.

Pandian M.S.S. "One Step Outside Modernity." *Economic and Political Weekly*. Vol. 37, No. 18, May 4, 2002.

Parikh, Sunita. *The Politics of Preference: Democratic Institutions and Affirmative Action in the United States and India*. Ann Arbor: University of Michigan Press. 1997.

Parvathamma. *Scheduled Castes and Tribes: A Socio-economic Survey*, Ashish, Delhi. 1984.

Pauline Kolenda. *Caste in Contemporary India: Beyond Organic Solidarity* Menlo Park. Benjamin/Cumming Publishing Co. 1978.

Pieter H. Streefland, *The Sweepers of the Slaughterhouse: Conflict and Survival in a Karachi Neighborhood*. Assen, the Netherlands: Van Gorcum. 1979.

Pinto, Amrose. "U.N. Conference Against Racism – Is Caste Race?" *Economic and Political Weekly*. Vol.36, No. 30, July 28, 2001.

Radhakrishnan P. "Sensitising Officials on Dalits and Reservations." *Economic and Political Weekly*. Vol. 37, No. 7, Feb. 16, 2002.

Rajendra Kalidas Wimala Goonesekere, "Prevention of Discrimination and Protection of Indigenous Peoples and Minorities". New York: United Nations. 2001.

Report of the Commissioner for Scheduled Castes and Scheduled Tribes, 1974. New Delhi: Government of India Press. 1977.

Rudolph, Lloyd I. and Susanne Hoeber Rudolph. *In Pursuit of Lakshmi: The Political Economy of the Indian State*. Chicago: University of Chicago Press. 1987.

Shah, Ghanshyam (ed.) *Dalit Identity and Politics.* Sage Publications. New Delhi. 2001.

Srinivas, M. N. (ed.). *Caste: Its Twentieth Century Avatar.* New Delhi: Viking, 1996.

Srinivas, M. N. *Religion and Society among the Coorgs of South India.* Oxford. 1952.

Susan Bayly. *Caste, Society and Politics in India.* Cambridge. Cambridge University Press. 1999.

Thorat S.K., "Passage to Adulthood : Perceptions from Below", in Sudhir Kakar (ed.), *Identity and Adulthood,* Oxford University Press, Delhi. 1979.

Index